INDONESIAN
VOCABULARY

FOR ENGLISH SPEAKERS

ENGLISH-INDONESIAN

The most useful words
To expand your lexicon and sharpen
your language skills

7000 words

Indonesian vocabulary for English speakers - 7000 words

By Andrey Taranov

T&P Books vocabularies are intended for helping you learn, memorize and review foreign words. The dictionary is divided into themes, covering all major spheres of everyday activities, business, science, culture, etc.

The process of learning words using T&P Books' theme-based dictionaries gives you the following advantages:

- Correctly grouped source information predetermines success at subsequent stages of word memorization
- Availability of words derived from the same root allowing memorization of word units (rather than separate words)
- Small units of words facilitate the process of establishing associative links needed for consolidation of vocabulary
- Level of language knowledge can be estimated by the number of learned words

T&P Books Publishing
www.tpbooks.com

ISBN: 978-1-78616-481-0

This book is also available in E-book formats.
Please visit www.tpbooks.com or the major online bookstores.

INDONESIAN VOCABULARY
for English speakers

T&P Books vocabularies are intended to help you learn, memorize, and review foreign words. The vocabulary contains over 7000 commonly used words arranged thematically.

- Vocabulary contains the most commonly used words
- Recommended as an addition to any language course
- Meets the needs of beginners and advanced learners of foreign languages
- Convenient for daily use, revision sessions, and self-testing activities
- Allows you to assess your vocabulary

Special features of the vocabulary

- Words are organized according to their meaning, not alphabetically
- Words are presented in three columns to facilitate the reviewing and self-testing processes
- Words in groups are divided into small blocks to facilitate the learning process
- The vocabulary offers a convenient and simple transcription of each foreign word

The vocabulary has 198 topics including:

Basic Concepts, Numbers, Colors, Months, Seasons, Units of Measurement, Clothing & Accessories, Food & Nutrition, Restaurant, Family Members, Relatives, Character, Feelings, Emotions, Diseases, City, Town, Sightseeing, Shopping, Money, House, Home, Office, Working in the Office, Import & Export, Marketing, Job Search, Sports, Education, Computer, Internet, Tools, Nature, Countries, Nationalities and more ...

T&P BOOKS' THEME-BASED DICTIONARIES

The Correct System for Memorizing Foreign Words

Acquiring vocabulary is one of the most important elements of learning a foreign language, because words allow us to express our thoughts, ask questions, and provide answers. An inadequate vocabulary can impede communication with a foreigner and make it difficult to understand a book or movie well.

The pace of activity in all spheres of modern life, including the learning of modern languages, has increased. Today, we need to memorize large amounts of information (grammar rules, foreign words, etc.) within a short period. However, this does not need to be difficult. All you need to do is to choose the right training materials, learn a few special techniques, and develop your individual training system.

Having a system is critical to the process of language learning. Many people fail to succeed in this regard; they cannot master a foreign language because they fail to follow a system comprised of selecting materials, organizing lessons, arranging new words to be learned, and so on. The lack of a system causes confusion and eventually, lowers self-confidence.

T&P Books' theme-based dictionaries can be included in the list of elements needed for creating an effective system for learning foreign words. These dictionaries were specially developed for learning purposes and are meant to help students effectively memorize words and expand their vocabulary.

Generally speaking, the process of learning words consists of three main elements:

- Reception (creation or acquisition) of a training material, such as a word list
- Work aimed at memorizing new words
- Work aimed at reviewing the learned words, such as self-testing

All three elements are equally important since they determine the quality of work and the final result. All three processes require certain skills and a well-thought-out approach.

New words are often encountered quite randomly when learning a foreign language and it may be difficult to include them all in a unified list. As a result, these words remain written on scraps of paper, in book margins, textbooks, and so on. In order to systematize such words, we have to create and continually update a "book of new words." A paper notebook, a netbook, or a tablet PC can be used for these purposes.

This "book of new words" will be your personal, unique list of words. However, it will only contain the words that you came across during the learning process. For example, you might have written down the words "Sunday," "Tuesday," and "Friday." However, there are additional words for days of the week, for example, "Saturday," that are missing, and your list of words would be incomplete. Using a theme dictionary, in addition to the "book of new words," is a reasonable solution to this problem.

The theme-based dictionary may serve as the basis for expanding your vocabulary.

It will be your big "book of new words" containing the most frequently used words of a foreign language already included. There are quite a few theme-based dictionaries available, and you should ensure that you make the right choice in order to get the maximum benefit from your purchase.

Therefore, we suggest using theme-based dictionaries from T&P Books Publishing as an aid to learning foreign words. Our books are specially developed for effective use in the sphere of vocabulary systematization, expansion and review.

Theme-based dictionaries are not a magical solution to learning new words. However, they can serve as your main database to aid foreign-language acquisition. Apart from theme dictionaries, you can have copybooks for writing down new words, flash cards, glossaries for various texts, as well as other resources; however, a good theme dictionary will always remain your primary collection of words.

T&P Books' theme-based dictionaries are specialty books that contain the most frequently used words in a language.

The main characteristic of such dictionaries is the division of words into themes. For example, the *City* theme contains the words "street," "crossroads," "square," "fountain," and so on. The *Talking* theme might contain words like "to talk," "to ask," "question," and "answer".

All the words in a theme are divided into smaller units, each comprising 3–5 words. Such an arrangement improves the perception of words and makes the learning process less tiresome. Each unit contains a selection of words with similar meanings or identical roots. This allows you to learn words in small groups and establish other associative links that have a positive effect on memorization.

The words on each page are placed in three columns: a word in your native language, its translation, and its transcription. Such positioning allows for the use of techniques for effective memorization. After closing the translation column, you can flip through and review foreign words, and vice versa. "This is an easy and convenient method of review – one that we recommend you do often."

Our theme-based dictionaries contain transcriptions for all the foreign words. Unfortunately, none of the existing transcriptions are able to convey the exact nuances of foreign pronunciation. That is why we recommend using the transcriptions only as a supplementary learning aid. Correct pronunciation can only be acquired with the help of sound. Therefore our collection includes audio theme-based dictionaries.

The process of learning words using T&P Books' theme-based dictionaries gives you the following advantages:

- You have correctly grouped source information, which predetermines your success at subsequent stages of word memorization
- Availability of words derived from the same root (lazy, lazily, lazybones), allowing you to memorize word units instead of separate words
- Small units of words facilitate the process of establishing associative links needed for consolidation of vocabulary
- You can estimate the number of learned words and hence your level of language knowledge
- The dictionary allows for the creation of an effective and high-quality revision process
- You can revise certain themes several times, modifying the revision methods and techniques
- Audio versions of the dictionaries help you to work out the pronunciation of words and develop your skills of auditory word perception

The T&P Books' theme-based dictionaries are offered in several variants differing in the number of words: 1.500, 3.000, 5.000, 7.000, and 9.000 words. There are also dictionaries containing 15,000 words for some language combinations. Your choice of dictionary will depend on your knowledge level and goals.

We sincerely believe that our dictionaries will become your trusty assistant in learning foreign languages and will allow you to easily acquire the necessary vocabulary.

TABLE OF CONTENTS

PRONUNCIATION GUIDE

Letter	Indonesian example	T&P phonetic alphabet	English example
Aa	zaman	[a]	shorter than in ask
Bb	besar	[b]	baby, book
Cc	kecil, cepat	[ʧ]	church, French
Dd	dugaan	[d]	day, doctor
Ee	segera, mencium	[e], [ə]	medal, elm
Ff	berfungsi	[f]	face, food
Gg	juga, lagi	[g]	game, gold
Hh	hanya, bahwa	[h]	home, have
Ii	izin, sebagai ganti	[i], [j]	Peter, yard
Jj	setuju, ijin	[dʒ]	jeans, gin
Kk	kemudian, tidak	[k], [ʔ]	kiss, glottal stop
Ll	dilarang	[l]	lace, people
Mm	melihat	[m]	magic, milk
Nn	berenang	[n], [ŋ]	name, ring
Oo	toko roti	[o:]	fall, bomb
Pp	peribahasa	[p]	pencil, private
Qq	Aquarius	[k]	clock, kiss
Rr	ratu, riang	[r]	trilled [r]
Ss	sendok, syarat	[s], [ʃ]	city, machine
Tt	tamu, adat	[t]	tourist, trip
Uu	ambulans	[u]	book
Vv	renovasi	[v]	very, river
Ww	pariwisata	[w]	vase, winter
Xx	boxer	[ks]	box, taxi
Yy	banyak, syarat	[j]	yes, New York
Zz	zamrud	[z]	zebra, please

Combinations of letters

aa	maaf	[aʔa]	a+glottal stop
kh	khawatir	[h]	home, have
th	Gereja Lutheran	[t]	tourist, trip
-k	tidak	[ʔ]	glottal stop

ABBREVIATIONS
used in the vocabulary

English abbreviations

ab.	-	about
adj	-	adjective
adv	-	adverb
anim.	-	animate
as adj	-	attributive noun used as adjective
e.g.	-	for example
etc.	-	et cetera
fam.	-	familiar
fem.	-	feminine
form.	-	formal
inanim.	-	inanimate
masc.	-	masculine
math	-	mathematics
mil.	-	military
n	-	noun
pl	-	plural
pron.	-	pronoun
sb	-	somebody
sing.	-	singular
sth	-	something
v aux	-	auxiliary verb
vi	-	intransitive verb
vi, vt	-	intransitive, transitive verb
vt	-	transitive verb

BASIC CONCEPTS

Basic concepts. Part 1

1. Pronouns

I, me	**saya, aku**	[saja], [aku]
you	**engkau, kamu**	[eŋkau], [kamu]
he, she, it	**beliau, dia, ia**	[beliau], [dia], [ia]
we	**kami, kita**	[kami], [kita]
you (to a group)	**kalian**	[kalian]
you (polite, sing.)	**Anda**	[anda]
you (polite, pl)	**Anda sekalian**	[anda sekalian]
they	**mereka**	[mereka]

2. Greetings. Salutations. Farewells

Hello! (fam.)	**Halo!**	[halo!]
Hello! (form.)	**Halo!**	[halo!]
Good morning!	**Selamat pagi!**	[slamat pagi!]
Good afternoon!	**Selamat siang!**	[slamat siaŋ!]
Good evening!	**Selamat sore!**	[slamat sore!]
to say hello	**menyapa**	[mənjapa]
Hi! (hello)	**Hai!**	[hey!]
greeting (n)	**sambutan, salam**	[sambutan], [salam]
to greet (vt)	**menyambut**	[mənjambut]
How are you?	**Apa kabar?**	[apa kabar?]
What's new?	**Apa yang baru?**	[apa yaŋ baru?]
Goodbye! (form.)	**Selamat tinggal!**	[slamat tiŋgal!],
	Selamat jalan!	[slamat dʒʲalan!]
Bye! (fam.)	**Dadah!**	[dadah!]
See you soon!	**Sampai bertemu lagi!**	[sampaj bərtemu lagi!]
Farewell! (to a friend)	**Sampai jumpa!**	[sampaj dʒʲumpa!]
Farewell! (form.)	**Selamat tinggal!**	[slamat tiŋgal!]
to say goodbye	**berpamitan**	[bərpamitan]
So long!	**Sampai nanti!**	[sampaj nanti!]
Thank you!	**Terima kasih!**	[tərima kasih!]
Thank you very much!	**Terima kasih banyak!**	[tərima kasih banjaʔ!]
You're welcome	**Kembali! Sama-sama!**	[kembali!], [sama-sama!]

| Don't mention it! | Kembali! | [kembali!] |
| It was nothing | Kembali! | [kembali!] |

| Excuse me! (apology) | Maaf, … | [ma'af, …] |
| to excuse (forgive) | memaafkan | [mema'afkan] |

to apologize (vi)	meminta maaf	[meminta ma'af]
My apologies	Maafkan saya	[ma'afkan saja]
I'm sorry!	Maaf!	[ma'af!]
to forgive (vt)	memaafkan	[mema'afkan]
It's okay! (that's all right)	Tidak apa-apa!	[tida' apa-apa!]
please (adv)	tolong	[toloŋ]

Don't forget!	Jangan lupa!	[dʒaŋan lupa!]
Certainly!	Tentu!	[tentu!]
Of course not!	Tentu tidak!	[tentu tida'!]
Okay! (I agree)	Baiklah! Baik!	[bajklah!], [baj'!]
That's enough!	Cukuplah!	[tʃukuplah!]

3. Cardinal numbers. Part 1

0 zero	nol	[nol]
1 one	satu	[satu]
2 two	dua	[dua]
3 three	tiga	[tiga]
4 four	empat	[empat]

5 five	lima	[lima]
6 six	enam	[enam]
7 seven	tujuh	[tudʒuh]
8 eight	delapan	[delapan]
9 nine	sembilan	[sembilan]

10 ten	sepuluh	[sepuluh]
11 eleven	sebelas	[sebelas]
12 twelve	dua belas	[dua belas]
13 thirteen	tiga belas	[tiga belas]
14 fourteen	empat belas	[empat belas]

15 fifteen	lima belas	[lima belas]
16 sixteen	enam belas	[enam belas]
17 seventeen	tujuh belas	[tudʒuh belas]
18 eighteen	delapan belas	[delapan belas]
19 nineteen	sembilan belas	[sembilan belas]

20 twenty	dua puluh	[dua puluh]
21 twenty-one	dua puluh satu	[dua puluh satu]
22 twenty-two	dua puluh dua	[dua puluh dua]
23 twenty-three	dua puluh tiga	[dua puluh tiga]
30 thirty	tiga puluh	[tiga puluh]

31 thirty-one	tiga puluh satu	[tiga puluh satu]
32 thirty-two	tiga puluh dua	[tiga puluh dua]
33 thirty-three	tiga puluh tiga	[tiga puluh tiga]
40 forty	empat puluh	[empat puluh]
41 forty-one	empat puluh satu	[empat puluh satu]
42 forty-two	empat puluh dua	[empat puluh dua]
43 forty-three	empat puluh tiga	[empat puluh tiga]
50 fifty	lima puluh	[lima puluh]
51 fifty-one	lima puluh satu	[lima puluh satu]
52 fifty-two	lima puluh dua	[lima puluh dua]
53 fifty-three	lima puluh tiga	[lima puluh tiga]
60 sixty	enam puluh	[enam puluh]
61 sixty-one	enam puluh satu	[enam puluh satu]
62 sixty-two	enam puluh dua	[enam puluh dua]
63 sixty-three	enam puluh tiga	[enam puluh tiga]
70 seventy	tujuh puluh	[tudʒʲuh puluh]
71 seventy-one	tujuh puluh satu	[tudʒʲuh puluh satu]
72 seventy-two	tujuh puluh dua	[tudʒʲuh puluh dua]
73 seventy-three	tujuh puluh tiga	[tudʒʲuh puluh tiga]
80 eighty	delapan puluh	[delapan puluh]
81 eighty-one	delapan puluh satu	[delapan puluh satu]
82 eighty-two	delapan puluh dua	[delapan puluh dua]
83 eighty-three	delapan puluh tiga	[delapan puluh tiga]
90 ninety	sembilan puluh	[sembilan puluh]
91 ninety-one	sembulan puluh satu	[sembulan puluh satu]
92 ninety-two	sembilan puluh dua	[sembilan puluh dua]
93 ninety-three	sembilan puluh tiga	[sembilan puluh tiga]

4. Cardinal numbers. Part 2

100 one hundred	seratus	[seratus]
200 two hundred	dua ratus	[dua ratus]
300 three hundred	tiga ratus	[tiga ratus]
400 four hundred	empat ratus	[empat ratus]
500 five hundred	lima ratus	[lima ratus]
600 six hundred	enam ratus	[enam ratus]
700 seven hundred	tujuh ratus	[tudʒʲuh ratus]
800 eight hundred	delapan ratus	[delapan ratus]
900 nine hundred	sembilan ratus	[sembilan ratus]
1000 one thousand	seribu	[seribu]
2000 two thousand	dua ribu	[dua ribu]
3000 three thousand	tiga ribu	[tiga ribu]

10000 ten thousand	sepuluh ribu	[sepuluh ribu]
one hundred thousand	seratus ribu	[seratus ribu]
million	juta	[dʒuta]
billion	miliar	[miliar]

5. Numbers. Fractions

fraction	pecahan	[petʃahan]
one half	seperdua	[seperdua]
one third	sepertiga	[sepertiga]
one quarter	seperempat	[seperempat]

one eighth	seperdelapan	[seperdelapan]
one tenth	sepersepuluh	[sepersepuluh]
two thirds	dua pertiga	[dua pərtiga]
three quarters	tiga perempat	[tiga pərempat]

6. Numbers. Basic operations

subtraction	pengurangan	[peŋuraŋan]
to subtract (vi, vt)	mengurangkan	[məŋuraŋkan]
division	pembagian	[pembagian]
to divide (vt)	membagi	[membagi]

addition	penambahan	[penambahan]
to add up (vt)	menambahkan	[mənambahkan]
to add (vi, vt)	menambahkan	[mənambahkan]
multiplication	pengalian	[peŋalian]
to multiply (vt)	mengalikan	[məŋalikan]

7. Numbers. Miscellaneous

digit, figure	angka	[aŋka]
number	nomor	[nomor]
numeral	kata bilangan	[kata bilaŋan]
minus sign	minus	[minus]
plus sign	plus	[plus]
formula	rumus	[rumus]

calculation	perhitungan	[pərhituŋan]
to count (vi, vt)	menghitung	[məŋhituŋ]
to count up	menghitung	[məŋhituŋ]
to compare (vt)	membandingkan	[membandiŋkan]

| How much? | Berapa? | [bərapa?] |
| sum, total | jumlah | [dʒumlah] |

result	hasil	[hasil]
remainder	sisa, baki	[sisa], [baki]

a few (a.g., = years ago)	beberapa	[beberapa]
little (I had ~ time)	sedikit	[sedikit]
the rest	selebihnya, sisanya	[selebihnja], [sisanja]
one and a half	satu setengah	[satu seteŋah]
dozen	lusin	[lusin]

in half (adv)	dua bagian	[dua bagian]
equally (evenly)	rata	[rata]
half	setengah	[seteŋah]
time (three ~s)	kali	[kali]

8. The most important verbs. Part 1

to advise (vt)	menasihati	[mənasihati]
to agree (say yes)	setuju	[setudʒʲu]
to answer (vi, vt)	menjawab	[məndʒʲawab]
to apologize (vi)	meminta maaf	[meminta ma'af]
to arrive (vi)	datang	[dataŋ]

to ask (~ oneself)	bertanya	[bərtanja]
to ask (~ sb to do sth)	meminta	[meminta]
to be (~ a teacher)	ialah, adalah	[ialah], [adalah]
to be (~ on a diet)	sedang	[sedaŋ]

to be afraid	takut	[takut]
to be hungry	lapar	[lapar]
to be interested in …	menaruh minat pada …	[mənaruh minat pada …]
to be needed	dibutuhkan	[dibutuhkan]
to be surprised	heran	[heran]

to be thirsty	haus	[haus]
to begin (vt)	memulai, membuka	[memulaj], [membuka]
to belong to …	kepunyaan …	[kepunja'an …]
to boast (vi)	membual	[membual]
to break (split into pieces)	memecahkan	[memetʃahkan]

to call (~ for help)	memanggil	[memaŋgil]
can (v aux)	bisa	[bisa]
to catch (vt)	menangkap	[mənaŋkap]
to change (vt)	mengubah	[məŋubah]
to choose (select)	memilih	[memilih]

to come down (the stairs)	turun	[turun]
to compare (vt)	membandingkan	[membandiŋkan]
to complain (vi, vt)	mengeluh	[məŋeluh]
to confuse (mix up)	bingung membedakan	[biŋuŋ membedakan]
to continue (vt)	meneruskan	[mənəruskan]

to control (vt)	mengontrol	[məŋontrol]
to cook (dinner)	memasak	[memasaʔ]
to cost (vt)	berharga	[bərharga]
to count (add up)	menghitung	[məŋhituŋ]
to count on ...	mengharapkan ...	[məŋharapkan ...]
to create (vt)	menciptakan	[məntʃiptakan]
to cry (weep)	menangis	[mənaŋis]

9. The most important verbs. Part 2

to deceive (vi, vt)	menipu	[mənipu]
to decorate (tree, street)	menghiasi	[məŋhiasi]
to defend (a country, etc.)	membela	[membela]
to demand (request firmly)	menuntut	[mənuntut]
to dig (vt)	menggali	[məŋgali]

to discuss (vt)	membicarakan	[membitʃarakan]
to do (vt)	membuat	[membuat]
to doubt (have doubts)	ragu-ragu	[ragu-ragu]
to drop (let fall)	tercecer	[tərtʃetʃer]
to enter (room, house, etc.)	masuk, memasuki	[masuk], [memasuki]

to excuse (forgive)	memaafkan	[memaʔafkan]
to exist (vi)	ada	[ada]
to expect (foresee)	menduga	[mənduga]
to explain (vt)	menjelaskan	[məndʒˈelaskan]
to fall (vi)	jatuh	[dʒˈatuh]

to find (vt)	menemukan	[mənemukan]
to finish (vt)	mengakhiri	[məŋahiri]
to fly (vi)	terbang	[tərbaŋ]
to follow ... (come after)	mengikuti ...	[məŋikuti ...]
to forget (vi, vt)	melupakan	[melupakan]

to forgive (vt)	memaafkan	[memaʔafkan]
to give (vt)	memberi	[memberi]
to give a hint	memberi petunjuk	[memberi petundʒˈuʔ]
to go (on foot)	berjalan	[bərdʒˈalan]

to go for a swim	berenang	[bərenaŋ]
to go out (for dinner, etc.)	keluar	[keluar]
to guess (the answer)	menerka	[mənerka]

to have (vt)	mempunyai	[mempunjaj]
to have breakfast	sarapan	[sarapan]
to have dinner	makan malam	[makan malam]
to have lunch	makan siang	[makan siaŋ]
to hear (vt)	mendengar	[məndeŋar]
to help (vt)	membantu	[membantu]

to hide (vt)	menyembunyikan	[mənjembunjikan]
to hope (vi, vt)	berharap	[bərharap]
to hunt (vi, vt)	berburu	[bərburu]
to hurry (vi)	tergesa-gesa	[tərgesa-gesa]

10. The most important verbs. Part 3

to inform (vt)	menginformasikan	[məninformasikan]
to insist (vi, vt)	mendesak	[məndesaʔ]
to insult (vt)	menghina	[mənhina]
to invite (vt)	mengundang	[məŋundaŋ]
to joke (vi)	bergurau	[bərgurau]

to keep (vt)	menyimpan	[mənjimpan]
to keep silent	diam	[diam]
to kill (vt)	membunuh	[membunuh]
to know (sb)	kenal	[kenal]
to know (sth)	tahu	[tahu]
to laugh (vi)	tertawa	[tərtawa]

to liberate (city, etc.)	membebaskan	[membebaskan]
to like (I like …)	suka	[suka]
to look for … (search)	mencari …	[məntʃari …]
to love (sb)	mencintai	[məntʃintaj]
to make a mistake	salah	[salah]
to manage, to run	memimpin	[memimpin]
to mean (signify)	berarti	[bərarti]
to mention (talk about)	menyebut	[mənjebut]
to miss (school, etc.)	absen	[absen]
to notice (see)	memperhatikan	[memperhatikan]

to object (vi, vt)	keberatan	[keberatan]
to observe (see)	mengamati	[məŋamati]
to open (vt)	membuka	[membuka]
to order (meal, etc.)	memesan	[memesan]
to order (mil.)	memerintahkan	[memerintahkan]
to own (possess)	memiliki	[memiliki]

to participate (vi)	turut serta	[turut serta]
to pay (vi, vt)	membayar	[membajar]
to permit (vt)	mengizinkan	[mənizinkan]
to plan (vt)	merencanakan	[merentʃanakan]
to play (children)	bermain	[bərmajn]

to pray (vi, vt)	bersembahyang, berdoa	[bərsembahjaŋ], [bərdoa]
to prefer (vt)	lebih suka	[lebih suka]
to promise (vt)	berjanji	[bərdʒ'andʒi]
to pronounce (vt)	melafalkan	[melafalkan]
to propose (vt)	mengusulkan	[məŋusulkan]
to punish (vt)	menghukum	[mənhukum]

11. The most important verbs. Part 4

to read (vi, vt)	**membaca**	[membatʃa]
to recommend (vt)	**merekomendasi**	[merekomendasi]
to refuse (vi, vt)	**menolak**	[mənolaʔ]
to regret (be sorry)	**menyesal**	[mənjesal]
to rent (sth from sb)	**menyewa**	[mənjewa]
to repeat (say again)	**mengulangi**	[məŋulaŋi]
to reserve, to book	**memesan**	[memesan]
to run (vi)	**lari**	[lari]
to save (rescue)	**menyelamatkan**	[mənjelamatkan]
to say (~ thank you)	**berkata**	[bərkata]
to scold (vt)	**memarahi, menegur**	[memarahi], [menegur]
to see (vt)	**melihat**	[melihat]
to sell (vt)	**menjual**	[məndʒiual]
to send (vt)	**mengirim**	[məɲirim]
to shoot (vi)	**menembak**	[mənembaʔ]
to shout (vi)	**berteriak**	[bərteriaʔ]
to show (vt)	**menunjukkan**	[mənundʒiuʔkan]
to sign (document)	**menandatangani**	[mənandataŋani]
to sit down (vi)	**duduk**	[duduʔ]
to smile (vi)	**tersenyum**	[tərsenyum]
to speak (vi, vt)	**berbicara**	[bərbitʃara]
to steal (money, etc.)	**mencuri**	[məntʃuri]
to stop (for pause, etc.)	**berhenti**	[bərhenti]
to stop (please ~ calling me)	**menghentikan**	[mənhentikan]
to study (vt)	**mempelajari**	[mempeladʒiari]
to swim (vi)	**berenang**	[bərenaŋ]
to take (vt)	**mengambil**	[məŋambil]
to think (vi, vt)	**berpikir**	[bərpikir]
to threaten (vt)	**mengancam**	[mənantʃam]
to touch (with hands)	**menyentuh**	[mənjentuh]
to translate (vt)	**menerjemahkan**	[mənerdʒiemahkan]
to trust (vt)	**mempercayai**	[mempertʃajaj]
to try (attempt)	**mencoba**	[məntʃoba]
to turn (e.g., ~ left)	**membelok**	[membeloʔ]
to underestimate (vt)	**meremehkan**	[meremehkan]
to understand (vt)	**mengerti**	[məɲerti]
to unite (vt)	**menyatukan**	[mənjatukan]
to wait (vt)	**menunggu**	[mənuŋgu]
to want (wish, desire)	**mau, ingin**	[mau], [iŋin]
to warn (vt)	**memperingatkan**	[memperiŋatkan]

to work (vi)	bekerja	[bekerdʒʲa]
to write (vt)	menulis	[mənulis]
to write down	mencatat	[məntʃatat]

12. Colors

color	warna	[warna]
shade (tint)	nuansa	[nuansa]
hue	warna	[warna]
rainbow	pelangi	[pelaɲi]

white (adj)	putih	[putih]
black (adj)	hitam	[hitam]
gray (adj)	kelabu	[kelabu]

green (adj)	hijau	[hidʒʲau]
yellow (adj)	kuning	[kuniŋ]
red (adj)	merah	[merah]
blue (adj)	biru	[biru]
light blue (adj)	biru muda	[biru muda]
pink (adj)	pink	[pinʔ]
orange (adj)	oranye, jingga	[oranje], [dʒiŋga]
violet (adj)	violet, ungu muda	[violet], [uŋu muda]
brown (adj)	cokelat	[tʃokelat]

golden (adj)	keemasan	[keemasan]
silvery (adj)	keperakan	[keperakan]
beige (adj)	abu-abu kecokelatan	[abu-abu ketʃokelatan]
cream (adj)	krem	[krem]
turquoise (adj)	pirus	[pirus]
cherry red (adj)	merah tua	[merah tua]
lilac (adj)	ungu	[uŋu]
crimson (adj)	merah lembayung	[merah lembajuŋ]

light (adj)	terang	[teraŋ]
dark (adj)	gelap	[gelap]
bright, vivid (adj)	terang	[teraŋ]

colored (pencils)	berwarna	[bərwarna]
color (e.g., ~ film)	warna	[warna]
black-and-white (adj)	hitam-putih	[hitam-putih]
plain (one-colored)	polos, satu warna	[polos], [satu warna]
multicolored (adj)	berwarna-warni	[bərwarna-warni]

13. Questions

| Who? | Siapa? | [siapa?] |
| What? | Apa? | [apa?] |

Where? (at, in)	Di mana?	[di mana?]
Where (to)?	Ke mana?	[ke mana?]
From where?	Dari mana?	[dari mana?]
When?	Kapan?	[kapan?]
Why? (What for?)	Mengapa?	[mənapa?]
Why? (~ are you crying?)	Mengapa?	[mənapa?]

What for?	Untuk apa?	[untu' apa?]
How? (in what way)	Bagaimana?	[bagajmana?]
What? (What kind of ...?)	Apa? Yang mana?	[apa?], [yaŋ mana?]
Which?	Yang mana?	[yaŋ mana?]

To whom?	Kepada siapa? Untuk siapa?	[kepada siapa?], [untu' siapa?]
About whom?	Tentang siapa?	[tentaŋ siapa?]
About what?	Tentang apa?	[tentaŋ apa?]
With whom?	Dengan siapa?	[deŋan siapa?]

| How many? How much? | Berapa? | [bərapa?] |
| Whose? | Milik siapa? | [mili' siapa?] |

14. Function words. Adverbs. Part 1

Where? (at, in)	Di mana?	[di mana?]
here (adv)	di sini	[di sini]
there (adv)	di sana	[di sana]

| somewhere (to be) | di suatu tempat | [di suatu tempat] |
| nowhere (not anywhere) | tak ada di mana pun | [ta' ada di mana pun] |

| by (near, beside) | dekat | [dekat] |
| by the window | dekat jendela | [dekat dʒʲendela] |

Where (to)?	Ke mana?	[ke mana?]
here (e.g., come ~!)	ke sini	[ke sini]
there (e.g., to go ~)	ke sana	[ke sana]
from here (adv)	dari sini	[dari sini]
from there (adv)	dari sana	[dari sana]

| close (adv) | dekat | [dekat] |
| far (adv) | jauh | [dʒʲauh] |

near (e.g., ~ Paris)	dekat	[dekat]
nearby (adv)	dekat	[dekat]
not far (adv)	tidak jauh	[tida' dʒʲauh]

left (adj)	kiri	[kiri]
on the left	di kiri	[di kiri]
to the left	ke kiri	[ke kiri]
right (adj)	kanan	[kanan]

on the right	di kanan	[di kanan]
to the right	ke kanan	[ke kanan]
in front (adv)	di depan	[di depan]
front (as adj)	depan	[depan]
ahead (the kids ran ~)	ke depan	[ke depan]
behind (adv)	di belakang	[di belakaŋ]
from behind	dari belakang	[dari belakaŋ]
back (towards the rear)	mundur	[mundur]
middle	tengah	[teŋah]
in the middle	di tengah	[di teŋah]
at the side	di sisi, di samping	[di sisi], [di sampiŋ]
everywhere (adv)	di mana-mana	[di mana-mana]
around (in all directions)	di sekitar	[di sekitar]
from inside	dari dalam	[dari dalam]
somewhere (to go)	ke suatu tempat	[ke suatu tempat]
straight (directly)	terus	[terus]
back (e.g., come ~)	kembali	[kembali]
from anywhere	dari mana pun	[dari mana pun]
from somewhere	dari suatu tempat	[dari suatu tempat]
firstly (adv)	pertama	[pertama]
secondly (adv)	kedua	[kedua]
thirdly (adv)	ketiga	[ketiga]
suddenly (adv)	tiba-tiba	[tiba-tiba]
at first (in the beginning)	mula-mula	[mula-mula]
for the first time	untuk pertama kalinya	[untu' pertama kalinja]
long before …	jauh sebelum …	[dʒauh sebelum …]
anew (over again)	kembali	[kembali]
for good (adv)	untuk selama-lamanya	[untu' selama-lamanja]
never (adv)	tidak pernah	[tida' pernah]
again (adv)	lagi, kembali	[lagi], [kembali]
now (adv)	sekarang	[sekaraŋ]
often (adv)	sering, seringkali	[seriŋ], [seriŋkali]
then (adv)	ketika itu	[ketika itu]
urgently (quickly)	segera	[segera]
usually (adv)	biasanya	[biasanja]
by the way, …	ngomong-ngomong …	[ŋomoŋ-ŋomoŋ …]
possible (that is ~)	mungkin	[muŋkin]
probably (adv)	mungkin	[muŋkin]
maybe (adv)	mungkin	[muŋkin]
besides …	selain itu …	[selajn itu …]
that's why …	karena itu …	[karena itu …]
in spite of …	meskipun …	[meskipun …]

thanks to ...	berkat ...	[berkat ...]
what (pron.)	apa	[apa]
that (conj.)	bahwa	[bahwa]
something	sesuatu	[sesuatu]
anything (something)	sesuatu	[sesuatu]
nothing	tidak sesuatu pun	[tida' sesuatu pun]
who (pron.)	siapa	[siapa]
someone	seseorang	[seseoraŋ]
somebody	seseorang	[seseoraŋ]
nobody	tidak seorang pun	[tida' seoraŋ pun]
nowhere (a voyage to ~)	tidak ke mana pun	[tida' ke mana pun]
nobody's	tidak milik siapa pun	[tida' mili' siapa pun]
somebody's	milik seseorang	[mili' seseoraŋ]
so (I'm ~ glad)	sangat	[saŋat]
also (as well)	juga	[dʒiuga]
too (as well)	juga	[dʒiuga]

15. Function words. Adverbs. Part 2

Why?	Mengapa?	[meŋapa?]
for some reason	entah mengapa	[entah meŋapa]
because ...	karena ...	[karena ...]
for some purpose	untuk tujuan tertentu	[untu' tudʒiuan tertentu]
and	dan	[dan]
or	atau	[atau]
but	tetapi, namun	[tetapi], [namun]
for (e.g., ~ me)	untuk	[untu']
too (~ many people)	terlalu	[terlalu]
only (exclusively)	hanya	[hanja]
exactly (adv)	tepat	[tepat]
about (more or less)	sekitar	[sekitar]
approximately (adv)	kira-kira	[kira-kira]
approximate (adj)	kira-kira	[kira-kira]
almost (adv)	hampir	[hampir]
the rest	selebihnya, sisanya	[selebihnja], [sisanja]
the other (second)	kedua	[kedua]
other (different)	lain	[lain]
each (adj)	setiap	[setiap]
any (no matter which)	sebarang	[sebaraŋ]
many, much (a lot of)	banyak	[banja']
many people	banyak orang	[banja' oraŋ]
all (everyone)	semua	[semua]
in return for ...	sebagai ganti ...	[sebagaj ganti ...]

in exchange (adv)	**sebagai gantinya**	[sebagaj gantinja]
by hand (made)	**dengan tangan**	[deŋan taŋan]
hardly (negative opinion)	**hampir tidak**	[hampir tidaʔ]

probably (adv)	**mungkin**	[muŋkin]
on purpose (intentionally)	**sengaja**	[seŋadʒʲa]
by accident (adv)	**tidak sengaja**	[tidaʔ seŋadʒʲa]

very (adv)	**sangat**	[saŋat]
for example (adv)	**misalnya**	[misalnja]
between	**antara**	[antara]
among	**di antara**	[di antara]
so much (such a lot)	**banyak sekali**	[banjaʔ sekali]
especially (adv)	**terutama**	[tərutama]

Basic concepts. Part 2

16. Weekdays

Monday	**Hari Senin**	[hari senin]
Tuesday	**Hari Selasa**	[hari selasa]
Wednesday	**Hari Rabu**	[hari rabu]
Thursday	**Hari Kamis**	[hari kamis]
Friday	**Hari Jumat**	[hari dʒʲumat]
Saturday	**Hari Sabtu**	[hari sabtu]
Sunday	**Hari Minggu**	[hari miŋgu]
today (adv)	**hari ini**	[hari ini]
tomorrow (adv)	**besok**	[besoʔ]
the day after tomorrow	**besok lusa**	[besoʔ lusa]
yesterday (adv)	**kemarin**	[kemarin]
the day before yesterday	**kemarin dulu**	[kemarin dulu]
day	**hari**	[hari]
working day	**hari kerja**	[hari kerdʒʲa]
public holiday	**hari libur**	[hari libur]
day off	**hari libur**	[hari libur]
weekend	**akhir pekan**	[ahir pekan]
all day long	**seharian**	[seharian]
the next day (adv)	**hari berikutnya**	[hari berikutnja]
two days ago	**dua hari lalu**	[dua hari lalu]
the day before	**hari sebelumnya**	[hari sebelumnja]
daily (adj)	**harian**	[harian]
every day (adv)	**tiap hari**	[tiap hari]
week	**minggu**	[miŋgu]
last week (adv)	**minggu lalu**	[miŋgu lalu]
next week (adv)	**minggu berikutnya**	[miŋgu berikutnja]
weekly (adj)	**mingguan**	[miŋguan]
every week (adv)	**tiap minggu**	[tiap miŋgu]
twice a week	**dua kali seminggu**	[dua kali semiŋgu]
every Tuesday	**tiap Hari Selasa**	[tiap hari selasa]

17. Hours. Day and night

morning	**pagi**	[pagi]
in the morning	**pada pagi hari**	[pada pagi hari]
noon, midday	**tengah hari**	[teŋah hari]

in the afternoon	**pada sore hari**	[pada sore hari]
evening	**sore, malam**	[sore], [malam]
in the evening	**waktu sore**	[waktu sore]
night	**malam**	[malam]
at night	**pada malam hari**	[pada malam hari]
midnight	**tengah malam**	[teŋah malam]

second	**detik**	[detiʔ]
minute	**menit**	[menit]
hour	**jam**	[dʒⁱam]
half an hour	**setengah jam**	[seteŋah dʒⁱam]
a quarter-hour	**seperempat jam**	[seperempat dʒⁱam]
fifteen minutes	**lima belas menit**	[lima belas menit]
24 hours	**siang-malam**	[siaŋ-malam]

sunrise	**matahari terbit**	[matahari tərbit]
dawn	**subuh**	[subuh]
early morning	**dini pagi**	[dini pagi]
sunset	**matahari terbenam**	[matahari tərbenam]

early in the morning	**pagi-pagi**	[pagi-pagi]
this morning	**pagi ini**	[pagi ini]
tomorrow morning	**besok pagi**	[besoʔ pagi]
this afternoon	**sore ini**	[sore ini]
in the afternoon	**pada sore hari**	[pada sore hari]
tomorrow afternoon	**besok sore**	[besoʔ sore]
tonight (this evening)	**sore ini**	[sore ini]
tomorrow night	**besok malam**	[besoʔ malam]

at 3 o'clock sharp	**pukul 3 tepat**	[pukul tiga tepat]
about 4 o'clock	**sekitar pukul 4**	[sekitar pukul empat]
by 12 o'clock	**pada pukul 12**	[pada pukul belas]

in 20 minutes	**dalam 20 menit**	[dalam dua puluh menit]
in an hour	**dalam satu jam**	[dalam satu dʒⁱam]
on time (adv)	**tepat waktu**	[tepat waktu]

a quarter of …	**… kurang seperempat**	[… kuraŋ seperempat]
within an hour	**selama sejam**	[selama sedʒⁱam]
every 15 minutes	**tiap 15 menit**	[tiap lima belas menit]
round the clock	**siang-malam**	[siaŋ-malam]

18. Months. Seasons

January	**Januari**	[dʒⁱanuari]
February	**Februari**	[februari]
March	**Maret**	[maret]
April	**April**	[april]
May	**Mei**	[mei]
June	**Juni**	[dʒⁱuni]

July	Juli	[dʒuli]
August	**Augustus**	[augustus]
September	**September**	[september]
October	**Oktober**	[oktober]
November	**November**	[november]
December	**Desember**	[desember]
spring	**musim semi**	[musim semi]
in spring	**pada musim semi**	[pada musim semi]
spring (as adj)	**musim semi**	[musim semi]
summer	**musim panas**	[musim panas]
in summer	**pada musim panas**	[pada musim panas]
summer (as adj)	**musim panas**	[musim panas]
fall	**musim gugur**	[musim gugur]
in fall	**pada musim gugur**	[pada musim gugur]
fall (as adj)	**musim gugur**	[musim gugur]
winter	**musim dingin**	[musim diŋin]
in winter	**pada musim dingin**	[pada musim diŋin]
winter (as adj)	**musim dingin**	[musim diŋin]
month	**bulan**	[bulan]
this month	**bulan ini**	[bulan ini]
next month	**bulan depan**	[bulan depan]
last month	**bulan lalu**	[bulan lalu]
a month ago	**sebulan lalu**	[sebulan lalu]
in a month (a month later)	**dalam satu bulan**	[dalam satu bulan]
in 2 months (2 months later)	**dalam 2 bulan**	[dalam dua bulan]
the whole month	**sepanjang bulan**	[sepandʒiaŋ bulan]
all month long	**sebulan penuh**	[sebulan penuh]
monthly (~ magazine)	**bulanan**	[bulanan]
monthly (adv)	**tiap bulan**	[tiap bulan]
every month	**tiap bulan**	[tiap bulan]
twice a month	**dua kali sebulan**	[dua kali sebulan]
year	**tahun**	[tahun]
this year	**tahun ini**	[tahun ini]
next year	**tahun depan**	[tahun depan]
last year	**tahun lalu**	[tahun lalu]
a year ago	**setahun lalu**	[setahun lalu]
in a year	**dalam satu tahun**	[dalam satu tahun]
in two years	**dalam 2 tahun**	[dalam dua tahun]
the whole year	**sepanjang tahun**	[sepandʒiaŋ tahun]
all year long	**setahun penuh**	[setahun penuh]
every year	**tiap tahun**	[tiap tahun]

annual (adj)	tahunan	[tahunan]
annually (adv)	tiap tahun	[tiap tahun]
4 times a year	empat kali setahun	[empat kali setahun]

date (e.g., today's ~)	tanggal	[taŋgal]
date (e.g., ~ of birth)	tanggal	[taŋgal]
calendar	kalender	[kalender]

half a year	setengah tahun	[seteŋah tahun]
six months	enam bulan	[enam bulan]
season (summer, etc.)	musim	[musim]
century	abad	[abad]

19. Time. Miscellaneous

time	waktu	[waktu]
moment	sekejap	[sekedʒⁱap]
instant (n)	saat, waktu	[sa'at], [waktu]
instant (adj)	seketika	[seketika]
lapse (of time)	jangka waktu	[dʒⁱaŋka waktu]
life	kehidupan, hidup	[kehidupan], [hidup]
eternity	keabadiaan	[keabadia'an]

epoch	zaman	[zaman]
era	era	[era]
cycle	siklus	[siklus]
period	periode, kurun waktu	[periode], [kurun waktu]
term (short-~)	jangka waktu	[dʒⁱaŋka waktu]

the future	masa depan	[masa depan]
future (as adj)	yang akan datang	[yaŋ akan dataŋ]
next time	lain kali	[lain kali]
the past	masa lalu	[masa lalu]
past (recent)	lalu	[lalu]
last time	terakhir kali	[terahir kali]

later (adv)	kemudian	[kemudian]
after (prep.)	sesudah	[sesudah]
nowadays (adv)	sekarang	[sekaraŋ]
now (adv)	saat ini	[sa'at ini]
immediately (adv)	segera	[segera]
soon (adv)	segera	[segera]
in advance (beforehand)	sebelumnya	[sebelumnja]

a long time ago	dahulu kala	[dahulu kala]
recently (adv)	baru-baru ini	[baru-baru ini]
destiny	nasib	[nasib]
memories (childhood ~)	kenang-kenangan	[kenaŋ-kenaŋan]
archives	arsip	[arsip]
during ...	selama ...	[selama ...]

long, a long time (adv)	lama	[lama]
not long (adv)	tidak lama	[tida' lama]
early (in the morning)	pagi-pagi	[pagi-pagi]
late (not early)	terlambat	[tərlambat]

forever (for good)	untuk selama-lamanya	[untu' selama-lamanja]
to start (begin)	memulai	[memulaj]
to postpone (vt)	menunda	[mənunda]

at the same time	serentak	[serenta']
permanently (adv)	tetap	[tetap]
constant (noise, pain)	terus menerus	[terus menerus]
temporary (adj)	sementara	[sementara]
sometimes (adv)	kadang-kadang	[kadaŋ-kadaŋ]
rarely (adv)	jarang	[dʒ'araŋ]
often (adv)	sering, seringkali	[seriŋ], [seriŋkali]

20. Opposites

| rich (adj) | kaya | [kaja] |
| poor (adj) | miskin | [miskin] |

| ill, sick (adj) | sakit | [sakit] |
| well (not sick) | sehat | [sehat] |

| big (adj) | besar | [besar] |
| small (adj) | kecil | [ketʃil] |

| quickly (adv) | cepat | [tʃepat] |
| slowly (adv) | perlahan-lahan | [perlahan-lahan] |

| fast (adj) | cepat | [tʃepat] |
| slow (adj) | lambat | [lambat] |

| glad (adj) | riang | [riaŋ] |
| sad (adj) | sedih | [sedih] |

| together (adv) | bersama | [bersama] |
| separately (adv) | terpisah | [terpisah] |

| aloud (to read) | dengan keras | [deŋan keras] |
| silently (to oneself) | dalam hati | [dalam hati] |

| tall (adj) | tinggi | [tiŋgi] |
| low (adj) | rendah | [rendah] |

| deep (adj) | dalam | [dalam] |
| shallow (adj) | dangkal | [daŋkal] |

| yes | ya | [ya] |

no	**tidak**	[tidaʔ]

distant (in space)	**jauh**	[dʒ͡auh]
nearby (adj)	**dekat**	[dekat]

far (adv)	**jauh**	[dʒ͡auh]
nearby (adv)	**dekat**	[dekat]

long (adj)	**panjang**	[pandʒ͡aŋ]
short (adj)	**pendek**	[pendeʔ]

good (kindhearted)	**baik hati**	[bajʔ hati]
evil (adj)	**jahat**	[dʒ͡ahat]

married (adj)	**menikah**	[mənikah]
single (adj)	**bujang**	[budʒ͡aŋ]

to forbid (vt)	**melarang**	[melaraŋ]
to permit (vt)	**mengizinkan**	[məŋizinkan]

end	**akhir**	[ahir]
beginning	**permulaan**	[pərmulaʔan]

left (adj)	**kiri**	[kiri]
right (adj)	**kanan**	[kanan]

first (adj)	**pertama**	[pərtama]
last (adj)	**terakhir**	[tərahir]

crime	**kejahatan**	[kedʒ͡ahatan]
punishment	**hukuman**	[hukuman]

to order (vt)	**memerintahkan**	[memerintahkan]
to obey (vi, vt)	**mematuhi**	[mematuhi]

straight (adj)	**lurus**	[lurus]
curved (adj)	**melengkung**	[meleŋkuŋ]

paradise	**surga**	[surga]
hell	**neraka**	[neraka]

to be born	**lahir**	[lahir]
to die (vi)	**mati, meninggal**	[mati], [meniŋgal]

strong (adj)	**kuat**	[kuat]
weak (adj)	**lemah**	[lemah]

old (adj)	**tua**	[tua]
young (adj)	**muda**	[muda]

old (adj)	**tua**	[tua]
new (adj)	**baru**	[baru]

| hard (adj) | keras | [keras] |
| soft (adj) | lunak | [lunaʔ] |

| warm (tepid) | hangat | [haŋat] |
| cold (adj) | dingin | [diŋin] |

| fat (adj) | gemuk | [gemuʔ] |
| thin (adj) | kurus | [kurus] |

| narrow (adj) | sempit | [sempit] |
| wide (adj) | lebar | [lebar] |

| good (adj) | baik | [bajʔ] |
| bad (adj) | buruk | [buruʔ] |

| brave (adj) | pemberani | [pemberani] |
| cowardly (adj) | penakut | [penakut] |

21. Lines and shapes

square	bujur sangkar	[budʒʲur saŋkar]
square (as adj)	persegi	[pərsegi]
circle	lingkaran	[liŋkaran]
round (adj)	bundar	[bundar]
triangle	segi tiga	[segi tiga]
triangular (adj)	segi tiga	[segi tiga]

oval	oval	[oval]
oval (as adj)	oval	[oval]
rectangle	segi empat	[segi empat]
rectangular (adj)	siku-siku	[siku-siku]

pyramid	piramida	[piramida]
rhombus	rombus	[rombus]
trapezoid	trapesium	[trapesium]
cube	kubus	[kubus]
prism	prisma	[prisma]

circumference	lingkar	[liŋkar]
sphere	bulatan	[bulatan]
ball (solid sphere)	bola	[bola]
diameter	diameter	[diameter]
radius	radius, jari-jari	[radius], [dʒʲari-dʒʲari]
perimeter (circle's ~)	perimeter	[perimeter]
center	pusat	[pusat]

horizontal (adj)	horizontal, mendatar	[horizontal], [mendatar]
vertical (adj)	vertikal, tegak lurus	[vertikal], [tegaʔ lurus]
parallel (n)	sejajar	[sedʒʲadʒʲar]
parallel (as adj)	sejajar	[sedʒʲadʒʲar]

line	garis	[garis]
stroke	garis	[garis]
straight line	garis lurus	[garis lurus]
curve (curved line)	garis lengkung	[garis leŋkuŋ]
thin (line, etc.)	tipis	[tipis]
contour (outline)	kontur	[kontur]

intersection	titik potong	[titiʔ potoŋ]
right angle	sudut siku-siku	[sudut siku-siku]
segment	segmen	[segmen]
sector	sektor	[sektor]
side (of triangle)	segi	[segi]
angle	sudut	[sudut]

22. Units of measurement

weight	berat	[berat]
length	panjang	[pandʒaŋ]
width	lebar	[lebar]
height	ketinggian	[ketiŋgian]
depth	kedalaman	[kedalaman]
volume	volume, isi	[volume], [isi]
area	luas	[luas]

gram	gram	[gram]
milligram	miligram	[miligram]
kilogram	kilogram	[kilogram]
ton	ton	[ton]
pound	pon	[pon]
ounce	ons	[ons]

meter	meter	[meter]
millimeter	milimeter	[milimeter]
centimeter	sentimeter	[sentimeter]
kilometer	kilometer	[kilometer]
mile	mil	[mil]

inch	inci	[intʃi]
foot	kaki	[kaki]
yard	yard	[yard]

| square meter | meter persegi | [meter pərsegi] |
| hectare | hektar | [hektar] |

liter	liter	[liter]
degree	derajat	[deradʒat]
volt	volt	[volt]
ampere	ampere	[ampere]
horsepower	tenaga kuda	[tenaga kuda]
quantity	kuantitas	[kuantitas]

a little bit of ...	sedikit ...	[sedikit ...]
half	setengah	[seteŋah]
dozen	lusin	[lusin]
piece (item)	buah	[buah]
size	ukuran	[ukuran]
scale (map ~)	skala	[skala]
minimal (adj)	minimal	[minimal]
the smallest (adj)	terkecil	[tərketʃil]
medium (adj)	sedang	[sedaŋ]
maximal (adj)	maksimal	[maksimal]
the largest (adj)	terbesar	[tərbesar]

23. Containers

canning jar (glass ~)	gelas	[gelas]
can	kaleng	[kaleŋ]
bucket	ember	[ember]
barrel	tong	[toŋ]
wash basin (e.g., plastic ~)	baskom	[baskom]
tank (100L water ~)	tangki	[taŋki]
hip flask	pelples	[pelples]
jerrycan	jeriken	[dʒ'eriken]
tank (e.g., tank car)	tangki	[taŋki]
mug	mangkuk	[maŋkuʔ]
cup (of coffee, etc.)	cangkir	[tʃaŋkir]
saucer	alas cangkir	[alas tʃaŋkir]
glass (tumbler)	gelas	[gelas]
wine glass	gelas anggur	[gelas aŋgur]
stock pot (soup pot)	panci	[pantʃi]
bottle (~ of wine)	botol	[botol]
neck (of the bottle, etc.)	leher	[leher]
carafe (decanter)	karaf	[karaf]
pitcher	kendi	[kendi]
vessel (container)	wadah	[wadah]
pot (crock, stoneware ~)	pot	[pot]
vase	vas	[vas]
bottle (perfume ~)	botol	[botol]
vial, small bottle	botol kecil	[botol ketʃil]
tube (of toothpaste)	tabung	[tabuŋ]
sack (bag)	karung	[karuŋ]
bag (paper ~, plastic ~)	kantong	[kantoŋ]
pack (of cigarettes, etc.)	bungkus	[buŋkus]

box (e.g., shoebox)	kotak, kardus	[kotak], [kardus]
crate	kotak	[kotaʔ]
basket	bakul	[bakul]

24. Materials

material	bahan	[bahan]
wood (n)	kayu	[kaju]
wood-, wooden (adj)	kayu	[kaju]

| glass (n) | kaca | [katʃa] |
| glass (as adj) | kaca | [katʃa] |

| stone (n) | batu | [batu] |
| stone (as adj) | batu | [batu] |

| plastic (n) | plastik | [plastiʔ] |
| plastic (as adj) | plastik | [plastiʔ] |

| rubber (n) | karet | [karet] |
| rubber (as adj) | karet | [karet] |

| cloth, fabric (n) | kain | [kain] |
| fabric (as adj) | kain | [kain] |

| paper (n) | kertas | [kertas] |
| paper (as adj) | kertas | [kertas] |

| cardboard (n) | karton | [karton] |
| cardboard (as adj) | karton | [karton] |

polyethylene	polietilena	[polietilena]
cellophane	selofana	[selofana]
linoleum	linoleum	[linoleum]
plywood	kayu lapis	[kaju lapis]

porcelain (n)	porselen	[porselen]
porcelain (as adj)	porselen	[porselen]
clay (n)	tanah liat	[tanah liat]
clay (as adj)	gerabah	[gerabah]
ceramic (n)	keramik	[keramiʔ]
ceramic (as adj)	keramik	[keramiʔ]

25. Metals

metal (n)	logam	[logam]
metal (as adj)	logam	[logam]
alloy (n)	aloi, lakur	[aloy], [lakur]

gold (n)	**emas**	[əmɑɑ]
gold, golden (adj)	**emas**	[emas]
silver (n)	**perak**	[peraʔ]
silver (as adj)	**perak**	[peraʔ]
iron (n)	**besi**	[besi]
iron-, made of iron (adj)	**besi**	[besi]
steel (n)	**baja**	[badʒʲa]
steel (as adj)	**baja**	[badʒʲa]
copper (n)	**tembaga**	[tembaga]
copper (as adj)	**tembaga**	[tembaga]
aluminum (n)	**aluminium**	[aluminium]
aluminum (as adj)	**aluminium**	[aluminium]
bronze (n)	**perunggu**	[perungu]
bronze (as adj)	**perunggu**	[perungu]
brass	**kuningan**	[kuniŋan]
nickel	**nikel**	[nikel]
platinum	**platinum**	[platinum]
mercury	**air raksa**	[air raksa]
tin	**timah**	[timah]
lead	**timbal**	[timbal]
zinc	**seng**	[seŋ]

HUMAN BEING

Human being. The body

26. Humans. Basic concepts

human being	**manusia**	[manusia]
man (adult male)	**laki-laki, pria**	[laki-laki], [pria]
woman	**perempuan, wanita**	[pərempuan], [wanita]
child	**anak**	[anaʔ]
girl	**anak perempuan**	[anaʔ pərempuan]
boy	**anak laki-laki**	[anaʔ laki-laki]
teenager	**remaja**	[remadʒʲa]
old man	**lelaki tua**	[lelaki tua]
old woman	**perempuan tua**	[pərempuan tua]

27. Human anatomy

organism (body)	**organisme**	[organisme]
heart	**jantung**	[dʒʲantuŋ]
blood	**darah**	[darah]
artery	**arteri, pembuluh darah**	[arteri], [pembuluh darah]
vein	**vena**	[vena]
brain	**otak**	[otaʔ]
nerve	**saraf**	[saraf]
nerves	**saraf**	[saraf]
vertebra	**ruas**	[ruas]
spine (backbone)	**tulang belakang**	[tulaŋ belakaŋ]
stomach (organ)	**lambung**	[lambuŋ]
intestines, bowels	**usus**	[usus]
intestine (e.g., large ~)	**usus**	[usus]
liver	**hati**	[hati]
kidney	**ginjal**	[gindʒʲal]
bone	**tulang**	[tulaŋ]
skeleton	**skelet, rangka**	[skelet], [raŋka]
rib	**tulang rusuk**	[tulaŋ rusuʔ]
skull	**tengkorak**	[teŋkoraʔ]
muscle	**otot**	[otot]
biceps	**bisep**	[bisep]

triceps	**trisep**	[trisep]
tendon	**tendon**	[tendon]
joint	**sendi**	[sendi]
lungs	**paru-paru**	[paru-paru]
genitals	**kemaluan**	[kemaluan]
skin	**kulit**	[kulit]

28. Head

head	**kepala**	[kepala]
face	**wajah**	[waʤah]
nose	**hidung**	[hiduŋ]
mouth	**mulut**	[mulut]

eye	**mata**	[mata]
eyes	**mata**	[mata]
pupil	**pupil, biji mata**	[pupil], [biʤi mata]
eyebrow	**alis**	[alis]
eyelash	**bulu mata**	[bulu mata]
eyelid	**kelopak mata**	[kelopaʔ mata]

tongue	**lidah**	[lidah]
tooth	**gigi**	[gigi]
lips	**bibir**	[bibir]
cheekbones	**tulang pipi**	[tulaŋ pipi]
gum	**gusi**	[gusi]
palate	**langit-langit mulut**	[laŋit-laŋit mulut]

nostrils	**lubang hidung**	[lubaŋ hiduŋ]
chin	**dagu**	[dagu]
jaw	**rahang**	[rahaŋ]
cheek	**pipi**	[pipi]

forehead	**dahi**	[dahi]
temple	**pelipis**	[pelipis]
ear	**telinga**	[teliŋa]
back of the head	**tengkuk**	[teŋkuʔ]
neck	**leher**	[leher]
throat	**tenggorok**	[teŋgoroʔ]

hair	**rambut**	[rambut]
hairstyle	**tatanan rambut**	[tatanan rambut]
haircut	**potongan rambut**	[potoŋan rambut]
wig	**wig, rambut palsu**	[wig], [rambut palsu]

mustache	**kumis**	[kumis]
beard	**janggut**	[ʤaŋgut]
to have (a beard, etc.)	**memelihara**	[memelihara]
braid	**kepang**	[kepaŋ]
sideburns	**brewok**	[brewoʔ]

red-haired (adj)	merah pirang	[merah piraŋ]
gray (hair)	beruban	[bəruban]
bald (adj)	botak, plontos	[botak], [plontos]
bald patch	botak	[botaʔ]
ponytail	ekor kuda	[ekor kuda]
bangs	poni rambut	[poni rambut]

29. Human body

hand	tangan	[taŋan]
arm	lengan	[leŋan]
finger	jari	[dʒˈari]
toe	jari	[dʒˈari]
thumb	jempol	[dʒˈempol]
little finger	jari kelingking	[dʒˈari keliŋkiŋ]
nail	kuku	[kuku]
fist	kepalan tangan	[kepalan taŋan]
palm	telapak	[telapaʔ]
wrist	pergelangan	[pərgelaŋan]
forearm	lengan bawah	[leŋan bawah]
elbow	siku	[siku]
shoulder	bahu	[bahu]
leg	kaki	[kaki]
foot	telapak kaki	[telapaʔ kaki]
knee	lutut	[lutut]
calf (part of leg)	betis	[betis]
hip	paha	[paha]
heel	tumit	[tumit]
body	tubuh	[tubuh]
stomach	perut	[perut]
chest	dada	[dada]
breast	payudara	[pajudara]
flank	rusuk	[rusuʔ]
back	punggung	[puŋguŋ]
lower back	pinggang bawah	[piŋgan bawah]
waist	pinggang	[piŋgaŋ]
navel (belly button)	pusar	[pusar]
buttocks	pantat	[pantat]
bottom	pantat	[pantat]
beauty mark	tanda lahir	[tanda lahir]
birthmark (café au lait spot)	tanda lahir	[tanda lahir]
tattoo	tato	[tato]
scar	parut luka	[parut luka]

Clothing & Accessories

30. Outerwear. Coats

clothes	**pakaian**	[pakajan]
outerwear	**pakaian luar**	[pakajan luar]
winter clothing	**pakaian musim dingin**	[pakajan musim diŋin]
coat (overcoat)	**mantel**	[mantel]
fur coat	**mantel bulu**	[mantel bulu]
fur jacket	**jaket bulu**	[ʤʲaket bulu]
down coat	**jaket bulu halus**	[ʤʲaket bulu halus]
jacket (e.g., leather ~)	**jaket**	[ʤʲaket]
raincoat (trenchcoat, etc.)	**jas hujan**	[ʤʲas huʤʲan]
waterproof (adj)	**kedap air**	[kedap air]

31. Men's & women's clothing

shirt (button shirt)	**kemeja**	[kemeʤʲa]
pants	**celana**	[ʧelana]
jeans	**celana jins**	[ʧelana ʤins]
suit jacket	**jas**	[ʤʲas]
suit	**setelan**	[setelan]
dress (frock)	**gaun**	[gaun]
skirt	**rok**	[roʔ]
blouse	**blus**	[blus]
knitted jacket (cardigan, etc.)	**jaket wol**	[ʤʲaket wol]
jacket (of woman's suit)	**jaket**	[ʤʲaket]
T-shirt	**baju kaus**	[baʤʲu kaus]
shorts (short trousers)	**celana pendek**	[ʧelana pendeʔ]
tracksuit	**pakaian olahraga**	[pakajan olahraga]
bathrobe	**jubah mandi**	[ʤʲubah mandi]
pajamas	**piyama**	[piyama]
sweater	**sweter**	[sweter]
pullover	**pulover**	[pulover]
vest	**rompi**	[rompi]
tailcoat	**jas berbuntut**	[ʤʲas bərbuntut]
tuxedo	**jas malam**	[ʤʲas malam]

uniform	**seragam**	[seragam]
workwear	**pakaian kerja**	[pakajan kerdʒʲa]
overalls	**baju monyet**	[badʒʲu monjet]
coat (e.g. doctor's smock)	**jas**	[dʒʲas]

32. Clothing. Underwear

underwear	**pakaian dalam**	[pakajan dalam]
boxers, briefs	**celana dalam lelaki**	[tʃelana dalam lelaki]
panties	**celana dalam wanita**	[tʃelana dalam wanita]
undershirt (A-shirt)	**singlet**	[siŋlet]
socks	**kaus kaki**	[kaus kaki]

nightgown	**baju tidur**	[badʒʲu tidur]
bra	**beha**	[beha]
knee highs (knee-high socks)	**kaus kaki selutut**	[kaus kaki selutut]

pantyhose	**pantihos**	[pantihos]
stockings (thigh highs)	**kaus kaki panjang**	[kaus kaki pandʒʲaŋ]
bathing suit	**baju renang**	[badʒʲu renaŋ]

33. Headwear

hat	**topi**	[topi]
fedora	**topi bulat**	[topi bulat]
baseball cap	**topi bisbol**	[topi bisbol]
flatcap	**topi pet**	[topi pet]

beret	**baret**	[baret]
hood	**kerudung kepala**	[keruduŋ kepala]
panama hat	**topi panama**	[topi panama]
knit cap (knitted hat)	**topi rajut**	[topi radʒʲut]

headscarf	**tudung kepala**	[tuduŋ kepala]
women's hat	**topi wanita**	[topi wanita]
hard hat	**topi baja**	[topi badʒʲa]
garrison cap	**topi lipat**	[topi lipat]
helmet	**helm**	[helm]

| derby | **topi bulat** | [topi bulat] |
| top hat | **topi tinggi** | [topi tiŋgi] |

34. Footwear

| footwear | **sepatu** | [sepatu] |
| shoes (men's shoes) | **sepatu bot** | [sepatu bot] |

shoes (women's shoes)	sepatu wanita	[sepatu wanita]
boots (e.g., cowboy ~)	sepatu lars	[sepatu lars]
slippers	pantofel	[pantofel]
tennis shoes (e.g., Nike ~)	sepatu tenis	[sepatu tenis]
sneakers (e.g., Converse ~)	sepatu kets	[sepatu kets]
sandals	sandal	[sandal]
cobbler (shoe repairer)	tukang sepatu	[tukaŋ sepatu]
heel	tumit	[tumit]
pair (of shoes)	sepasang	[sepasaŋ]
shoestring	tali sepatu	[tali sepatu]
to lace (vt)	mengikat tali	[meŋikat tali]
shoehorn	sendok sepatu	[sendo' sepatu]
shoe polish	semir sepatu	[semir sepatu]

35. Textile. Fabrics

cotton (n)	katun	[katun]
cotton (as adj)	katun	[katun]
flax (n)	linen	[linen]
flax (as adj)	linen	[linen]
silk (n)	sutra	[sutra]
silk (as adj)	sutra	[sutra]
wool (n)	wol	[wol]
wool (as adj)	wol	[wol]
velvet	beledu	[beledu]
suede	suede	[suede]
corduroy	korduroi	[korduroy]
nylon (n)	nilon	[nilon]
nylon (as adj)	nilon	[nilon]
polyester (n)	poliester	[poliester]
polyester (as adj)	poliester	[poliester]
leather (n)	kulit	[kulit]
leather (as adj)	kulit	[kulit]
fur (n)	kulit berbulu	[kulit bərbulu]
fur (e.g., ~ coat)	bulu	[bulu]

36. Personal accessories

gloves	sarung tangan	[saruŋ taŋan]
mittens	sarung tangan	[saruŋ taŋan]

scarf (muffler)	selendang	[selendaŋ]
glasses (eyeglasses)	kacamata	[katʃamata]
frame (eyeglass ~)	bingkai	[biŋkaj]
umbrella	payung	[pajuŋ]
walking stick	tongkat jalan	[toŋkat dʒalan]
hairbrush	sikat rambut	[sikat rambut]
fan	kipas	[kipas]

tie (necktie)	dasi	[dasi]
bow tie	dasi kupu-kupu	[dasi kupu-kupu]
suspenders	bretel	[bretel]
handkerchief	sapu tangan	[sapu taŋan]

comb	sisir	[sisir]
barrette	jepit rambut	[dʒepit rambut]
hairpin	harnal	[harnal]
buckle	gesper	[gesper]

| belt | sabuk | [sabuʔ] |
| shoulder strap | tali tas | [tali tas] |

bag (handbag)	tas	[tas]
purse	tas tangan	[tas taŋan]
backpack	ransel	[ransel]

37. Clothing. Miscellaneous

fashion	mode	[mode]
in vogue (adj)	modis	[modis]
fashion designer	perancang busana	[pərantʃaŋ busana]

collar	kerah	[kerah]
pocket	saku	[saku]
pocket (as adj)	saku	[saku]
sleeve	lengan	[leŋan]
hanging loop	tali kait	[tali kait]
fly (on trousers)	golbi	[golbi]

zipper (fastener)	ritsleting	[ritsletiŋ]
fastener	kancing	[kantʃiŋ]
button	kancing	[kantʃiŋ]
buttonhole	lubang kancing	[lubaŋ kantʃiŋ]
to come off (ab. button)	terlepas	[tərlepas]

to sew (vi, vt)	menjahit	[məndʒahit]
to embroider (vi, vt)	membordir	[membordir]
embroidery	bordiran	[bordiran]
sewing needle	jarum	[dʒarum]
thread	benang	[benaŋ]
seam	setik	[setiʔ]

to get dirty (vi)	kena kotor	[kena kotɔr]
stain (mark, spot)	bercak	[bertʃaʔ]
to crease, crumple (vi)	kumal	[kumal]
to tear, to rip (vt)	merobek	[merobeʔ]
clothes moth	ngengat	[ŋeŋat]

38. Personal care. Cosmetics

toothpaste	pasta gigi	[pasta gigi]
toothbrush	sikat gigi	[sikat gigi]
to brush one's teeth	menggosok gigi	[meŋgosoʔ gigi]

razor	pisau cukur	[pisau tʃukur]
shaving cream	krim cukur	[krim tʃukur]
to shave (vi)	bercukur	[bertʃukur]

| soap | sabun | [sabun] |
| shampoo | sampo | [sampo] |

scissors	gunting	[guntiŋ]
nail file	kikir kuku	[kikir kuku]
nail clippers	pemotong kuku	[pemotoŋ kuku]
tweezers	pinset	[pinset]

cosmetics	kosmetik	[kosmetiʔ]
face mask	masker	[masker]
manicure	manikur	[manikur]
to have a manicure	melakukan manikur	[melakukan manikur]
pedicure	pedi	[pedi]

make-up bag	tas kosmetik	[tas kosmetiʔ]
face powder	bedak	[bedaʔ]
powder compact	kotak bedak	[kotaʔ bedaʔ]
blusher	perona pipi	[perona pipi]

perfume (bottled)	parfum	[parfum]
toilet water (lotion)	minyak wangi	[minjaʔ waŋi]
lotion	losion	[losjon]
cologne	kolonye	[kolone]

eyeshadow	pewarna mata	[pewarna mata]
eyeliner	pensil alis	[pensil alis]
mascara	celak	[tʃelaʔ]

lipstick	lipstik	[lipstiʔ]
nail polish, enamel	kuteks, cat kuku	[kuteks], [tʃat kuku]
hair spray	semprotan rambut	[semprotan rambut]
deodorant	deodoran	[deodoran]
cream	krim	[krim]
face cream	krim wajah	[krim wadʒjah]

hand cream	**krim tangan**	[krim taŋan]
anti-wrinkle cream	**krim antikerut**	[krim antikerut]
day cream	**krim siang**	[krim siaŋ]
night cream	**krim malam**	[krim malam]
day (as adj)	**siang**	[siaŋ]
night (as adj)	**malam**	[malam]

tampon	**tampon**	[tampon]
toilet paper (toilet roll)	**kertas toilet**	[kertas toylet]
hair dryer	**pengering rambut**	[peŋeriŋ rambut]

39. Jewelry

jewelry	**perhiasan**	[pərhiasan]
precious (e.g., ~ stone)	**mulia, berharga**	[mulia], [bərharga]
hallmark stamp	**tanda kadar**	[tanda kadar]

ring	**cincin**	[tʃintʃin]
wedding ring	**cincin kawin**	[tʃintʃin kawin]
bracelet	**gelang**	[gelaŋ]

earrings	**anting-anting**	[antiŋ-antiŋ]
necklace (~ of pearls)	**kalung**	[kaluŋ]
crown	**mahkota**	[mahkota]
bead necklace	**kalung manik-manik**	[kaluŋ maniʔ-maniʔ]

diamond	**berlian**	[bərlian]
emerald	**zamrud**	[zamrud]
ruby	**batu mirah delima**	[batu mirah delima]
sapphire	**nilakandi**	[nilakandi]
pearl	**mutiara**	[mutiara]
amber	**batu amber**	[batu amber]

40. Watches. Clocks

watch (wristwatch)	**arloji**	[arlodʒi]
dial	**piringan jam**	[piriŋan dʒam]
hand (of clock, watch)	**jarum**	[dʒarum]
metal watch band	**rantai arloji**	[rantaj arlodʒi]
watch strap	**tali arloji**	[tali arlodʒi]

battery	**baterai**	[bateraj]
to be dead (battery)	**mati**	[mati]
to change a battery	**mengganti baterai**	[məŋganti bateraj]
to run fast	**cepat**	[tʃepat]
to run slow	**terlambat**	[tərlambat]
wall clock	**jam dinding**	[dʒam dindiŋ]
hourglass	**jam pasir**	[dʒam pasir]

sundial	jam matahari	[ʤam matahari]
alarm clock	weker	[weker]
watchmaker	tukang jam	[tukaŋ ʤam]
to repair (vt)	mereparasi, memperbaiki	[mereparasi], [memperbajki]

Food. Nutricion

41. Food

meat	**daging**	[daɲiŋ]
chicken	**ayam**	[ajam]
Rock Cornish hen (poussin)	**anak ayam**	[ana' ajam]
duck	**bebek**	[bebe']
goose	**angsa**	[aŋsa]
game	**binatang buruan**	[binataŋ buruan]
turkey	**kalkun**	[kalkun]
pork	**daging babi**	[daɲiŋ babi]
veal	**daging anak sapi**	[daɲiŋ ana' sapi]
lamb	**daging domba**	[daɲiŋ domba]
beef	**daging sapi**	[daɲiŋ sapi]
rabbit	**kelinci**	[kelintʃi]
sausage (bologna, pepperoni, etc.)	**sosis**	[sosis]
vienna sausage (frankfurter)	**sosis**	[sosis]
bacon	**bakon**	[beykon]
ham	**ham, daging kornet**	[ham], [daɲiŋ kornet]
gammon	**ham**	[ham]
pâté	**pasta**	[pasta]
liver	**hati**	[hati]
hamburger (ground beef)	**daging giling**	[daɲiŋ giliŋ]
tongue	**lidah**	[lidah]
egg	**telur**	[telur]
eggs	**telur**	[telur]
egg white	**putih telur**	[putih telur]
egg yolk	**kuning telur**	[kuniŋ telur]
fish	**ikan**	[ikan]
seafood	**makanan laut**	[makanan laut]
crustaceans	**krustasea**	[krustasea]
caviar	**caviar**	[kaviar]
crab	**kepiting**	[kepitiŋ]
shrimp	**udang**	[udaŋ]
oyster	**tiram**	[tiram]
spiny lobster	**lobster berduri**	[lobster berduri]

squid	cumi-cumi	[ʧumi-ʧumi]
sturgeon	ikan sturgeon	[ikan sturdʒien]
salmon	salmon	[salmon]
halibut	ikan turbot	[ikan turbot]
cod	ikan kod	[ikan kod]
mackerel	ikan kembung	[ikan kembuŋ]
tuna	tuna	[tuna]
eel	belut	[belut]
trout	ikan forel	[ikan forel]
sardine	sarden	[sarden]
pike	ikan pike	[ikan paik]
herring	ikan haring	[ikan hariŋ]
bread	roti	[roti]
cheese	keju	[kedʒiu]
sugar	gula	[gula]
salt	garam	[garam]
rice	beras, nasi	[beras], [nasi]
pasta (macaroni)	makaroni	[makaroni]
noodles	mi	[mi]
butter	mentega	[məntega]
vegetable oil	minyak nabati	[minja' nabati]
sunflower oil	minyak bunga matahari	[minja' buɲa matahari]
margarine	margarin	[margarin]
olives	buah zaitun	[buah zajtun]
olive oil	minyak zaitun	[minja' zajtun]
milk	susu	[susu]
condensed milk	susu kental	[susu kental]
yogurt	yogurt	[yogurt]
sour cream	krim asam	[krim asam]
cream (of milk)	krim, kepala susu	[krim], [kepala susu]
mayonnaise	mayones	[majones]
buttercream	krim	[krim]
cereal grains (wheat, etc.)	menir	[menir]
flour	tepung	[tepuŋ]
canned food	makanan kalengan	[makanan kaleŋan]
cornflakes	emping jagung	[empiŋ dʒiaguŋ]
honey	madu	[madu]
jam	selai	[selaj]
chewing gum	permen karet	[pərmen karet]

42. Drinks

water	air	[air]
drinking water	air minum	[air minum]
mineral water	air mineral	[air mineral]
still (adj)	tanpa gas	[tanpa gas]
carbonated (adj)	berkarbonasi	[bərkarbonasi]
sparkling (adj)	bergas	[bərgas]
ice	es	[es]
with ice	dengan es	[deŋan es]
non-alcoholic (adj)	tanpa alkohol	[tanpa alkohol]
soft drink	minuman ringan	[minuman riŋan]
refreshing drink	minuman penygar	[minuman penigar]
lemonade	limun	[limun]
liquors	minoman beralkohol	[minoman bəralkohol]
wine	anggur	[aŋgur]
white wine	anggur putih	[aŋgur putih]
red wine	anggur merah	[aŋgur merah]
liqueur	likeur	[likeur]
champagne	sampanye	[sampanje]
vermouth	vermouth	[vermut]
whiskey	wiski	[wiski]
vodka	vodka	[vodka]
gin	jin, jenewer	[dʒin], [dʒʲenewer]
cognac	konyak	[konjaʔ]
rum	rum	[rum]
coffee	kopi	[kopi]
black coffee	kopi pahit	[kopi pahit]
coffee with milk	kopi susu	[kopi susu]
cappuccino	cappuccino	[kaputʃino]
instant coffee	kopi instan	[kopi instan]
milk	susu	[susu]
cocktail	koktail	[koktajl]
milkshake	susu kocok	[susu kotʃoʔ]
juice	jus	[dʒʲus]
tomato juice	jus tomat	[dʒʲus tomat]
orange juice	jus jeruk	[dʒʲus dʒʲeruʔ]
freshly squeezed juice	jus peras	[dʒʲus pəras]
beer	bir	[bir]
light beer	bir putih	[bir putih]
dark beer	bir hitam	[bir hitam]
tea	teh	[teh]

| black tea | teh hitam | [teh hitam] |
| green tea | teh hijau | [teh hiʤau] |

43. Vegetables

vegetables	sayuran	[sajuran]
greens	sayuran hijau	[sajuran hiʤau]
tomato	tomat	[tomat]
cucumber	mentimun, ketimun	[məntimun], [ketimun]
carrot	wortel	[wortel]
potato	kentang	[kentaŋ]
onion	bawang	[bawaŋ]
garlic	bawang putih	[bawaŋ putih]
cabbage	kol	[kol]
cauliflower	kembang kol	[kembaŋ kol]
Brussels sprouts	kol Brussels	[kol brusels]
broccoli	brokoli	[brokoli]
beetroot	ubi bit merah	[ubi bit merah]
eggplant	terung, terong	[teruŋ], [təroŋ]
zucchini	labu siam	[labu siam]
pumpkin	labu	[labu]
turnip	turnip	[turnip]
parsley	peterseli	[peterseli]
dill	adas sowa	[adas sowa]
lettuce	selada	[selada]
celery	seledri	[seledri]
asparagus	asparagus	[asparagus]
spinach	bayam	[bajam]
pea	kacang polong	[kaʧaŋ poloŋ]
beans	kacang-kacangan	[kaʧaŋ-kaʧaŋan]
corn (maize)	jagung	[ʤaguŋ]
kidney bean	kacang buncis	[kaʧaŋ bunʧis]
bell pepper	cabai	[ʧabaj]
radish	radis	[radis]
artichoke	artisyok	[artiʃoʔ]

44. Fruits. Nuts

fruit	buah	[buah]
apple	apel	[apel]
pear	pir	[pir]
lemon	jeruk sitrun	[ʤeruʔ sitrun]

orange	**jeruk manis**	[dʒʲeruˀ manis]
strawberry (garden ~)	**stroberi**	[stroberi]
mandarin	**jeruk mandarin**	[dʒʲeruˀ mandarin]
plum	**plum**	[plum]
peach	**persik**	[persiˀ]
apricot	**aprikot**	[aprikot]
raspberry	**buah frambus**	[buah frambus]
pineapple	**nanas**	[nanas]
banana	**pisang**	[pisaŋ]
watermelon	**semangka**	[semaŋka]
grape	**buah anggur**	[buah aŋgur]
sour cherry	**buah ceri asam**	[buah tʃeri asam]
sweet cherry	**buah ceri manis**	[buah tʃeri manis]
melon	**melon**	[melon]
grapefruit	**jeruk Bali**	[dʒʲeruˀ bali]
avocado	**avokad**	[avokad]
papaya	**pepaya**	[pepaja]
mango	**mangga**	[maŋga]
pomegranate	**buah delima**	[buah delima]
redcurrant	**redcurrant**	[redkaren]
blackcurrant	**blackcurrant**	[bleˀkaren]
gooseberry	**buah arbei hijau**	[buah arbei hidʒʲau]
bilberry	**buah bilberi**	[buah bilberi]
blackberry	**beri hitam**	[beri hitam]
raisin	**kismis**	[kismis]
fig	**buah ara**	[buah ara]
date	**buah kurma**	[buah kurma]
peanut	**kacang tanah**	[katʃaŋ tanah]
almond	**badam**	[badam]
walnut	**buah walnut**	[buah walnut]
hazelnut	**kacang hazel**	[katʃaŋ hazel]
coconut	**buah kelapa**	[buah kelapa]
pistachios	**badam hijau**	[badam hidʒʲau]

45. Bread. Candy

bakers' confectionery (pastry)	**kue-mue**	[kue-mue]
bread	**roti**	[roti]
cookies	**biskuit**	[biskuit]
chocolate (n)	**cokelat**	[tʃokelat]
chocolate (as adj)	**cokelat**	[tʃokelat]
candy (wrapped)	**permen**	[pərmen]

cake (н џ , cupcake)	kue	[kue]
cake (e.g., birthday ~)	kue tar	[kue tar]
pie (e.g., apple ~)	pai	[pai]
filling (for cake, pie)	inti	[inti]
jam (whole fruit jam)	selai buah utuh	[selaj buah utuh]
marmalade	marmelade	[marmelade]
waffles	wafel	[wafel]
ice-cream	es krim	[es krim]
pudding	puding	[pudiŋ]

46. Cooked dishes

course, dish	masakan, hidangan	[masakan], [hidaŋan]
cuisine	masakan	[masakan]
recipe	resep	[resep]
portion	porsi	[porsi]
salad	salada	[salada]
soup	sup	[sup]
clear soup (broth)	kaldu	[kaldu]
sandwich (bread)	roti lapis	[roti lapis]
fried eggs	telur mata sapi	[telur mata sapi]
hamburger (beefburger)	hamburger	[hamburger]
beefsteak	bistik	[bisti']
side dish	lauk	[lau']
spaghetti	spageti	[spageti]
mashed potatoes	kentang tumbuk	[kentaŋ tumbu']
pizza	piza	[piza]
porridge (oatmeal, etc.)	bubur	[bubur]
omelet	telur dadar	[telur dadar]
boiled (e.g., ~ beef)	rebus	[rebus]
smoked (adj)	asap	[asap]
fried (adj)	goreng	[goreŋ]
dried (adj)	kering	[keriŋ]
frozen (adj)	beku	[beku]
pickled (adj)	marinade	[marinade]
sweet (sugary)	manis	[manis]
salty (adj)	asin	[asin]
cold (adj)	dingin	[diŋin]
hot (adj)	panas	[panas]
bitter (adj)	pahit	[pahit]
tasty (adj)	enak	[ena']
to cook in boiling water	merebus	[merebus]

to cook (dinner)	memasak	[memasaʔ]
to fry (vt)	menggoreng	[məŋgoreŋ]
to heat up (food)	memanaskan	[memanaskan]

to salt (vt)	menggarami	[məŋgarami]
to pepper (vt)	membubuh merica	[membubuh meritʃa]
to grate (vt)	memarut	[memarut]
peel (n)	kulit	[kulit]
to peel (vt)	mengupas	[məŋupas]

47. Spices

salt	garam	[garam]
salty (adj)	asin	[asin]
to salt (vt)	menggarami	[məŋgarami]

black pepper	merica	[meritʃa]
red pepper (milled ~)	cabai merah	[tʃabaj merah]
mustard	mustar	[mustar]
horseradish	lobak pedas	[lobaʔ pedas]

condiment	bumbu	[bumbu]
spice	rempah-rempah	[rempah-rempah]
sauce	saus	[saus]
vinegar	cuka	[tʃuka]

anise	adas manis	[adas manis]
basil	selasih	[selasih]
cloves	cengkih	[tʃeŋkih]
ginger	jahe	[dʒʲahe]
coriander	ketumbar	[ketumbar]
cinnamon	kayu manis	[kaju manis]

sesame	wijen	[widʒʲen]
bay leaf	daun salam	[daun salam]
paprika	cabai	[tʃabaj]
caraway	jintan	[dʒintan]
saffron	kuma-kuma	[kuma-kuma]

48. Meals

| food | makanan | [makanan] |
| to eat (vi, vt) | makan | [makan] |

breakfast	makan pagi, sarapan	[makan pagi], [sarapan]
to have breakfast	sarapan	[sarapan]
lunch	makan siang	[makan siaŋ]
to have lunch	makan siang	[makan siaŋ]

dinner	makan malam	[makan malam]
to have dinner	makan malam	[makan malam]
appetite	nafsu makan	[nafsu makan]
Enjoy your meal!	Selamat makan!	[selamat makan!]
to open (~ a bottle)	membuka	[membuka]
to spill (liquid)	menumpahkan	[mɜnumpahkan]
to boil (vi)	mendidih	[mɜndidih]
to boil (vt)	mendidihkan	[mɜndidihkan]
boiled (~ water)	masak	[masaʔ]
to chill, cool down (vt)	mendinginkan	[mɜndiŋinkan]
to chill (vi)	mendingin	[mɜndiŋin]
taste, flavor	rasa	[rasa]
aftertaste	nuansa rasa	[nuansa rasa]
to slim down (lose weight)	berdiet	[berdiet]
diet	diet, pola makan	[diet], [pola makan]
vitamin	vitamin	[vitamin]
calorie	kalori	[kalori]
vegetarian (n)	vegetarian	[vegetarian]
vegetarian (adj)	vegetarian	[vegetarian]
fats (nutrient)	lemak	[lemaʔ]
proteins	protein	[protein]
carbohydrates	karbohidrat	[karbohidrat]
slice (of lemon, ham)	irisan	[irisan]
piece (of cake, pie)	potongan	[potoŋan]
crumb	remah	[remah]
(of bread, cake, etc.)		

49. Table setting

spoon	sendok	[sendoʔ]
knife	pisau	[pisau]
fork	garpu	[garpu]
cup (e.g., coffee ~)	cangkir	[ʧaŋkir]
plate (dinner ~)	piring	[piriŋ]
saucer	alas cangkir	[alas ʧaŋkir]
napkin (on table)	serbet	[serbet]
toothpick	tusuk gigi	[tusuʔ gigi]

50. Restaurant

restaurant	restoran	[restoran]
coffee house	warung kopi	[waruŋ kopi]

pub, bar	**bar**	[bar]
tearoom	**warung teh**	[waruŋ teh]
waiter	**pelayan lelaki**	[pelajan lelaki]
waitress	**pelayan perempuan**	[pelajan perempuan]
bartender	**pelayan bar**	[pelajan bar]
menu	**menu**	[menu]
wine list	**daftar anggur**	[daftar aŋgur]
to book a table	**memesan meja**	[memesan medʒ′a]
course, dish	**masakan, hidangan**	[masakan], [hidaŋan]
to order (meal)	**memesan**	[memesan]
to make an order	**memesan**	[memesan]
aperitif	**aperitif**	[aperitif]
appetizer	**makanan ringan**	[makanan riŋan]
dessert	**hidangan penutup**	[hidaŋan penutup]
check	**bon**	[bon]
to pay the check	**membayar bon**	[membajar bon]
to give change	**memberikan**	[memberikan
	uang kembalian	uaŋ kembalian]
tip	**tip**	[tip]

Family, relatives and friends

51. Personal information. Forms

name (first name)	**nama, nama depan**	[nama], [nama depan]
surname (last name)	**nama keluarga**	[nama keluarga]
date of birth	**tanggal lahir**	[taŋgal lahir]
place of birth	**tempat lahir**	[tempat lahir]
nationality	**kebangsaan**	[kebaŋsa'an]
place of residence	**tempat tinggal**	[tempat tiŋgal]
country	**negara, negeri**	[negara], [negeri]
profession (occupation)	**profesi**	[profesi]
gender, sex	**jenis kelamin**	[dʒenis kelamin]
height	**tinggi badan**	[tiŋgi badan]
weight	**berat**	[berat]

52. Family members. Relatives

mother	**ibu**	[ibu]
father	**ayah**	[ajah]
son	**anak lelaki**	[ana' lelaki]
daughter	**anak perempuan**	[ana' perempuan]
younger daughter	**anak perempuan bungsu**	[ana' perempuan buŋsu]
younger son	**anak lelaki bungsu**	[ana' lelaki buŋsu]
eldest daughter	**anak perempuan sulung**	[ana' perempuan suluŋ]
eldest son	**anak lelaki sulung**	[ana' lelaki suluŋ]
brother	**saudara lelaki**	[saudara lelaki]
elder brother	**kakak lelaki**	[kaka' lelaki]
younger brother	**adik lelaki**	[adi' lelaki]
sister	**saudara perempuan**	[saudara perempuan]
elder sister	**kakak perempuan**	[kaka' perempuan]
younger sister	**adik perempuan**	[adi' perempuan]
cousin (masc.)	**sepupu lelaki**	[sepupu lelaki]
cousin (fem.)	**sepupu perempuan**	[sepupu perempuan]
mom, mommy	**mama, ibu**	[mama], [ibu]
dad, daddy	**papa, ayah**	[papa], [ajah]
parents	**orang tua**	[oraŋ tua]
child	**anak**	[ana']
children	**anak-anak**	[ana'-ana']

grandmother	**nenek**	[nene⁷]
grandfather	**kakek**	[kake⁷]
grandson	**cucu laki-laki**	[ʧuʧu laki-laki]
granddaughter	**cucu perempuan**	[ʧuʧu pərəmpuan]
grandchildren	**cucu**	[ʧuʧu]

uncle	**paman**	[paman]
aunt	**bibi**	[bibi]
nephew	**keponakan laki-laki**	[keponakan laki-laki]
niece	**keponakan perempuan**	[keponakan pərempuan]

mother-in-law (wife's mother)	**ibu mertua**	[ibu mertua]
father-in-law (husband's father)	**ayah mertua**	[ajah mertua]
son-in-law (daughter's husband)	**menantu laki-laki**	[mənantu laki-laki]
stepmother	**ibu tiri**	[ibu tiri]
stepfather	**ayah tiri**	[ajah tiri]
infant	**bayi**	[baji]
baby (infant)	**bayi**	[baji]
little boy, kid	**bocah cilik**	[boʧah ʧili⁷]

wife	**istri**	[istri]
husband	**suami**	[suami]
spouse (husband)	**suami**	[suami]
spouse (wife)	**istri**	[istri]

married (masc.)	**menikah, beristri**	[mənikah], [bəristri]
married (fem.)	**menikah, bersuami**	[mənikah], [bərsuami]
single (unmarried)	**bujang**	[budʒʲaŋ]
bachelor	**bujang**	[budʒʲaŋ]
divorced (masc.)	**bercerai**	[bərʧeraj]
widow	**janda**	[dʒʲanda]
widower	**duda**	[duda]

relative	**kerabat**	[kerabat]
close relative	**kerabat dekat**	[kerabat dekat]
distant relative	**kerabat jauh**	[kerabat dʒʲauh]
relatives	**kerabat, sanak saudara**	[kerabat], [sana⁷ saudara]

orphan (boy or girl)	**yatim piatu**	[yatim piatu]
guardian (of a minor)	**wali**	[wali]
to adopt (a boy)	**mengadopsi**	[məŋadopsi]
to adopt (a girl)	**mengadopsi**	[məŋadopsi]

53. Friends. Coworkers

| friend (masc.) | **sahabat** | [sahabat] |
| friend (fem.) | **sahabat** | [sahabat] |

| friendship | persahabatan | [pərsahabatan] |
| to be friends | bersahabat | [bərsahabat] |

buddy (masc.)	teman	[teman]
buddy (fem.)	teman	[teman]
partner	mitra	[mitra]

chief (boss)	atasan	[atasan]
superior (n)	atasan	[atasan]
owner, proprietor	pemilik	[pemiliʔ]
subordinate (n)	bawahan	[bawahan]
colleague	kolega	[kolega]

acquaintance (person)	kenalan	[kenalan]
fellow traveler	rekan seperjalanan	[rekan seperdʒʲalanan]
classmate	teman sekelas	[teman sekelas]

neighbor (masc.)	tetangga	[tetaŋga]
neighbor (fem.)	tetangga	[tetaŋga]
neighbors	para tetangga	[para tetaŋga]

54. Man. Woman

woman	perempuan, wanita	[perempuan], [wanita]
girl (young woman)	gadis	[gadis]
bride	mempelai perempuan	[mempelaj perempuan]

beautiful (adj)	cantik	[tʃantiʔ]
tall (adj)	tinggi	[tiŋgi]
slender (adj)	ramping	[rampiŋ]
short (adj)	pendek	[pendeʔ]

| blonde (n) | orang berambut pirang | [oraŋ berambut piraŋ] |
| brunette (n) | orang berambut cokelat | [oraŋ berambut tʃokelat] |

ladies' (adj)	wanita	[wanita]
virgin (girl)	perawan	[perawan]
pregnant (adj)	hamil	[hamil]

man (adult male)	laki-laki, pria	[laki-laki], [pria]
blond (n)	orang berambut pirang	[oraŋ berambut piraŋ]
brunet (n)	orang berambut cokelat	[oraŋ berambut tʃokelat]
tall (adj)	tinggi	[tiŋgi]
short (adj)	pendek	[pendeʔ]

rude (rough)	kasar	[kasar]
stocky (adj)	kekar	[kekar]
robust (adj)	tegap	[tegap]
strong (adj)	kuat	[kuat]
strength	kekuatan	[kekuatan]

stout, fat (adj)   gemuk   [gemu']
swarthy (adj)   berkulit hitam   [berkulit hitam]
slender (well-built)   ramping   [rampiŋ]
elegant (adj)   anggun   [ɔŋgun]

55. Age

age   umur   [umur]
youth (young age)   usia muda   [usia muda]
young (adj)   muda   [muda]

younger (adj)   lebih muda   [lebih muda]
older (adj)   lebih tua   [lebih tua]

young man   pemuda   [pemuda]
teenager   remaja   [remadʒʲa]
guy, fellow   cowok   [tʃowo']

old man   lelaki tua   [lelaki tua]
old woman   perempuan tua   [perempuan tua]

adult (adj)   dewasa   [dewasa]
middle-aged (adj)   paruh baya   [paruh baja]
elderly (adj)   lansia   [lansia]
old (adj)   tua   [tua]

retirement   pensiun   [pensiun]
to retire (from job)   pensiun   [pensiun]
retiree   pensiunan   [pensiunan]

56. Children

child   anak   [ana']
children   anak-anak   [ana'-ana']
twins   kembar   [kembar]

cradle   buaian   [buajan]
rattle   ocehan   [otʃehan]
diaper   popok   [popo']

pacifier   dot   [dot]
baby carriage   kereta bayi   [kereta baji]
kindergarten   taman kanak-kanak [taman kana'-kana']
babysitter   pengasuh anak   [peŋasuh ana']

childhood   masa kanak-kanak   [masa kana'-kana']
doll   boneka   [boneka]
toy   mainan   [majnan]

construction set (toy)	**alat permainan bongkah**	[alat pərmajnan boŋkah]
well-bred (adj)	**beradab**	[bəradab]
ill-bred (adj)	**biadab**	[biadab]
spoiled (adj)	**manja**	[mandʒia]
to be naughty	**nakal**	[nakal]
mischievous (adj)	**nakal**	[nakal]
mischievousness	**kenakalan**	[kenakalan]
mischievous child	**anak nakal**	[ana' nakal]
obedient (adj)	**patuh**	[patuh]
disobedient (adj)	**tidak patuh**	[tida' patuh]
docile (adj)	**penurut**	[penurut]
clever (smart)	**pandai, pintar**	[pandaj], [pintar]
child prodigy	**anak ajaib**	[ana' adʒiajb]

57. Married couples. Family life

to kiss (vt)	**mencium**	[mənt͡ʃium]
to kiss (vi)	**berciuman**	[bərt͡ʃiuman]
family (n)	**keluarga**	[keluarga]
family (as adj)	**keluarga**	[keluarga]
couple	**pasangan**	[pasaŋan]
marriage (state)	**pernikahan**	[pərnikahan]
hearth (home)	**rumah tangga**	[rumah taŋga]
dynasty	**dinasti**	[dinasti]
date	**kencan**	[kent͡ʃan]
kiss	**ciuman**	[t͡ʃiuman]
love (for sb)	**cinta**	[t͡ʃinta]
to love (sb)	**mencintai**	[mənt͡ʃintaj]
beloved	**kekasih**	[kekasih]
tenderness	**kelembutan**	[kelembutan]
tender (affectionate)	**lembut**	[lembut]
faithfulness	**kesetiaan**	[kesetia'an]
faithful (adj)	**setia**	[setia]
care (attention)	**perhatian**	[pərhatian]
caring (~ father)	**penuh perhatian**	[penuh pərhatian]
newlyweds	**pengantin baru**	[peŋantin baru]
honeymoon	**bulan madu**	[bulan madu]
to get married (ab. woman)	**menikah, bersuami**	[mənikah], [bərsuami]
to get married (ab. man)	**menikah, beristri**	[mənikah], [beristri]
wedding	**pernikahan**	[pərnikahan]
golden wedding	**pernikahan emas**	[pərnikahan emas]

anniversary	hari jadi, HUT	[hari dʒ'adi], [ha-u-te]
lover (masc.)	pria idaman lain	[pria idaman lajn]
mistress (lover)	wanita idaman lain	[wanita idaman lajn]

| adultery | perselingkuhan | [pərseliŋkuhan] |
| to cheat on ... (commit adultery) | berselingkuh dari ... | [bərseliŋkuh dari ...] |

jealous (adj)	cemburu	[tʃemburu]
to be jealous	cemburu	[tʃemburu]
divorce	perceraian	[pərtʃerajan]
to divorce (vi)	bercerai	[bərtʃeraj]

to quarrel (vi)	bertengkar	[bərteŋkar]
to be reconciled (after an argument)	berdamai	[bərdamaj]
together (adv)	bersama	[bərsama]
sex	seks	[seks]

happiness	kebahagiaan	[kebahagia'an]
happy (adj)	berbahagia	[bərbahagia]
misfortune (accident)	kemalangan	[kemalaŋan]
unhappy (adj)	malang	[malaŋ]

Character. Feelings. Emotions

58. Feelings. Emotions

feeling (emotion)	**perasaan**	[pərasa'an]
feelings	**perasaan**	[pərasa'an]
to feel (vt)	**merasa**	[merasa]
hunger	**kelaparan**	[kelaparan]
to be hungry	**lapar**	[lapar]
thirst	**kehausan**	[kehausan]
to be thirsty	**haus**	[haus]
sleepiness	**kantuk**	[kantu']
to feel sleepy	**mengantuk**	[mənŋantu']
tiredness	**rasa lelah**	[rasa lelah]
tired (adj)	**lelah**	[lelah]
to get tired	**lelah**	[lelah]
mood (humor)	**suasana hati**	[suasana hati]
boredom	**kebosanan**	[kebosanan]
to be bored	**bosan**	[bosan]
seclusion	**kesendirian**	[kesendirian]
to seclude oneself	**menyendiri**	[mənjendiri]
to worry (make anxious)	**membuat khawatir**	[membuat hawatir]
to be worried	**khawatir**	[hawatir]
worrying (n)	**kekhawatiran**	[kehawatiran]
anxiety	**kegelisahan**	[kegelisahan]
preoccupied (adj)	**prihatin**	[prihatin]
to be nervous	**gugup, gelisah**	[gugup], [gelisah]
to panic (vi)	**panik**	[pani']
hope	**harapan**	[harapan]
to hope (vi, vt)	**berharap**	[bərharap]
certainty	**kepastian**	[kepastian]
certain, sure (adj)	**pasti**	[pasti]
uncertainty	**ketidakpastian**	[ketidakpastian]
uncertain (adj)	**tidak pasti**	[tida' pasti]
drunk (adj)	**mabuk**	[mabu']
sober (adj)	**sadar, tidak mabuk**	[sadar], [tida' mabu']
weak (adj)	**lemah**	[lemah]
happy (adj)	**berbahagia**	[bərbahagia]
to scare (vt)	**menakuti**	[mənakuti]

| fury (madness) | kemarahan | [kemarahan] |
| rage (fury) | kemarahan | [kemarahan] |

depression	depresi	[depresi]
discomfort (unease)	ketidaknyamanan	[kɔtidaknjamanan]
comfort	kenyamanan	[kenjamanan]
to regret (be sorry)	menyesal	[mənjesal]
regret	penyesalan	[penjesalan]
bad luck	kesialan	[kesialan]
sadness	kekesalan	[kekesalan]

shame (remorse)	rasa malu	[rasa malu]
gladness	kegirangan	[kegiraŋan]
enthusiasm, zeal	antusiasme	[antusiasme]
enthusiast	antusias	[antusias]
to show enthusiasm	memperlihatkan antusiasme	[memperlihatkan antusiasme]

59. Character. Personality

character	watak	[wata']
character flaw	kepincangan	[kepintʃaŋan]
mind	otak	[ota']
reason	akal	[akal]

conscience	nurani	[nurani]
habit (custom)	kebiasaan	[kebiasa'an]
ability (talent)	kemampuan, bakat	[kemampuan], [bakat]
can (e.g., ~ swim)	dapat	[dapat]

patient (adj)	sabar	[sabar]
impatient (adj)	tidak sabar	[tida' sabar]
curious (inquisitive)	ingin tahu	[iŋin tahu]
curiosity	rasa ingin tahu	[rasa iŋin tahu]

modesty	kerendahan hati	[kerendahan hati]
modest (adj)	rendah hati	[rendah hati]
immodest (adj)	tidak tahu malu	[tida' tahu malu]

laziness	kemalasan	[kemalasan]
lazy (adj)	malas	[malas]
lazy person (masc.)	pemalas	[pemalas]

cunning (n)	kelicikan	[kelitʃikan]
cunning (as adj)	licik	[litʃi']
distrust	ketidakpercayaan	[ketidakpertʃaja'an]
distrustful (adj)	tidak percaya	[tida' pertʃaja]

| generosity | kemurahan hati | [kemurahan hati] |
| generous (adj) | murah hati | [murah hati] |

| talented (adj) | berbakat | [bərbakat] |
| talent | bakat | [bakat] |

courageous (adj)	berani	[bərani]
courage	keberanian	[keberanian]
honest (adj)	jujur	[dʒ'udʒ'ur]
honesty	kejujuran	[kedʒ'udʒ'uran]

careful (cautious)	berhati-hati	[bərhati-hati]
brave (courageous)	berani	[bərani]
serious (adj)	serius	[serius]
strict (severe, stern)	keras	[keras]

decisive (adj)	tegas	[tegas]
indecisive (adj)	ragu-ragu	[ragu-ragu]
shy, timid (adj)	malu	[malu]
shyness, timidity	sifat pemalu	[sifat pemalu]

confidence (trust)	kepercayaan	[kepertʃaja'an]
to believe (trust)	percaya	[pərtʃaja]
trusting (credulous)	mudah percaya	[mudah pərtʃaja]

sincerely (adv)	ikhlas	[ihlas]
sincere (adj)	ikhlas	[ihlas]
sincerity	keikhlasan	[keihlasan]
open (person)	terbuka	[tərbuka]

calm (adj)	tenang	[tenaŋ]
frank (sincere)	terus terang	[terus təraŋ]
naïve (adj)	naif	[naif]
absent-minded (adj)	lalai	[lalaj]
funny (odd)	lucu	[lutʃu]

greed	kerakusan	[kerakusan]
greedy (adj)	rakus	[rakus]
stingy (adj)	pelit, kikir	[pelit], [kikir]
evil (adj)	jahat	[dʒ'ahat]
stubborn (adj)	keras kepala, degil	[keras kepala], [degil]
unpleasant (adj)	tidak menyenangkan	[tida' menjenaŋkan]

selfish person (masc.)	egois	[egois]
selfish (adj)	egoistis	[egoistis]
coward	penakut	[penakut]
cowardly (adj)	penakut	[penakut]

60. Sleep. Dreams

to sleep (vi)	tidur	[tidur]
sleep, sleeping	tidur	[tidur]
dream	mimpi	[mimpi]

| to dream (in sleep) | bermimpi | [bərmimpi] |
| sleepy (adj) | mengantuk | [məŋantuʔ] |

bed	ranjang	[randʒⁱaŋ]
mattress	kasur	[kasur]
blanket (comforter)	selimut	[selimut]
pillow	bantal	[bantal]
sheet	seprai	[sepraj]

insomnia	insomnia	[insomnia]
sleepless (adj)	tanpa tidur	[tanpa tidur]
sleeping pill	obat tidur	[obat tidur]
to take a sleeping pill	meminum obat tidur	[meminum obat tidur]

to feel sleepy	mengantuk	[məŋantuʔ]
to yawn (vi)	menguap	[məŋuap]
to go to bed	tidur	[tidur]
to make up the bed	menyiapkan ranjang	[mənjiapkan randʒⁱaŋ]
to fall asleep	tertidur	[tərtidur]

nightmare	mimpi buruk	[mimpi buruʔ]
snore, snoring	dengkuran	[deŋkuran]
to snore (vi)	berdengkur	[bərdeŋkur]

alarm clock	weker	[weker]
to wake (vt)	membangunkan	[membaŋunkan]
to wake up	bangun	[baŋun]
to get up (vi)	bangun	[baŋun]
to wash up (wash face)	mencuci muka	[mənt͡ʃut͡ʃi muka]

61. Humour. Laughter. Gladness

humor (wit, fun)	humor	[humor]
sense of humor	rasa humor	[rasa humor]
to enjoy oneself	bersukaria	[bərsukaria]
cheerful (merry)	riang, gembira	[riaŋ], [gembira]
merriment (gaiety)	keriangan, kegembiraan	[kerianan], [kegembiraʔan]

smile	senyuman	[senyuman]
to smile (vi)	tersenyum	[tərsenyum]
to start laughing	tertawa	[tərtawa]
to laugh (vi)	tertawa	[tərtawa]
laugh, laughter	gelak tawa	[gelaʔ tawa]

anecdote	anekdot, lelucon	[anekdot], [lelut͡ʃon]
funny (anecdote, etc.)	lucu	[lut͡ʃu]
funny (odd)	lucu	[lut͡ʃu]

| to joke (vi) | bergurau | [bərgurau] |
| joke (verbal) | lelucon | [lelut͡ʃon] |

joy (emotion)	kegembiraan	[kegembira'an]
to rejoice (vi)	bergembira	[bərgembira]
joyful (adj)	gembira	[gembira]

62. Discussion, conversation. Part 1

| communication | komunikasi | [komunikasi] |
| to communicate | berkomunikasi | [bərkomunikasi] |

conversation	pembicaraan	[pembitʃara'an]
dialog	dialog	[dialog]
discussion (discourse)	diskusi	[diskusi]
dispute (debate)	perdebatan	[pərdebatan]
to dispute	berdebat	[bərdebat]

interlocutor	lawan bicara	[lawan bitʃara]
topic (theme)	topik, tema	[topik], [tema]
point of view	sudut pandang	[sudut pandaŋ]
opinion (point of view)	opini, pendapat	[opini], [pendapat]
speech (talk)	pidato, tuturan	[pidato], [tuturan]

discussion (of report, etc.)	pembicaraan	[pembitʃara'an]
to discuss (vt)	membicarakan	[membitʃarakan]
talk (conversation)	pembicaraan	[pembitʃara'an]
to talk (to chat)	berbicara	[bərbitʃara]
meeting	pertemuan	[pərtemuan]
to meet (vi, vt)	bertemu	[bərtemu]

proverb	peribahasa	[pəribahasa]
saying	peribahasa	[pəribahasa]
riddle (poser)	teka-teki	[teka-teki]
to pose a riddle	memberi teka-teki	[memberi teka-teki]
password	kata sandi	[kata sandi]
secret	rahasia	[rahasia]

oath (vow)	sumpah	[sumpah]
to swear (an oath)	bersumpah	[bersumpah]
promise	janji	[dʒˈandʒi]
to promise (vt)	berjanji	[bərdʒˈandʒi]

advice (counsel)	nasihat	[nasihat]
to advise (vt)	menasihati	[mənasihati]
to follow one's advice	mengikuti nasihat	[məŋikuti nasihat]
to listen to ... (obey)	mendengar ...	[məndeŋar ...]

news	berita	[berita]
sensation (news)	sensasi	[sensasi]
information (data)	data, informasi	[data], [informasi]
conclusion (decision)	kesimpulan	[kesimpulan]
voice	suara	[suara]

compliment	**pujian**	[pudʒian]
kind (nice)	**ramah**	[ramah]
word	**kata**	[kata]
phrase	**frasa**	[frasa]
answer	**jawaban**	[dʒawaban]
truth	**kebenaran**	[kebenaran]
lie	**kebohongan**	[kebohoŋan]
thought	**pikiran**	[pikiran]
idea (inspiration)	**ide**	[ide]
fantasy	**fantasi**	[fantasi]

63. Discussion, conversation. Part 2

respected (adj)	**terhormat**	[tərhormat]
to respect (vt)	**menghormati**	[məŋhormati]
respect	**penghormatan**	[peŋhormatan]
Dear ... (letter)	**Yth. ... (Yang Terhormat)**	[yaŋ tərhormat]
to introduce (sb to sb)	**memperkenalkan**	[memperkenalkan]
to make acquaintance	**berkenalan**	[bərkenalan]
intention	**niat**	[niat]
to intend (have in mind)	**berniat**	[bərniat]
wish	**pengharapan**	[peŋharapan]
to wish (~ good luck)	**mengharapkan**	[məŋharapkan]
surprise (astonishment)	**keheranan**	[keheranan]
to surprise (amaze)	**mengherankan**	[məŋherankan]
to be surprised	**heran**	[heran]
to give (vt)	**memberi**	[memberi]
to take (get hold of)	**mengambil**	[məŋambil]
to give back	**mengembalikan**	[məŋembalikan]
to return (give back)	**mengembalikan**	[məŋembalikan]
to apologize (vi)	**meminta maaf**	[meminta maʔaf]
apology	**permintaan maaf**	[pərmintaʔan maʔaf]
to forgive (vt)	**memaafkan**	[memaʔafkan]
to talk (speak)	**berbicara**	[bərbitʃara]
to listen (vi)	**mendengarkan**	[məndeŋarkan]
to hear out	**mendengar**	[məndeŋar]
to understand (vt)	**mengerti**	[məŋerti]
to show (to display)	**menunjukkan**	[mənundʒuʔkan]
to look at ...	**melihat ...**	[melihat ...]
to call (yell for sb)	**memanggil**	[memaŋgil]

to distract (disturb)	mengganggu	[məŋgaŋgu]
to disturb (vt)	mengganggu	[məŋgaŋgu]
to pass (to hand sth)	menyampaikan	[mənjampajkan]
demand (request)	permintaan	[pərminta'an]
to request (ask)	meminta	[meminta]
demand (firm request)	tuntutan	[tuntutan]
to demand (request firmly)	menuntut	[mənuntut]
to tease (call names)	mengejek	[məŋedʒ'e']
to mock (make fun of)	mencemooh	[məntʃemooh]
mockery, derision	cemoohan	[tʃemoohan]
nickname	nama panggilan	[nama paŋgilan]
insinuation	isyarat	[iʃarat]
to insinuate (imply)	mengisyaratkan	[məŋiʃaratkan]
to mean (vt)	berarti	[bərarti]
description	penggambaran	[pəŋgambaran]
to describe (vt)	menggambarkan	[məŋgambarkan]
praise (compliments)	pujian	[pudʒian]
to praise (vt)	memuji	[memudʒi]
disappointment	kekecewaan	[keketʃewa'an]
to disappoint (vt)	mengecewakan	[məŋetʃewakan]
to be disappointed	kecewa	[ketʃewa]
supposition	dugaan	[duga'an]
to suppose (assume)	menduga	[mənduga]
warning (caution)	peringatan	[periŋatan]
to warn (vt)	memperingatkan	[memperiŋatkan]

64. Discussion, conversation. Part 3

to talk into (convince)	meyakinkan	[meyakinkan]
to calm down (vt)	menenangkan	[mənenaŋkan]
silence (~ is golden)	kebisuan	[kebisuan]
to be silent (not speaking)	membisu	[membisu]
to whisper (vi, vt)	berbisik	[bərbisi']
whisper	bisikan	[bisikan]
frankly, sincerely (adv)	terus terang	[terus teraŋ]
in my opinion ...	menurut saya ...	[mənurut saja ...]
detail (of the story)	detail, perincian	[detajl], [pərintʃian]
detailed (adj)	mendetail	[məndetajl]
in detail (adv)	dengan mendetail	[deŋan mendetajl]
hint, clue	petunjuk	[petundʒ'u']
to give a hint	memberi petunjuk	[memberi petundʒ'u']

look (glance)	melihat	[melihat]
to have a look	melihat	[melihat]
fixed (look)	kaku	[kaku]
to blink (vi)	berkedip	[bərkedip]
to wink (vi)	mengedipkan mata	[məŋedipkan mata]
to nod (in assent)	mengangguk	[məŋaŋgu']
sigh	desah	[desah]
to sigh (vi)	mendesah	[məndesah]
to shudder (vi)	tersentak	[tərsenta']
gesture	gerak tangan	[gera' taŋan]
to touch (one's arm, etc.)	menyentuh	[mənjentuh]
to seize	memegang	[memegaŋ]
(e.g., ~ by the arm)		
to tap (on the shoulder)	menepuk	[mənepu']
Look out!	Awas! Hati-hati!	[awas!], [hati-hati!]
Really?	Sungguh?	[suŋguh?]
Are you sure?	Kamu yakin?	[kamu yakin?]
Good luck!	Semoga behasil!	[semoga behasil!]
I see!	Begitu!	[begitu!]
What a pity!	Sayang sekali!	[sajaŋ sekali!]

65. Agreement. Refusal

consent	persetujuan	[pərsetudʒʲuan]
to consent (vi)	setuju, ijin	[setudʒʲu], [idʒin]
approval	persetujuan	[pərsetudʒʲuan]
to approve (vt)	menyetujui	[mənjetudʒʲui]
refusal	penolakan	[penolakan]
to refuse (vi, vt)	menolak	[mənola']
Great!	Bagus!	[bagus!]
All right!	Baiklah! Baik!	[bajklah!], [baj'!]
Okay! (I agree)	Baiklah! Baik!	[bajklah!], [baj'!]
forbidden (adj)	larangan	[laraŋan]
it's forbidden	dilarang	[dilaraŋ]
it's impossible	mustahil	[mustahil]
incorrect (adj)	salah	[salah]
to reject (~ a demand)	menolak	[mənola']
to support (cause, idea)	mendukung	[məndukuŋ]
to accept (~ an apology)	menerima	[mənerima]
to confirm (vt)	mengonfirmasi	[məŋonfirmasi]
confirmation	konfirmasi	[konfirmasi]
permission	izin	[izin]
to permit (vt)	mengizinkan	[məŋizinkan]
decision	keputusan	[keputusan]

to say nothing (hold one's tongue)	membisu	[membisu]
condition (term)	syarat	[ʃarat]
excuse (pretext)	alasan, dalih	[alasan], [dalih]
praise (compliments)	pujian	[pudʒian]
to praise (vt)	memuji	[memudʒi]

66. Success. Good luck. Failure

success	sukses, berhasil	[sukses], [bərhasil]
successfully (adv)	dengan sukses	[deŋan sukses]
successful (adj)	sukses, berhasil	[sukses], [bərhasil]
luck (good luck)	keberuntungan	[keberuntuŋan]
Good luck!	Semoga behasil!	[semoga behasil!]
lucky (e.g., ~ day)	beruntung	[bəruntuŋ]
lucky (fortunate)	beruntung	[bəruntuŋ]
failure	kegagalan	[kegagalan]
misfortune	kesialan	[kesialan]
bad luck	kesialan	[kesialan]
unsuccessful (adj)	gagal	[gagal]
catastrophe	gagal total	[gagal total]
pride	kebanggaan	[kebaŋga'an]
proud (adj)	bangga	[baŋga]
to be proud	bangga	[baŋga]
winner	pemenang	[pemenaŋ]
to win (vi)	menang	[menaŋ]
to lose (not win)	kalah	[kalah]
try	percobaan	[pərtʃoba'an]
to try (vi)	mencoba	[məntʃoba]
chance (opportunity)	kans, peluang	[kans], [peluaŋ]

67. Quarrels. Negative emotions

shout (scream)	teriakan	[teriakan]
to shout (vi)	berteriak	[bərteria']
to start to cry out	berteriak	[bərteria']
quarrel	pertengkaran	[pərteŋkaran]
to quarrel (vi)	bertengkar	[bərteŋkar]
fight (squabble)	pertengkaran	[pərteŋkaran]
to make a scene	bertengkar	[bərteŋkar]
conflict	konflik	[konfli']
misunderstanding	kesalahpahaman	[kesalahpahaman]
insult	penghinaan	[peŋhina'an]

to insult (vt)	menghina	[məŋhina]
insulted (adj)	terhina	[tərhina]
resentment	perasaan tersinggung	[pərasa'an tərsiŋguŋ]
to offend (vt)	menyinggung	[mənjiŋguŋ]
to take offense	tersinggung	[tərsiŋguŋ]

indignation	kemarahan	[kemarahan]
to be indignant	marah	[marah]
complaint	komplain, pengaduan	[kompleyn], [peŋaduan]
to complain (vi, vt)	mengeluh	[məŋeluh]

apology	permintaan maaf	[pərminta'an ma'af]
to apologize (vi)	meminta maaf	[meminta ma'af]
to beg pardon	minta maaf	[minta ma'af]

criticism	kritik	[kriti']
to criticize (vt)	mengkritik	[məŋkriti']
accusation	tuduhan	[tuduhan]
to accuse (vt)	menuduh	[mənuduh]

revenge	dendam	[dendam]
to avenge (get revenge)	membalas dendam	[membalas dendam]
to pay back	membalas	[membalas]

disdain	penghinaan	[peŋhina'an]
to despise (vt)	benci, membenci	[bentʃi], [membentʃi]
hatred, hate	rasa benci	[rasa bentʃi]
to hate (vt)	membenci	[membentʃi]

nervous (adj)	gugup, grogi	[gugup], [grogi]
to be nervous	gugup, gelisah	[gugup], [gelisah]
angry (mad)	marah	[marah]
to make angry	membuat marah	[membuat marah]

humiliation	penghinaan	[peŋhina'an]
to humiliate (vt)	merendahkan	[merendahkan]
to humiliate oneself	merendahkan diri sendiri	[merendahkan diri sendiri]

| shock | keterkejutan | [keterkedʒ'utan] |
| to shock (vt) | mengejutkan | [məŋedʒ'utkan] |

| trouble (e.g., serious ~) | kesulitan | [kesulitan] |
| unpleasant (adj) | tidak menyenangkan | [tida' menjenaŋkan] |

fear (dread)	ketakutan	[ketakutan]
terrible (storm, heat)	dahsyat	[dahʃat]
scary (e.g., ~ story)	menakutkan	[mənakutkan]
horror	horor, ketakutan	[horor], [ketakutan]
awful (crime, news)	buruk, parah	[buruk], [parah]

| to begin to tremble | gemetar | [gemetar] |
| to cry (weep) | menangis | [mənaŋis] |

| to start crying | menangis | [mənaŋis] |
| tear | air mata | [air mata] |

fault	kesalahan	[kesalahan]
guilt (feeling)	rasa bersalah	[rasa bərsalah]
dishonor (disgrace)	aib	[aib]
protest	protes	[protes]
stress	stres	[stres]

to disturb (vt)	mengganggu	[məŋgaŋgu]
to be furious	marah	[marah]
mad, angry (adj)	marah	[marah]
to end (~ a relationship)	menghentikan	[məŋhentikan]
to swear (at sb)	menyumpahi	[mənyumpahi]

to scare (become afraid)	takut	[takut]
to hit (strike with hand)	memukul	[memukul]
to fight (street fight, etc.)	berkelahi	[bərkelahi]

to settle (a conflict)	menyelesaikan	[mənjelesajkan]
discontented (adj)	tidak puas	[tida' puas]
furious (adj)	garam	[garam]

| It's not good! | Tidak baik! | [tida' bai'!] |
| It's bad! | Jelek! Buruk! | [dʒ'ele'!], [buru'!] |

Medicine

68. Diseases

sickness	penyakit	[penjakit]
to be sick	sakit	[sakit]
health	kesehatan	[kesehatan]

runny nose (coryza)	hidung meler	[hiduŋ meler]
tonsillitis	radang tonsil	[radaŋ tonsil]
cold (illness)	pilek, selesma	[pilek], [selesma]
to catch a cold	masuk angin	[masuʔ aŋin]

bronchitis	bronkitis	[bronkitis]
pneumonia	radang paru-paru	[radaŋ paru-paru]
flu, influenza	flu	[flu]

nearsighted (adj)	rabun jauh	[rabun dʒ'auh]
farsighted (adj)	rabun dekat	[rabun dekat]
strabismus (crossed eyes)	mata juling	[mata dʒ'uliŋ]
cross-eyed (adj)	bermata juling	[bərmata dʒ'uliŋ]
cataract	katarak	[kataraʔ]
glaucoma	glaukoma	[glaukoma]

stroke	stroke	[stroke]
heart attack	infark	[infarʔ]
myocardial infarction	serangan jantung	[seraŋan dʒ'antuŋ]
paralysis	kelumpuhan	[kelumpuhan]
to paralyze (vt)	melumpuhkan	[melumpuhkan]

allergy	alergi	[alergi]
asthma	asma	[asma]
diabetes	diabetes	[diabetes]

| toothache | sakit gigi | [sakit gigi] |
| caries | karies | [karies] |

diarrhea	diare	[diare]
constipation	konstipasi, sembelit	[konstipasi], [sembelit]
stomach upset	gangguan pencernaan	[gaŋuan pentʃarnaʔan]
food poisoning	keracunan makanan	[keratʃunan makanan]
to get food poisoning	keracunan makanan	[keratʃunan makanan]

arthritis	artritis	[artritis]
rickets	rakitis	[rakitis]
rheumatism	rematik	[rematiʔ]

atherosclerosis	aterosklerosis	[aterosklorosis]
gastritis	radang perut	[radaŋ pərut]
appendicitis	apendisitis	[apendisitis]
cholecystitis	radang pundi empedu	[radaŋ pundi empedu]
ulcer	tukak lambung	[tuka' lambuŋ]
measles	penyakit campak	[penjakit tʃampa']
rubella (German measles)	penyakit campak Jerman	[penjakit tʃampa' dʒʲerman]
jaundice	sakit kuning	[sakit kuniŋ]
hepatitis	hepatitis	[hepatitis]
schizophrenia	skizofrenia	[skizofrenia]
rabies (hydrophobia)	rabies	[rabies]
neurosis	neurosis	[neurosis]
concussion	gegar otak	[gegar ota']
cancer	kanker	[kanker]
sclerosis	sklerosis	[sklerosis]
multiple sclerosis	sklerosis multipel	[sklerosis multipel]
alcoholism	alkoholisme	[alkoholisme]
alcoholic (n)	alkoholik	[alkoholi']
syphilis	sifilis	[sifilis]
AIDS	AIDS	[ajds]
tumor	tumor	[tumor]
malignant (adj)	ganas	[ganas]
benign (adj)	jinak	[dʒina']
fever	demam	[demam]
malaria	malaria	[malaria]
gangrene	gangren	[gaŋren]
seasickness	mabuk laut	[mabu' laut]
epilepsy	epilepsi	[epilepsi]
epidemic	epidemi	[epidemi]
typhus	tifus	[tifus]
tuberculosis	tuberkulosis	[tuberkulosis]
cholera	kolera	[kolera]
plague (bubonic ~)	penyakit pes	[penjakit pes]

69. Symptoms. Treatments. Part 1

symptom	gejala	[gedʒʲala]
temperature	temperatur, suhu	[temperatur], [suhu]
high temperature (fever)	temperatur tinggi	[temperatur tiŋgi]
pulse	denyut nadi	[denyut nadi]
dizziness (vertigo)	rasa pening	[rasa peniŋ]
hot (adj)	panas	[panas]

| shivering | menggigil | [məŋgigil] |
| pale (e.g., ~ face) | pucat | [putʃat] |

cough	batuk	[batuʔ]
to cough (vi)	batuk	[batuʔ]
to sneeze (vi)	bersin	[bersin]
faint	pingsan	[piŋsan]
to faint (vi)	jatuh pingsan	[dʒatuh piŋsan]

bruise (hématome)	luka memar	[luka memar]
bump (lump)	bengkak	[beŋkaʔ]
to bang (bump)	terantuk	[tərantuʔ]
contusion (bruise)	luka memar	[luka memar]
to get a bruise	kena luka memar	[kena luka memar]

to limp (vi)	pincang	[pintʃaŋ]
dislocation	keseleo	[keseleo]
to dislocate (vt)	keseleo	[keseleo]
fracture	fraktura, patah tulang	[fraktura], [patah tulaŋ]
to have a fracture	patah tulang	[patah tulaŋ]

cut (e.g., paper ~)	teriris	[təriris]
to cut oneself	teriris	[təriris]
bleeding	perdarahan	[pərdarahan]

| burn (injury) | luka bakar | [luka bakar] |
| to get burned | menderita luka bakar | [mənderita luka bakar] |

to prick (vt)	menusuk	[mənusuʔ]
to prick oneself	tertusuk	[tərtusuʔ]
to injure (vt)	melukai	[melukaj]
injury	cedera	[tʃedera]
wound	luka	[luka]
trauma	trauma	[trauma]

to be delirious	mengigau	[məŋigau]
to stutter (vi)	gagap	[gagap]
sunstroke	sengatan matahari	[seŋatan matahari]

70. Symptoms. Treatments. Part 2

| pain, ache | sakit | [sakit] |
| splinter (in foot, etc.) | selumbar | [selumbar] |

sweat (perspiration)	keringat	[keriŋat]
to sweat (perspire)	berkeringat	[bərkeriŋat]
vomiting	muntah	[muntah]
convulsions	kram	[kram]
pregnant (adj)	hamil	[hamil]
to be born	lahir	[lahir]

delivery, labor	persalinan	[persalinan]
to deliver (~ a baby)	melahirkan	[melahirkan]
abortion	aborsi	[aborsi]

breathing, respiration	pernapasan	[pernapasan]
in-breath (inhalation)	tarikan napas	[tarikan napas]
out-breath (exhalation)	napas keluar	[napas keluar]
to exhale (breathe out)	mengembuskan napas	[menembuskan napas]
to inhale (vi)	menarik napas	[menariʔ napas]

disabled person	penderita cacat	[penderita t∫at∫at]
cripple	penderita cacat	[penderita t∫at∫at]
drug addict	pecandu narkoba	[pet∫andu narkoba]

deaf (adj)	tunarungu	[tunaruŋu]
mute (adj)	tunawicara	[tunawit∫ara]
deaf mute (adj)	tunarungu-wicara	[tunaruŋu-wit∫ara]

mad, insane (adj)	gila	[gila]
madman (demented person)	lelaki gila	[lelaki gila]
madwoman	perempuan gila	[perempuan gila]
to go insane	menggila	[meŋgila]

gene	gen	[gen]
immunity	imunitas	[imunitas]
hereditary (adj)	turun-temurun	[turun-temurun]
congenital (adj)	bawaan	[bawa'an]

virus	virus	[virus]
microbe	mikroba	[mikroba]
bacterium	bakteri	[bakteri]
infection	infeksi	[infeksi]

71. Symptoms. Treatments. Part 3

| hospital | rumah sakit | [rumah sakit] |
| patient | pasien | [pasien] |

diagnosis	diagnosis	[diagnosis]
cure	perawatan	[perawatan]
medical treatment	pengobatan medis	[peŋobatan medis]
to get treatment	berobat	[berobat]
to treat (~ a patient)	merawat	[merawat]
to nurse (look after)	merawat	[merawat]
care (nursing ~)	pengasuhan	[peŋasuhan]

operation, surgery	operasi, pembedahan	[operasi], [pembedahan]
to bandage (head, limb)	membalut	[membalut]
bandaging	pembalutan	[pembalutan]

vaccination	**vaksinasi**	[vaksinasi]
to vaccinate (vt)	**memvaksinasi**	[memvaksinasi]
injection, shot	**suntikan**	[suntikan]
to give an injection	**menyuntik**	[mənyuntiʔ]
attack	**serangan**	[seraŋan]
amputation	**amputasi**	[amputasi]
to amputate (vt)	**mengamputasi**	[mənʲamputasi]
coma	**koma**	[koma]
to be in a coma	**dalam keadaan koma**	[dalam keadaʔan koma]
intensive care	**perawatan intensif**	[perawatan intensif]
to recover (~ from flu)	**sembuh**	[sembuh]
condition (patient's ~)	**keadaan**	[keadaʔan]
consciousness	**kesadaran**	[kesadaran]
memory (faculty)	**memori, daya ingat**	[memori], [daja iŋat]
to pull out (tooth)	**mencabut**	[mentʃabut]
filling	**tambalan**	[tambalan]
to fill (a tooth)	**menambal**	[mənambal]
hypnosis	**hipnosis**	[hipnosis]
to hypnotize (vt)	**menghipnosis**	[məŋhipnosis]

72. Doctors

doctor	**dokter**	[dokter]
nurse	**suster, juru rawat**	[suster], [dʒʲuru rawat]
personal doctor	**dokter pribadi**	[dokter pribadi]
dentist	**dokter gigi**	[dokter gigi]
eye doctor	**dokter mata**	[dokter mata]
internist	**ahli penyakit dalam**	[ahli penjakit dalam]
surgeon	**dokter bedah**	[dokter bedah]
psychiatrist	**psikiater**	[psikiater]
pediatrician	**dokter anak**	[dokter anaʔ]
psychologist	**psikolog**	[psikolog]
gynecologist	**ginekolog**	[ginekolog]
cardiologist	**kardiolog**	[kardiolog]

73. Medicine. Drugs. Accessories

medicine, drug	**obat**	[obat]
remedy	**obat**	[obat]
to prescribe (vt)	**meresepkan**	[meresepkan]
prescription	**resep**	[resep]
tablet, pill	**pil, tablet**	[pil], [tablet]

ointment	salep	[salep]
ampule	ampul	[ampul]
mixture	obat cair	[obat tʃajr]
syrup	sirop	[sirop]
pill	pil	[pil]
powder	bubuk	[bubuʔ]
gauze bandage	perban	[perban]
cotton wool	kapas	[kapas]
iodine	iodium	[iodium]
Band-Aid	plester obat	[plester obat]
eyedropper	tetes mata	[tetes mata]
thermometer	termometer	[termometer]
syringe	alat suntik	[alat suntiʔ]
wheelchair	kursi roda	[kursi roda]
crutches	kruk	[kruʔ]
painkiller	obat bius	[obat bius]
laxative	laksatif, obat pencuci perut	[laksatif], [obat pentʃutʃi perut]
spirits (ethanol)	spiritus, alkohol	[spiritus], [alkohol]
medicinal herbs	tanaman obat	[tanaman obat]
herbal (~ tea)	herbal	[herbal]

74. Smoking. Tobacco products

tobacco	tembakau	[tembakau]
cigarette	rokok	[rokoʔ]
cigar	cerutu	[tʃerutu]
pipe	pipa	[pipa]
pack (of cigarettes)	bungkus	[buŋkus]
matches	korek api	[koreʔ api]
matchbox	kotak korek api	[kotaʔ koreʔ api]
lighter	pemantik	[pemantiʔ]
ashtray	asbak	[asbaʔ]
cigarette case	selepa	[selepa]
cigarette holder	pemegang rokok	[pemegaŋ rokoʔ]
filter (cigarette tip)	filter	[filter]
to smoke (vi, vt)	merokok	[merokoʔ]
to light a cigarette	menyulut rokok	[menyulut rokoʔ]
smoking	merokok	[merokoʔ]
smoker	perokok	[perokoʔ]
stub, butt (of cigarette)	puntung rokok	[puntuŋ rokoʔ]
smoke, fumes	asap	[asap]
ash	abu	[abu]

HUMAN HABITAT

City

city, town	**kota**	[kota]
capital city	**ibu kota**	[ibu kota]
village	**desa**	[desa]
city map	**peta kota**	[peta kota]
downtown	**pusat kota**	[pusat kota]
suburb	**pinggir kota**	[piŋgir kota]
suburban (adj)	**pinggir kota**	[piŋgir kota]
outskirts	**pinggir**	[piŋgir]
environs (suburbs)	**daerah sekitarnya**	[daerah sekitarnja]
city block	**blok**	[bloʔ]
residential block (area)	**blok perumahan**	[bloʔ pərumahan]
traffic	**lalu lintas**	[lalu lintas]
traffic lights	**lampu lalu lintas**	[lampu lalu lintas]
public transportation	**angkot**	[aŋkot]
intersection	**persimpangan**	[pərsimpaŋan]
crosswalk	**penyeberangan**	[penjeberaŋan]
pedestrian underpass	**terowongan**	[tərowoŋan
	penyeberangan	penjeberaŋan]
to cross (~ the street)	**menyeberang**	[mənjeberaŋ]
pedestrian	**pejalan kaki**	[pedʒʲalan kaki]
sidewalk	**trotoar**	[trotoar]
bridge	**jembatan**	[dʒʲembatan]
embankment (river walk)	**tepi sungai**	[tepi suŋaj]
fountain	**air mancur**	[air mantʃur]
allée (garden walkway)	**jalan kecil**	[dʒʲalan ketʃil]
park	**taman**	[taman]
boulevard	**bulevar, adimarga**	[bulevar], [adimarga]
square	**lapangan**	[lapaŋan]
avenue (wide street)	**jalan raya**	[dʒʲalan raja]
street	**jalan**	[dʒʲalan]
side street	**gang**	[gaŋ]
dead end	**jalan buntu**	[dʒʲalan buntu]
house	**rumah**	[rumah]

building	**gedung**	[gɔduŋ]
skyscraper	**pencakar langit**	[pentʃakar laŋit]
facade	**bagian depan**	[bagian depan]
roof	**atap**	[atap]
window	**jendela**	[dʒ'endela]
arch	**lengkungan**	[leŋkuŋan]
column	**pilar**	[pilar]
corner	**sudut**	[sudut]
store window	**etalase**	[etalase]
signboard (store sign, etc.)	**papan nama**	[papan nama]
poster	**poster**	[poster]
advertising poster	**poster iklan**	[poster iklan]
billboard	**papan iklan**	[papan iklan]
garbage, trash	**sampah**	[sampah]
trashcan (public ~)	**tong sampah**	[toŋ sampah]
to litter (vi)	**menyampah**	[mənjampah]
garbage dump	**tempat pemrosesan akhir (TPA)**	[tempat pemrosesan ahir]
phone booth	**gardu telepon umum**	[gardu telepon umum]
lamppost	**tiang lampu**	[tiaŋ lampu]
bench (park ~)	**bangku**	[baŋku]
police officer	**polisi**	[polisi]
police	**polisi, kepolisian**	[polisi], [kepolisian]
beggar	**pengemis**	[peŋemis]
homeless (n)	**tuna wisma**	[tuna wisma]

76. Urban institutions

store	**toko**	[toko]
drugstore, pharmacy	**apotek, toko obat**	[apotek], [toko obat]
eyeglass store	**optik**	[optiʔ]
shopping mall	**toserba**	[toserba]
supermarket	**pasar swalayan**	[pasar swalajan]
bakery	**toko roti**	[toko roti]
baker	**pembuat roti**	[pembuat roti]
pastry shop	**toko kue**	[toko kue]
grocery store	**toko pangan**	[toko paŋan]
butcher shop	**toko daging**	[toko dagiŋ]
produce store	**toko sayur**	[toko sajur]
market	**pasar**	[pasar]
coffee house	**warung kopi**	[waruŋ kopi]
restaurant	**restoran**	[restoran]

pub, bar	**kedai bir**	[kedaj bir]
pizzeria	**kedai piza**	[kedaj piza]
hair salon	**salon rambut**	[salon rambut]
post office	**kantor pos**	[kantor pos]
dry cleaners	**penatu kimia**	[penatu kimia]
photo studio	**studio foto**	[studio foto]
shoe store	**toko sepatu**	[toko sepatu]
bookstore	**toko buku**	[toko buku]
sporting goods store	**toko alat olahraga**	[toko alat olahraga]
clothes repair shop	**reparasi pakaian**	[reparasi pakajan]
formal wear rental	**rental pakaian**	[rental pakajan]
video rental store	**rental film**	[rental film]
circus	**sirkus**	[sirkus]
zoo	**kebun binatang**	[kebun binataŋ]
movie theater	**bioskop**	[bioskop]
museum	**museum**	[museum]
library	**perpustakaan**	[pərpustakaʔan]
theater	**teater**	[teater]
opera (opera house)	**opera**	[opera]
nightclub	**klub malam**	[klub malam]
casino	**kasino**	[kasino]
mosque	**masjid**	[masdʒid]
synagogue	**sinagoga, kanisah**	[sinagoga], [kanisah]
cathedral	**katedral**	[katedral]
temple	**kuil, candi**	[kuil], [tʃandi]
church	**gereja**	[geredʒʲa]
college	**institut, perguruan tinggi**	[institut], [pərguruan tiŋgi]
university	**universitas**	[universitas]
school	**sekolah**	[sekolah]
prefecture	**prefektur, distrik**	[prefektur], [distriʔ]
city hall	**balai kota**	[balaj kota]
hotel	**hotel**	[hotel]
bank	**bank**	[banʔ]
embassy	**kedutaan besar**	[kedutaʔan besar]
travel agency	**kantor pariwisata**	[kantor pariwisata]
information office	**kantor penerangan**	[kantor peneraŋan]
currency exchange	**kantor penukaran uang**	[kantor penukaran uaŋ]
subway	**kereta api bawah tanah**	[kereta api bawah tanah]
hospital	**rumah sakit**	[rumah sakit]
gas station	**SPBU,**	[es-pe-be-u],
	stasiun bensin	[stasjun bensin]
parking lot	**tempat parkir**	[tempat parkir]

77. Urban transportation

bus	**bus**	[bus]
streetcar	**trem**	[trem]
trolley bus	**bus listrik**	[bus listriʔ]
route (of bus, etc.)	**trayek**	[traeʔ]
number (e.g., bus ~)	**nomor**	[nomor]
to go by ...	**naik ...**	[naiʔ ...]
to get on (~ the bus)	**naik**	[naiʔ]
to get off ...	**turun ...**	[turun ...]
stop (e.g., bus ~)	**halte, pemberhentian**	[halte], [pemberhentian]
next stop	**halte berikutnya**	[halte berikutnja]
terminus	**halte terakhir**	[halte terahir]
schedule	**jadwal**	[dʒadwal]
to wait (vt)	**menunggu**	[menungu]
ticket	**tiket**	[tiket]
fare	**harga karcis**	[harga kartʃis]
cashier (ticket seller)	**kasir**	[kasir]
ticket inspection	**pemeriksaan tiket**	[pemeriksaʔan tiket]
ticket inspector	**kondektur**	[kondektur]
to be late (for ...)	**terlambat ...**	[terlambat ...]
to miss (~ the train, etc.)	**ketinggalan**	[ketingalan]
to be in a hurry	**tergesa-gesa**	[tergesa-gesa]
taxi, cab	**taksi**	[taksi]
taxi driver	**sopir taksi**	[sopir taksi]
by taxi	**naik taksi**	[naiʔ taksi]
taxi stand	**pangkalan taksi**	[pankalan taksi]
to call a taxi	**memanggil taksi**	[memangil taksi]
to take a taxi	**menaiki taksi**	[menajki taksi]
traffic	**lalu lintas**	[lalu lintas]
traffic jam	**kemacetan lalu lintas**	[kematʃetan lalu lintas]
rush hour	**jam sibuk**	[dʒam sibuʔ]
to park (vi)	**parkir**	[parkir]
to park (vt)	**memarkir**	[memarkir]
parking lot	**tempat parkir**	[tempat parkir]
subway	**kereta api bawah tanah**	[kereta api bawah tanah]
station	**stasiun**	[stasiun]
to take the subway	**naik kereta api bawah tanah**	[naiʔ kereta api bawah tanah]
train	**kereta api**	[kereta api]
train station	**stasiun kereta api**	[stasiun kereta api]

78. Sightseeing

monument	monumen, patung	[monumen], [patuŋ]
fortress	benteng	[benteŋ]
palace	istana	[istana]
castle	kastil	[kastil]
tower	menara	[mənara]
mausoleum	mausoleum	[mausoleum]
architecture	arsitektur	[arsitektur]
medieval (adj)	abad pertengahan	[abad pərteŋahan]
ancient (adj)	kuno	[kuno]
national (adj)	nasional	[nasional]
famous (monument, etc.)	terkenal	[tərkenal]
tourist	turis, wisatawan	[turis], [wisatawan]
guide (person)	pemandu wisata	[pemandu wisata]
excursion, sightseeing tour	ekskursi	[ekskursi]
to show (vt)	menunjukkan	[mənundʒ'uʔkan]
to tell (vt)	menceritakan	[məntʃeritakan]
to find (vt)	mendapatkan	[məndapatkan]
to get lost (lose one's way)	tersesat	[tərsesat]
map (e.g., subway ~)	denah	[denah]
map (e.g., city ~)	peta	[peta]
souvenir, gift	suvenir	[suvenir]
gift shop	toko suvenir	[toko suvenir]
to take pictures	memotret	[memotret]
to have one's picture taken	berfoto	[bərfoto]

79. Shopping

to buy (purchase)	membeli	[membeli]
purchase	belanjaan	[belandʒ'a'an]
to go shopping	berbelanja	[bərbelandʒ'a]
shopping	berbelanja	[bərbelandʒ'a]
to be open (ab. store)	buka	[buka]
to be closed	tutup	[tutup]
footwear, shoes	sepatu	[sepatu]
clothes, clothing	pakaian	[pakajan]
cosmetics	kosmetik	[kosmetiʔ]
food products	produk makanan	[produʔ makanan]
gift, present	hadiah	[hadiah]
salesman	pramuniaga	[pramuniaga]
saleswoman	pramuniaga perempuan	[pramuniaga pərempuan]

check out, cash desk	kas	[kas]
mirror	cermin	[tʃermin]
counter (store ~)	konter	[konter]
fitting room	kamar pas	[kamar pas]

to try on	mengepas	[məŋepas]
to fit (ab. dress, etc.)	pas, cocok	[pas], [tʃotʃoʔ]
to like (I like …)	suka	[suka]

price	harga	[harga]
price tag	label harga	[label harga]
to cost (vt)	berharga	[bərharga]
How much?	Berapa?	[bərapa?]
discount	diskon	[diskon]

inexpensive (adj)	tidak mahal	[tidaʔ mahal]
cheap (adj)	murah	[murah]
expensive (adj)	mahal	[mahal]
It's expensive	Ini mahal	[ini mahal]

rental (n)	rental, persewaan	[rental], [pərsewaʔan]
to rent (~ a tuxedo)	menyewa	[mənjewa]
credit (trade credit)	kredit	[kredit]
on credit (adv)	secara kredit	[setʃara kredit]

80. Money

money	uang	[uaŋ]
currency exchange	pertukaran mata uang	[pərtukaran mata uaŋ]
exchange rate	nilai tukar	[nilaj tukar]
ATM	Anjungan Tunai Mandiri, ATM	[andʒّuŋan tunaj mandiri], [a-te-em]
coin	koin	[koin]

dollar	dolar	[dolar]
euro	euro	[euro]

lira	lira	[lira]
Deutschmark	Mark Jerman	[marʔ dʒّerman]
franc	franc	[frantʃ]
pound sterling	poundsterling	[paundsterliŋ]
yen	yen	[yen]

debt	utang	[utaŋ]
debtor	pengutang	[pəŋutaŋ]
to lend (money)	meminjamkan	[memindʒّamkan]
to borrow (vi, vt)	meminjam	[memindʒّam]

bank	bank	[banʔ]
account	rekening	[rekeniŋ]

to deposit (vt)	memasukkan	[memasuʔkan]
to deposit into the account	memasukkan ke rekening	[memasuʔkan ke rekeniŋ]
to withdraw (vt)	menarik uang	[mənariʔ uaŋ]
credit card	kartu kredit	[kartu kredit]
cash	uang kontan, uang tunai	[uaŋ kontan], [uaŋ tunaj]
check	cek	[tʃeʔ]
to write a check	menulis cek	[mənulis tʃeʔ]
checkbook	buku cek	[buku tʃeʔ]
wallet	dompet	[dompet]
change purse	dompet, pundi-pundi	[dompet], [pundi-pundi]
safe	brankas	[brankas]
heir	pewaris	[pewaris]
inheritance	warisan	[warisan]
fortune (wealth)	kekayaan	[kekajaʔan]
lease	sewa	[sewa]
rent (money)	uang sewa	[uaŋ sewa]
to rent (sth from sb)	menyewa	[mənjewa]
price	harga	[harga]
cost	harga	[harga]
sum	jumlah	[dʒʲumlah]
to spend (vt)	menghabiskan	[məŋhabiskan]
expenses	ongkos	[oŋkos]
to economize (vi, vt)	menghemat	[məŋhemat]
economical	hemat	[hemat]
to pay (vi, vt)	membayar	[membajar]
payment	pembayaran	[pembajaran]
change (give the ~)	kembalian	[kembalian]
tax	pajak	[padʒʲaʔ]
fine	denda	[denda]
to fine (vt)	mendenda	[məndenda]

81. Post. Postal service

post office	kantor pos	[kantor pos]
mail (letters, etc.)	surat	[surat]
mailman	tukang pos	[tukaŋ pos]
opening hours	jam buka	[dʒʲam buka]
letter	surat	[surat]
registered letter	surat tercatat	[surat tərtʃatat]
postcard	kartu pos	[kartu pos]

telegram	telegram	[telegram]
package (parcel)	parsel, paket pos	[parsel], [paket pos]
money transfer	wesel pos	[wesel pos]
to receive (vt)	menerima	[mənerima]
to send (vt)	mengirim	[məŋirim]
sending	pengiriman	[peŋiriman]
address	alamat	[alamat]
ZIP code	kode pos	[kode pos]
sender	pengirim	[peŋirim]
receiver	penerima	[penerima]
name (first name)	nama	[nama]
surname (last name)	nama keluarga	[nama keluarga]
postage rate	tarif	[tarif]
standard (adj)	biasa, standar	[biasa], [standar]
economical (adj)	ekonomis	[ekonomis]
weight	berat	[berat]
to weigh (~ letters)	menimbang	[mənimban]
envelope	amplop	[amplop]
postage stamp	prangko	[praŋko]
to stamp an envelope	menempelkan prangko	[mənempelkan praŋko]

Dwelling. House. Home

82. House. Dwelling

house	**rumah**	[rumah]
at home (adv)	**di rumah**	[di rumah]
yard	**pekarangan**	[pekaraŋan]
fence (iron ~)	**pagar**	[pagar]
brick (n)	**bata, batu bata**	[bata], [batu bata]
brick (as adj)	**bata, batu bata**	[bata], [batu bata]
stone (n)	**batu**	[batu]
stone (as adj)	**batu**	[batu]
concrete (n)	**beton**	[beton]
concrete (as adj)	**beton**	[beton]
new (new-built)	**baru**	[baru]
old (adj)	**tua**	[tua]
decrepit (house)	**reyot**	[reyot]
modern (adj)	**modern**	[modern]
multistory (adj)	**susun**	[susun]
tall (~ building)	**tinggi**	[tiŋgi]
floor, story	**lantai**	[lantaj]
single-story (adj)	**berlantai satu**	[bərlantaj satu]
1st floor	**lantai bawah**	[lantaj bawah]
top floor	**lantai atas**	[lantaj atas]
roof	**atap**	[atap]
chimney	**cerobong**	[tʃeroboŋ]
roof tiles	**genting**	[gentiŋ]
tiled (adj)	**bergenting**	[bərgentiŋ]
attic (storage place)	**loteng**	[loteŋ]
window	**jendela**	[dʒʲendela]
glass	**kaca**	[katʃa]
window ledge	**ambang jendela**	[ambaŋ dʒʲendela]
shutters	**daun jendela**	[daun dʒʲendela]
wall	**dinding**	[dindiŋ]
balcony	**balkon**	[balkon]
downspout	**pipa talang**	[pipa talaŋ]
upstairs (to be ~)	**di atas**	[di atas]
to go upstairs	**naik**	[naiʔ]
to come down (the stairs)	**turun**	[turun]
to move (to new premises)	**pindah**	[pindah]

83. House. Entrance. Lift

entrance	**pintu masuk**	[pintu masuʔ]
stairs (stairway)	**tangga**	[taŋga]
steps	**anak tangga**	[anaʔ taŋga]
banister	**pegangan tangan**	[pegaŋan taŋan]
lobby (hotel ~)	**lobi, ruang depan**	[lobi], [ruaŋ depan]

mailbox	**kotak pos**	[kotaʔ pos]
garbage can	**tong sampah**	[toŋ sampah]
trash chute	**saluran pembuangan sampah**	[saluran pembuaŋan sampah]

elevator	**elevator**	[elevator]
freight elevator	**lift barang**	[lift baraŋ]
elevator cage	**kabin lift**	[kabin lift]
to take the elevator	**naik elevator**	[naiʔ elevator]

apartment	**apartemen**	[apartemen]
residents (~ of a building)	**penghuni**	[peŋhuni]
neighbor (masc.)	**tetangga**	[tetaŋga]
neighbor (fem.)	**tetangga**	[tetaŋga]
neighbors	**para tetangga**	[para tetaŋga]

84. House. Doors. Locks

door	**pintu**	[pintu]
gate (vehicle ~)	**pintu gerbang**	[pintu gerbaŋ]
handle, doorknob	**gagang pintu**	[gagaŋ pintu]
to unlock (unbolt)	**membuka kunci**	[membuka kunʧi]
to open (vt)	**membuka**	[membuka]
to close (vt)	**menutup**	[menutup]

key	**kunci**	[kunʧi]
bunch (of keys)	**serangkaian kunci**	[seraŋkajan kunʧi]
to creak (door, etc.)	**bergerit**	[bergerit]
creak	**gerit**	[gerit]
hinge (door ~)	**engsel**	[eŋsel]
doormat	**tikar**	[tikar]

door lock	**kunci pintu**	[kunʧi pintu]
keyhole	**lubang kunci**	[lubaŋ kunʧi]
crossbar (sliding bar)	**gerendel**	[gerendel]
door latch	**gerendel**	[gerendel]
padlock	**gembok**	[gemboʔ]

to ring (~ the door bell)	**membunyikan**	[membunjikan]
ringing (sound)	**dering**	[deriŋ]
doorbell	**bel**	[bel]

doorbell button	kenop	[kenop]
knock (at the door)	ketukan	[ketukan]
to knock (vi)	mengetuk	[məŋetuʔ]

code	kode	[kode]
combination lock	gembok berkode	[gemboʔ berkode]
intercom	interkom	[interkom]
number (on the door)	nomor	[nomor]
doorplate	papan tanda	[papan tanda]
peephole	lubang intip	[lubaŋ intip]

85. Country house

village	desa	[desa]
vegetable garden	kebun sayur	[kebun sajur]
fence	pagar	[pagar]
picket fence	pagar	[pagar]
wicket gate	pintu pagar	[pintu pagar]

granary	lumbung	[lumbuŋ]
root cellar	kelder	[kelder]
shed (garden ~)	gubuk	[gubuʔ]
well (water)	sumur	[sumur]

stove (wood-fired ~)	tungku	[tuŋku]
to stoke the stove	menyalakan tungku	[mənjalakan tuŋku]
firewood	kayu bakar	[kaju bakar]
log (firewood)	potongan kayu bakar	[potoŋan kaju bakar]

veranda	beranda	[bəranda]
deck (terrace)	teras	[teras]
stoop (front steps)	anjungan depan	[andʒiuŋan depan]
swing (hanging seat)	ayunan	[ajunan]

86. Castle. Palace

castle	kastil	[kastil]
palace	istana	[istana]
fortress	benteng	[benteŋ]

wall (round castle)	tembok	[temboʔ]
tower	menara	[mənara]
keep, donjon	menara utama	[mənara utama]

portcullis	jeruji pintu kota	[dʒierudʒi pintu kota]
underground passage	jalan bawah tanah	[dʒialan bawah tanah]
moat	parit	[parit]
chain	rantai	[rantaj]

arrow loop	laras panah, lop panah	[laras panah], [lop panah]
magnificent (adj)	megah	[megah]
majestic (adj)	megah sekali	[megah sekali]
impregnable (adj)	sulit dicapai	[sulit ditʃapaj]
medieval (adj)	abad pertengahan	[abad pertenahan]

87. Apartment

apartment	apartemen	[apartemen]
room	kamar	[kamar]
bedroom	kamar tidur	[kamar tidur]
dining room	ruang makan	[ruaŋ makan]
living room	ruang tamu	[ruaŋ tamu]
study (home office)	ruang kerja	[ruaŋ kerdʒʲa]
entry room	ruang depan	[ruaŋ depan]
bathroom (room with a bath or shower)	kamar mandi	[kamar mandi]
half bath	kamar kecil	[kamar ketʃil]
ceiling	plafon, langit-langit	[plafon], [laŋit-laŋit]
floor	lantai	[lantaj]
corner	sudut	[sudut]

88. Apartment. Cleaning

to clean (vi, vt)	membereskan	[membereskan]
to put away (to stow)	meletakkan	[meletaʔkan]
dust	debu	[debu]
dusty (adj)	debu	[debu]
to dust (vt)	menyapu debu	[menjapu debu]
vacuum cleaner	pengisap debu	[peɲisap debu]
to vacuum (vt)	membersihkan dengan pengisap debu	[membersihkan deŋan peɲisap debu]
to sweep (vi, vt)	menyapu	[menjapu]
sweepings	sampah	[sampah]
order	kerapian	[kerapian]
disorder, mess	berantakan	[berantakan]
mop	kain pel	[kain pel]
dust cloth	lap	[lap]
short broom	sapu lidi	[sapu lidi]
dustpan	pengki	[peŋki]

89. Furniture. Interior

furniture	**mebel**	[mebel]
table	**meja**	[medʒʲa]
chair	**kursi**	[kursi]
bed	**ranjang**	[randʒʲaŋ]
couch, sofa	**dipan**	[dipan]
armchair	**kursi malas**	[kursi malas]
bookcase	**lemari buku**	[lemari buku]
shelf	**rak**	[raʔ]
wardrobe	**lemari pakaian**	[lemari pakajan]
coat rack (wall-mounted ~)	**kapstok**	[kapstoʔ]
coat stand	**kapstok berdiri**	[kapstoʔ bərdiri]
bureau, dresser	**lemari laci**	[lemari latʃi]
coffee table	**meja kopi**	[medʒʲa kopi]
mirror	**cermin**	[tʃermin]
carpet	**permadani**	[pərmadani]
rug, small carpet	**karpet kecil**	[karpet ketʃil]
fireplace	**perapian**	[pərapian]
candle	**lilin**	[lilin]
candlestick	**kaki lilin**	[kaki lilin]
drapes	**gorden**	[gorden]
wallpaper	**kertas dinding**	[kertas dindiŋ]
blinds (jalousie)	**kerai**	[keraj]
table lamp	**lampu meja**	[lampu medʒʲa]
wall lamp (sconce)	**lampu dinding**	[lampu dindiŋ]
floor lamp	**lampu lantai**	[lampu lantaj]
chandelier	**lampu bercabang**	[lampu bərtʃabaŋ]
leg (of chair, table)	**kaki**	[kaki]
armrest	**lengan**	[leŋan]
back (backrest)	**sandaran**	[sandaran]
drawer	**laci**	[latʃi]

90. Bedding

bedclothes	**kain kasur**	[kain kasur]
pillow	**bantal**	[bantal]
pillowcase	**sarung bantal**	[saruŋ bantal]
duvet, comforter	**selimut**	[selimut]
sheet	**seprai**	[sepraj]
bedspread	**selubung kasur**	[selubuŋ kasur]

91. Kitchen

kitchen	**dapur**	[dapur]
gas	**gas**	[gas]
gas stove (range)	**kompor gas**	[kompor gas]
electric stove	**kompor listrik**	[kompor listriʔ]
oven	**oven**	[oven]
microwave oven	**microwave**	[majkrowav]
refrigerator	**lemari es, kulkas**	[lemari es], [kulkas]
freezer	**lemari pembeku**	[lemari pembeku]
dishwasher	**mesin pencuci piring**	[mesin pentʃutʃi piriŋ]
meat grinder	**alat pelumat daging**	[alat pelumat dagiŋ]
juicer	**mesin sari buah**	[mesin sari buah]
toaster	**alat pemanggang roti**	[alat pemaŋgaŋ roti]
mixer	**pencampur**	[pentʃampur]
coffee machine	**mesin pembuat kopi**	[mesin pembuat kopi]
coffee pot	**teko kopi**	[teko kopi]
coffee grinder	**mesin penggiling kopi**	[mesin peŋgiliŋ kopi]
kettle	**cerek**	[tʃereʔ]
teapot	**teko**	[teko]
lid	**tutup**	[tutup]
tea strainer	**saringan teh**	[sariŋan teh]
spoon	**sendok**	[sendoʔ]
teaspoon	**sendok teh**	[sendoʔ teh]
soup spoon	**sendok makan**	[sendoʔ makan]
fork	**garpu**	[garpu]
knife	**pisau**	[pisau]
tableware (dishes)	**piring mangkuk**	[piriŋ maŋkuʔ]
plate (dinner ~)	**piring**	[piriŋ]
saucer	**alas cangkir**	[alas tʃaŋkir]
shot glass	**seloki**	[seloki]
glass (tumbler)	**gelas**	[gelas]
cup	**cangkir**	[tʃaŋkir]
sugar bowl	**wadah gula**	[wadah gula]
salt shaker	**wadah garam**	[wadah garam]
pepper shaker	**wadah merica**	[wadah meritʃa]
butter dish	**wadah mentega**	[wadah mentega]
stock pot (soup pot)	**panci**	[pantʃi]
frying pan (skillet)	**kuali**	[kuali]
ladle	**sudu**	[sudu]
colander	**saringan**	[sariŋan]
tray (serving ~)	**talam**	[talam]

bottle	**botol**	[botol]
jar (glass)	**gelas**	[gelas]
can	**kaleng**	[kaleŋ]
bottle opener	**pembuka botol**	[pembuka botol]
can opener	**pembuka kaleng**	[pembuka kaleŋ]
corkscrew	**kotrek**	[kotreʔ]
filter	**saringan**	[sariŋan]
to filter (vt)	**saringan**	[sariŋan]
trash, garbage (food waste, etc.)	**sampah**	[sampah]
trash can (kitchen ~)	**tong sampah**	[toŋ sampah]

92. Bathroom

bathroom	**kamar mandi**	[kamar mandi]
water	**air**	[air]
faucet	**keran**	[keran]
hot water	**air panas**	[air panas]
cold water	**air dingin**	[air diŋin]
toothpaste	**pasta gigi**	[pasta gigi]
to brush one's teeth	**menggosok gigi**	[məŋgosoʔ gigi]
toothbrush	**sikat gigi**	[sikat gigi]
to shave (vi)	**bercukur**	[bərtʃukur]
shaving foam	**busa cukur**	[busa tʃukur]
razor	**pisau cukur**	[pisau tʃukur]
to wash (one's hands, etc.)	**mencuci**	[məntʃutʃi]
to take a bath	**mandi**	[mandi]
shower	**pancuran**	[pantʃuran]
to take a shower	**mandi pancuran**	[mandi pantʃuran]
bathtub	**bak mandi**	[baʔ mandi]
toilet (toilet bowl)	**kloset**	[kloset]
sink (washbasin)	**wastafel**	[wastafel]
soap	**sabun**	[sabun]
soap dish	**wadah sabun**	[wadah sabun]
sponge	**spons**	[spons]
shampoo	**sampo**	[sampo]
towel	**handuk**	[handuʔ]
bathrobe	**jubah mandi**	[dʒʲubah mandi]
laundry (process)	**pencucian**	[pentʃutʃian]
washing machine	**mesin cuci**	[mesin tʃutʃi]
to do the laundry	**mencuci**	[məntʃutʃi]
laundry detergent	**deterjen cuci**	[deterdʒʲen tʃutʃi]

93. Household appliances

TV set	**pesawat TV**	[pesawat ti-vi]
tape recorder	**alat perekam**	[alat pərekam]
VCR (video recorder)	**video, VCR**	[vidio], [vi-si-er]
radio	**radio**	[radio]
player (CD, MP3, etc.)	**pemutar**	[pemutar]
video projector	**proyektor video**	[proektor video]
home movie theater	**bioskop rumah**	[bioskop rumah]
DVD player	**pemutar DVD**	[pemutar di-vi-di]
amplifier	**penguat**	[peŋuat]
video game console	**konsol permainan video**	[konsol pərmajnan video]
video camera	**kamera video**	[kamera video]
camera (photo)	**kamera**	[kamera]
digital camera	**kamera digital**	[kamera digital]
vacuum cleaner	**pengisap debu**	[peɲisap debu]
iron (e.g., steam ~)	**setrika**	[setrika]
ironing board	**papan setrika**	[papan setrika]
telephone	**telepon**	[telepon]
cell phone	**ponsel**	[ponsel]
typewriter	**mesin ketik**	[mesin ketiʔ]
sewing machine	**mesin jahit**	[mesin dʒʲahit]
microphone	**mikrofon**	[mikrofon]
headphones	**headphone, fonkepala**	[headphone], [fonkepala]
remote control (TV)	**panel kendali**	[panel kendali]
CD, compact disc	**cakram kompak**	[tʃakram kompaʔ]
cassette, tape	**kaset**	[kaset]
vinyl record	**piringan hitam**	[piriŋan hitam]

94. Repairs. Renovation

renovations	**renovasi**	[renovasi]
to renovate (vt)	**merenovasi**	[merenovasi]
to repair, to fix (vt)	**mereparasi, memperbaiki**	[mereparasi], [memperbajki]
to put in order	**membereskan**	[membereskan]
to redo (do again)	**mengulangi**	[meŋulaŋi]
paint	**cat**	[tʃat]
to paint (~ a wall)	**mengecat**	[məŋetʃat]
house painter	**tukang cat**	[tukaŋ tʃat]
paintbrush	**kuas**	[kuas]
whitewash	**cat kapur**	[tʃat kapur]

to whitewash (vt)	mengapur	[məŋapur]
wallpaper	kertas dinding	[kertas dindiŋ]
to wallpaper (vt)	memasang kertas dinding	[memasaŋ kertas dindiŋ]
varnish	pernis	[pernis]
to varnish (vt)	memernis	[memernis]

95. Plumbing

water	air	[air]
hot water	air panas	[air panas]
cold water	air dingin	[air diŋin]
faucet	keran	[keran]
drop (of water)	tetes	[tetes]
to drip (vi)	menetes	[mənetes]
to leak (ab. pipe)	bocor	[botʃor]
leak (pipe ~)	kebocoran	[kebotʃoran]
puddle	kubangan	[kubaŋan]
pipe	pipa	[pipa]
valve (e.g., ball ~)	katup	[katup]
to be clogged up	tersumbat	[tərsumbat]
tools	peralatan	[pəralatan]
adjustable wrench	kunci inggris	[kuntʃi iŋgris]
to unscrew (lid, filter, etc.)	mengendurkan	[məŋendurkan]
to screw (tighten)	mengencangkan	[məŋentʃaŋkan]
to unclog (vt)	membersihkan	[membersihkan]
plumber	tukang pipa	[tukaŋ pipa]
basement	rubanah	[rubanah]
sewerage (system)	riol	[riol]

96. Fire. Conflagration

fire (accident)	kebakaran	[kebakaran]
flame	nyala api	[njala api]
spark	percikan api	[pərtʃikan api]
smoke (from fire)	asap	[asap]
torch (flaming stick)	obor	[obor]
campfire	api unggun	[api uŋgun]
gas, gasoline	bensin	[bensin]
kerosene (type of fuel)	minyak tanah	[minja' tanah]
flammable (adj)	mudah terbakar	[mudah tərbakar]
explosive (adj)	mudah meledak	[mudah meleda']
NO SMOKING	DILARANG MEROKOK!	[dilaraŋ meroko'!]

safety	**keamanan**	[keamanan]
danger	**bahaya**	[bahaja]
dangerous (adj)	**berbahaya**	[bərbahaja]
to catch fire	**menyala**	[mənjala]
explosion	**ledakan**	[ledakan]
to set fire	**membakar**	[membakar]
arsonist	**pelaku pembakaran**	[pelaku pembakaran]
arson	**pembakaran**	[pembakaran]
to blaze (vi)	**berkobar**	[bərkobar]
to burn (be on fire)	**menyala**	[mənjala]
to burn down	**terbakar**	[tərbakar]
to call the fire department	**memanggil pemadam kebakaran**	[memaŋgil pemadam kebakaran]
firefighter, fireman	**pemadam kebakaran**	[pemadam kebakaran]
fire truck	**branwir**	[branwir]
fire department	**pemadam kebakaran**	[pemadam kebakaran]
fire truck ladder	**tangga branwir**	[taŋga branwir]
fire hose	**selang pemadam**	[selaŋ pemadam]
fire extinguisher	**pemadam api**	[pemadam api]
helmet	**helm**	[helm]
siren	**sirene**	[sirene]
to cry (for help)	**berteriak**	[bərteria?]
to call for help	**meminta pertolongan**	[meminta pertoloŋan]
rescuer	**penyelamat**	[penjelamat]
to rescue (vt)	**menyelamatkan**	[mənjelamatkan]
to arrive (vi)	**datang**	[dataŋ]
to extinguish (vt)	**memadamkan**	[memadamkan]
water	**air**	[air]
sand	**pasir**	[pasir]
ruins (destruction)	**reruntuhan**	[reruntuhan]
to collapse (building, etc.)	**runtuh**	[runtuh]
to fall down (vi)	**roboh**	[roboh]
to cave in (ceiling, floor)	**roboh**	[roboh]
piece of debris	**serpihan**	[serpihan]
ash	**abu**	[abu]
to suffocate (die)	**mati lemas**	[mati lemas]
to be killed (perish)	**mati, tewas**	[mati], [tewas]

HUMAN ACTIVITIES

Job. Business. Part 1

97. Banking

bank	**bank**	[banʔ]
branch (of bank, etc.)	**cabang**	[ʧabaŋ]
bank clerk, consultant	**konsultan**	[konsultan]
manager (director)	**manajer**	[manadʒʲer]
bank account	**rekening**	[rekeniŋ]
account number	**nomor rekening**	[nomor rekeniŋ]
checking account	**rekening koran**	[rekeniŋ koran]
savings account	**rekening simpanan**	[rekeniŋ simpanan]
to open an account	**membuka rekening**	[membuka rekeniŋ]
to close the account	**menutup rekening**	[mənutup rekeniŋ]
to deposit into the account	**memasukkan ke rekening**	[memasuʔkan ke rekeniŋ]
to withdraw (vt)	**menarik uang**	[mənariʔ uaŋ]
deposit	**deposito**	[deposito]
to make a deposit	**melakukan setoran**	[melakukan setoran]
wire transfer	**transfer kawat**	[transfer kawat]
to wire, to transfer	**mentransfer**	[məntransfer]
sum	**jumlah**	[dʒʲumlah]
How much?	**Berapa?**	[bərapa?]
signature	**tanda tangan**	[tanda taŋan]
to sign (vt)	**menandatangani**	[mənandataŋani]
credit card	**kartu kredit**	[kartu kredit]
code (PIN code)	**kode**	[kode]
credit card number	**nomor kartu kredit**	[nomor kartu kredit]
ATM	**Anjungan Tunai Mandiri, ATM**	[andʒʲuŋan tunaj mandiri], [a-te-em]
check	**cek**	[ʧeʔ]
to write a check	**menulis cek**	[mənulis ʧeʔ]
checkbook	**buku cek**	[buku ʧeʔ]
loan (bank ~)	**kredit, pinjaman**	[kredit], [pindʒʲaman]
to apply for a loan	**meminta kredit**	[meminta kredit]

to get a loan	mendapatkan kredit	[məndapatkan kredit]
to give a loan	memberikan kredit	[memberikan kredit]
guarantee	jaminan	[dʒʲaminan]

98. Telephone. Phone conversation

telephone	telepon	[telepon]
cell phone	ponsel	[ponsel]
answering machine	mesin penjawab panggilan	[mesin pendʒʲawab paŋgilan]

| to call (by phone) | menelepon | [mənelepon] |
| phone call | panggilan telepon | [paŋgilan telepon] |

to dial a number	memutar nomor telepon	[memutar nomor telepon]
Hello!	Halo!	[halo!]
to ask (vt)	bertanya	[bərtanja]
to answer (vi, vt)	menjawab	[məndʒʲawab]

to hear (vt)	mendengar	[məndeŋar]
well (adv)	baik	[bajʔ]
not well (adv)	buruk, jelek	[buruk], [dʒʲeleʔ]
noises (interference)	bising, gangguan	[bisiŋ], [gaŋguan]

receiver	gagang	[gagaŋ]
to pick up (~ the phone)	mengangkat telepon	[məŋaŋkat telepon]
to hang up (~ the phone)	menutup telepon	[mənutup telepon]

busy (engaged)	sibuk	[sibuʔ]
to ring (ab. phone)	berdering	[bərderiŋ]
telephone book	buku telepon	[buku telepon]

local (adj)	lokal	[lokal]
local call	panggilan lokal	[paŋgilan lokal]
long distance (~ call)	interlokal	[interlokal]
long-distance call	panggilan interlokal	[paŋgilan interlokal]
international (adj)	internasional	[internasional]
international call	panggilan internasional	[paŋgilan internasional]

99. Cell phone

cell phone	ponsel	[ponsel]
display	layar	[lajar]
button	kenop	[kenop]
SIM card	kartu SIM	[kartu sim]

| battery | baterai | [bateraj] |
| to be dead (battery) | mati | [mati] |

charger	pengisi baterai, pengecas	[peɲisi bateraj], [peɲetʃas]
menu	menu	[menu]
settings	penyetelan	[peɲetelan]
tune (melody)	nada panggil	[nada paŋgil]
to select (vt)	memilih	[memilih]
calculator	kalkulator	[kalkulator]
voice mail	penjawab telepon	[pendʒawab telepon]
alarm clock	weker	[weker]
contacts	buku telepon	[buku telepon]
SMS (text message)	pesan singkat	[pesan siŋkat]
subscriber	pelanggan	[pelaŋgan]

100. Stationery

ballpoint pen	bolpen	[bolpen]
fountain pen	pena celup	[pena tʃelup]
pencil	pensil	[pensil]
highlighter	spidol	[spidol]
felt-tip pen	spidol	[spidol]
notepad	buku catatan	[buku tʃatatan]
agenda (diary)	agenda	[agenda]
ruler	mistar, penggaris	[mistar], [peŋgaris]
calculator	kalkulator	[kalkulator]
eraser	karet penghapus	[karet peŋhapus]
thumbtack	paku payung	[paku pajuŋ]
paper clip	penjepit kertas	[pendʒepit kertas]
glue	lem	[lem]
stapler	stapler	[stapler]
hole punch	alat pelubang kertas	[alat pelubaŋ kertas]
pencil sharpener	rautan pensil	[rautan pensil]

Job. Business. Part 2

101. Mass Media

newspaper	**koran**	[koran]
magazine	**majalah**	[madʒialah]
press (printed media)	**pers**	[pers]
radio	**radio**	[radio]
radio station	**stasiun radio**	[stasiun radio]
television	**televisi**	[televisi]
presenter, host	**pembawa acara**	[pembawa atʃara]
newscaster	**penyiar**	[penjiar]
commentator	**komentator**	[komentator]
journalist	**wartawan**	[wartawan]
correspondent (reporter)	**koresponden**	[koresponden]
press photographer	**fotografer pers**	[fotografer pers]
reporter	**reporter, pewarta**	[reporter], [pewarta]
editor	**editor, penyunting**	[editor], [penyuntiŋ]
editor-in-chief	**editor kepala**	[editor kepala]
to subscribe (to ...)	**berlangganan ...**	[bərlaŋganan ...]
subscription	**langganan**	[laŋganan]
subscriber	**pelanggan**	[pelaŋgan]
to read (vi, vt)	**membaca**	[membatʃa]
reader	**pembaca**	[pembatʃa]
circulation (of newspaper)	**oplah**	[oplah]
monthly (adj)	**bulanan**	[bulanan]
weekly (adj)	**mingguan**	[miŋguan]
issue (edition)	**edisi**	[edisi]
new (~ issue)	**baru**	[baru]
headline	**kepala berita**	[kepala bərita]
short article	**artikel singkat**	[artikel siŋkat]
column (regular article)	**kolom**	[kolom]
article	**artikel**	[artikel]
page	**halaman**	[halaman]
reportage, report	**reportase**	[reportase]
event (happening)	**peristiwa, kejadian**	[pəristiwa], [kedʒiadian]
sensation (news)	**sensasi**	[sensasi]
scandal	**skandal**	[skandal]
scandalous (adj)	**penuh skandal**	[penuh skandal]

great (~ scandal)	**besar**	[besar]
show (e.g., cooking ~)	**program**	[program]
interview	**wawancara**	[wawantʃara]
live broadcast	**siaran langsung**	[siaran laŋsuŋ]
channel	**saluran**	[saluran]

102. Agriculture

agriculture	**pertanian**	[pertanian]
peasant (masc.)	**petani**	[petani]
peasant (fem.)	**petani**	[petani]
farmer	**petani**	[petani]

| tractor (farm ~) | **traktor** | [traktor] |
| combine, harvester | **mesin pemanen** | [mesin pemanen] |

plow	**bajak**	[badʒ'aʔ]
to plow (vi, vt)	**membajak,**	[membadʒ'ak],
	menenggala	[meneŋgala]

| plowland | **tanah garapan** | [tanah garapan] |
| furrow (in field) | **alur** | [alur] |

to sow (vi, vt)	**menanam**	[menanam]
seeder	**mesin penanam**	[mesin penanam]
sowing (process)	**penanaman**	[penanaman]

| scythe | **sabit** | [sabit] |
| to mow, to scythe | **menyabit** | [menjabit] |

| spade (tool) | **sekop** | [sekop] |
| to till (vt) | **menggali** | [meŋgali] |

hoe	**cangkul**	[tʃaŋkul]
to hoe, to weed	**menyiangi**	[menjiaŋi]
weed (plant)	**gulma**	[gulma]

watering can	**kaleng penyiram**	[kaleŋ penjiram]
to water (plants)	**menyiram**	[menjiram]
watering (act)	**penyiraman**	[penjiraman]

| pitchfork | **garpu ramput** | [garpu ramput] |
| rake | **penggaruk** | [peŋgaruʔ] |

fertilizer	**pupuk**	[pupuʔ]
to fertilize (vt)	**memupuk**	[memupuʔ]
manure (fertilizer)	**pupuk kandang**	[pupuʔ kandaŋ]

field	**ladang**	[ladaŋ]
meadow	**padang rumput**	[padaŋ rumput]
vegetable garden	**kebun sayur**	[kebun sajur]

orchard (e.g., apple ~)	kebun buah	[kebun buah]
to graze (vt)	menggembalakan	[məŋgembalakan]
herder (herdsman)	penggembala	[peŋgembala]
pasture	padang penggembalaan	[padaŋ peŋgembala'an]

| cattle breeding | peternakan | [peternakan] |
| sheep farming | peternakan domba | [peternakan domba] |

plantation	perkebunan	[pərkebunan]
row (garden bed ~s)	bedeng	[bedeŋ]
hothouse	rumah kaca	[rumah katʃa]

| drought (lack of rain) | musim kering | [musim keriŋ] |
| dry (~ summer) | kering | [keriŋ] |

grain	biji	[bidʒi]
cereal crops	serealia	[serealia]
to harvest, to gather	memanen	[memanen]

miller (person)	penggiling	[peŋgiliŋ]
mill (e.g., gristmill)	kincir	[kintʃir]
to grind (grain)	menggiling	[məŋgiliŋ]
flour	tepung	[tepuŋ]
straw	jerami	[dʒ'erami]

103. Building. Building process

construction site	lokasi pembangunan	[lokasi pembaŋunan]
to build (vt)	membangun	[membaŋun]
construction worker	buruh bangunan	[buruh baŋunan]

project	proyek	[proe']
architect	arsitek	[arsite']
worker	buruh, pekerja	[buruh], [pekerdʒ'a]

foundation (of a building)	fondasi	[fondasi]
roof	atap	[atap]
foundation pile	tiang fondasi	[tiaŋ fondasi]
wall	dinding	[dindiŋ]

| reinforcing bars | kerangka besi | [keraŋka besi] |
| scaffolding | perancah | [pərantʃah] |

concrete	beton	[beton]
granite	granit	[granit]
stone	batu	[batu]
brick	bata, batu bata	[bata], [batu bata]

| sand | pasir | [pasir] |
| cement | semen | [semen] |

plaster (for walls)	lepa, plester	[lepa], [plester]
to plaster (vt)	melepa	[melepa]
paint	cat	[ʧat]
to paint (~ a wall)	mengecat	[maneʧfat]
barrel	tong	[toŋ]

crane	derek	[dereʔ]
to lift, to hoist (vt)	menaikkan	[mənajʔkan]
to lower (vt)	menurunkan	[mənurunkan]

bulldozer	buldoser	[buldozer]
excavator	ekskavator	[ekskavator]
scoop, bucket	sudu pengeruk	[sudu peɲeruʔ]
to dig (excavate)	menggali	[məŋgali]
hard hat	topi baja	[topi badʒʲa]

Professions and occupations

104. Job search. Dismissal

job	kerja, pekerjaan	[kerdʒʲa], [pekerdʒʲa'an]
staff (work force)	staf, personalia	[staf], [personalia]
personnel	staf, personel	[staf], [personel]
career	karier	[karier]
prospects (chances)	perspektif	[perspektif]
skills (mastery)	keterampilan	[keterampilan]
selection (screening)	pilihan	[pilihan]
employment agency	biro tenaga kerja	[biro tenaga kerdʒʲa]
résumé	resume	[resume]
job interview	wawancara kerja	[wawantʃara kerdʒʲa]
vacancy, opening	lowongan	[lowoŋan]
salary, pay	gaji, upah	[gadʒi], [upah]
fixed salary	gaji tetap	[gadʒi tetap]
pay, compensation	bayaran	[bajaran]
position (job)	jabatan	[dʒʲabatan]
duty (of employee)	tugas	[tugas]
range of duties	bidang tugas	[bidaŋ tugas]
busy (I'm ~)	sibuk	[sibu']
to fire (dismiss)	memecat	[memetʃat]
dismissal	pemecatan	[pemetʃatan]
unemployment	pengangguran	[peŋaŋguran]
unemployed (n)	pengganggur	[peŋgaŋgur]
retirement	pensiun	[pensiun]
to retire (from job)	pensiun	[pensiun]

105. Business people

director	direktur	[direktur]
manager (director)	manajer	[manadʒʲer]
boss	bos, atasan	[bos], [atasan]
superior	atasan	[atasan]
superiors	atasan	[atasan]
president	presiden	[presiden]

chairman	ketua, dirut	[ketua], [dirut]
deputy (substitute)	wakil	[wakil]
assistant	asisten	[asisten]
secretary	sekretaris	[sekretaris]
personal assistant	asisten pribadi	[asisten pribadi]

businessman	pengusaha, pebisnis	[peŋusaha], [pebisnis]
entrepreneur	pengusaha	[peŋusaha]
founder	pendiri	[pendiri]
to found (vt)	mendirikan	[məndirikan]

incorporator	pendiri	[pendiri]
partner	mitra	[mitra]
stockholder	pemegang saham	[pemegaŋ saham]

millionaire	jutawan	[dʒutawan]
billionaire	miliarder	[miliarder]
owner, proprietor	pemilik	[pemiliʔ]
landowner	tuan tanah	[tuan tanah]

client	klien	[klien]
regular client	klien tetap	[klien tetap]
buyer (customer)	pembeli	[pembeli]
visitor	tamu	[tamu]

professional (n)	profesional	[profesional]
expert	pakar, ahli	[pakar], [ahli]
specialist	spesialis, ahli	[spesialis], [ahli]

| banker | bankir | [bankir] |
| broker | broker, pialang | [broker], [pialaŋ] |

cashier, teller	kasir	[kasir]
accountant	akuntan	[akuntan]
security guard	satpam, pengawal	[satpam], [peŋawal]

investor	investor	[investor]
debtor	debitur	[debitur]
creditor	kreditor	[kreditor]
borrower	peminjam	[pemindʒam]

| importer | importir | [importir] |
| exporter | eksportir | [eksportir] |

manufacturer	produsen	[produsen]
distributor	penyalur	[penjalur]
middleman	perantara	[pərantara]

consultant	konsultan	[konsultan]
sales representative	perwakilan penjualan	[pərwakilan pendʒualan]
agent	agen	[agen]
insurance agent	agen asuransi	[agen asuransi]

106. Service professions

cook	koki, juru masak	[koki], [dʒ'uru masa']
chef (kitchen chef)	koki kepala	[koki kepala]
baker	pembuat roti	[pembuat roti]
bartender	pelayan bar	[pelajan bar]
waiter	pelayan lelaki	[pelajan lelaki]
waitress	pelayan perempuan	[pelajan perempuan]
lawyer, attorney	advokat, pengacara	[advokat], [peɲatʃara]
lawyer (legal expert)	ahli hukum	[ahli hukum]
notary	notaris	[notaris]
electrician	tukang listrik	[tukaŋ listri']
plumber	tukang pipa	[tukaŋ pipa]
carpenter	tukang kayu	[tukaŋ kaju]
masseur	tukang pijat lelaki	[tukaŋ pidʒ'at lelaki]
masseuse	tukang pijat perempuan	[tukaŋ pidʒ'at perempuan]
doctor	dokter	[dokter]
taxi driver	sopir taksi	[sopir taksi]
driver	sopir	[sopir]
delivery man	kurir	[kurir]
chambermaid	pelayan kamar	[pelajan kamar]
security guard	satpam, pengawal	[satpam], [peɲawal]
flight attendant (fem.)	pramugari	[pramugari]
schoolteacher	guru	[guru]
librarian	pustakawan	[pustakawan]
translator	penerjemah	[penerdʒ'emah]
interpreter	juru bahasa	[dʒ'uru bahasa]
guide	pemandu wisata	[pemandu wisata]
hairdresser	tukang cukur	[tukaŋ tʃukur]
mailman	tukang pos	[tukaŋ pos]
salesman (store staff)	pramuniaga	[pramuniaga]
gardener	tukang kebun	[tukaŋ kebun]
domestic servant	pramuwisma	[pramuwisma]
maid (female servant)	pramuwisma	[pramuwisma]
cleaner (cleaning lady)	pembersih ruangan	[pembersih ruaŋan]

107. Military professions and ranks

private	prajurit	[pradʒ'urit]
sergeant	sersan	[sersan]

| lieutenant | letnan | [letnan] |
| captain | kapten | [kapten] |

major	mayor	[major]
colonel	kolonel	[kolonel]
general	jenderal	[dʒenderal]
marshal	marsekal	[marsekal]
admiral	laksamana	[laksamana]

military (n)	anggota militer	[aŋgota militer]
soldier	tentara, serdadu	[tentara], [serdadu]
officer	perwira	[pərwira]
commander	komandan	[komandan]

border guard	penjaga perbatasan	[pendʒaga perbatasan]
radio operator	operator radio	[operator radio]
scout (searcher)	pengintai	[peɲintaj]
pioneer (sapper)	pencari ranjau	[pentʃari randʒau]
marksman	petembak	[petembaʔ]
navigator	navigator, penavigasi	[navigator], [penavigasi]

108. Officials. Priests

| king | raja | [radʒa] |
| queen | ratu | [ratu] |

| prince | pangeran | [paŋeran] |
| princess | putri | [putri] |

| czar | tsar, raja | [tsar], [radʒa] |
| czarina | tsarina, ratu | [tsarina], [ratu] |

president	presiden	[presiden]
Secretary (minister)	Menteri Sekretaris	[menteri sekretaris]
prime minister	perdana menteri	[pərdana menteri]
senator	senator	[senator]

diplomat	diplomat	[diplomat]
consul	konsul	[konsul]
ambassador	duta besar	[duta besar]
counsilor (diplomatic officer)	penasihat	[penasihat]

official, functionary (civil servant)	petugas	[petugas]
prefect	prefek	[prefeʔ]
mayor	walikota	[walikota]
judge	hakim	[hakim]
prosecutor (e.g., district attorney)	kejaksaan negeri	[kedʒaksaʔan negeri]

missionary	misionaris	[misionaris]
monk	biarawan, rahib	[biarawan], [rahib]
abbot	abbas	[abbas]
rabbi	rabbi	[rabbi]
vizier	wazir	[wazir]
shah	syah	[ʃah]
sheikh	syeikh	[ʃejh]

109. Agricultural professions

beekeeper	peternak lebah	[peterna' lebah]
herder, shepherd	penggembala	[peŋgembala]
agronomist	agronom	[agronom]
cattle breeder	peternak	[peterna']
veterinarian	dokter hewan	[dokter hewan]
farmer	petani	[petani]
winemaker	pembuat anggur	[pembuat aŋgur]
zoologist	zoolog	[zoolog]
cowboy	koboi	[koboi]

110. Art professions

actor	aktor	[aktor]
actress	aktris	[aktris]
singer (masc.)	biduan	[biduan]
singer (fem.)	biduanita	[biduanita]
dancer (masc.)	penari lelaki	[penari lelaki]
dancer (fem.)	penari perempuan	[penari perempuan]
performer (masc.)	artis	[artis]
performer (fem.)	artis	[artis]
musician	musisi, musikus	[musisi], [musikus]
pianist	pianis	[pianis]
guitar player	pemain gitar	[pemajn gitar]
conductor (orchestra ~)	konduktor	[konduktor]
composer	komposer, komponis	[komposer], [komponis]
impresario	impresario	[impresario]
film director	sutradara	[sutradara]
producer	produser	[produser]
scriptwriter	penulis skenario	[penulis skenario]
critic	kritikus	[kritikus]

writer	**penulis**	[penulis]
poet	**penyair**	[penjajr]
sculptor	**pematung**	[pematuŋ]
artist (painter)	**perupa**	[pərupa]

juggler	**juggler**	[dʒˈuggler]
clown	**badut**	[badut]
acrobat	**akrobat**	[akrobat]
magician	**pesulap**	[pesulap]

111. Various professions

doctor	**dokter**	[dokter]
nurse	**suster, juru rawat**	[suster], [dʒˈuru rawat]
psychiatrist	**psikiater**	[psikiater]
dentist	**dokter gigi**	[dokter gigi]
surgeon	**dokter bedah**	[dokter bedah]

astronaut	**astronaut**	[astronaut]
astronomer	**astronom**	[astronom]
pilot	**pilot**	[pilot]

driver (of taxi, etc.)	**sopir**	[sopir]
engineer (train driver)	**masinis**	[masinis]
mechanic	**mekanik**	[mekaniʔ]

miner	**penambang**	[penambaŋ]
worker	**buruh, pekerja**	[buruh], [pekerdʒˈa]
locksmith	**tukang kikir**	[tukaŋ kikir]
joiner (carpenter)	**tukang kayu**	[tukaŋ kaju]
turner (lathe machine operator)	**tukang bubut**	[tukaŋ bubut]
construction worker	**buruh bangunan**	[buruh baŋunan]
welder	**tukang las**	[tukaŋ las]

professor (title)	**profesor**	[profesor]
architect	**arsitek**	[arsiteʔ]
historian	**sejarawan**	[sedʒˈarawan]
scientist	**ilmuwan**	[ilmuwan]
physicist	**fisikawan**	[fisikawan]
chemist (scientist)	**kimiawan**	[kimiawan]

archeologist	**arkeolog**	[arkeolog]
geologist	**geolog**	[geolog]
researcher (scientist)	**periset, peneliti**	[pəriset], [peneliti]

babysitter	**pengasuh anak**	[peŋasuh anaʔ]
teacher, educator	**guru, pendidik**	[guru], [pendidiʔ]
editor	**editor, penyunting**	[editor], [penyuntiŋ]
editor-in-chief	**editor kepala**	[editor kepala]

| correspondent | korespondan | [kɔrɛspɔndɛn] |
| typist (fem.) | juru ketik | [dʒuru ketiʔ] |

designer	desainer, perancang	[desajner], [pərantʃaŋ]
computer expert	ahli komputer	[ahli komputer]
programmer	pemrogram	[pemrogram]
engineer (designer)	insinyur	[insinyur]

sailor	pelaut	[pelaut]
seaman	kelasi	[kelasi]
rescuer	penyelamat	[penjelamat]

fireman	pemadam kebakaran	[pemadam kebakaran]
police officer	polisi	[polisi]
watchman	penjaga	[pendʒʲaga]
detective	detektif	[detektif]

customs officer	petugas pabean	[petugas pabean]
bodyguard	pengawal pribadi	[peŋawal pribadi]
prison guard	sipir,	[sipir],
	penjaga penjara	[pendʒʲaga pendʒʲara]
inspector	inspektur	[inspektur]

sportsman	olahragawan	[olahragawan]
trainer, coach	pelatih	[pelatih]
butcher	tukang daging	[tukaŋ dagiŋ]
cobbler (shoe repairer)	tukang sepatu	[tukaŋ sepatu]
merchant	pedagang	[pedagaŋ]
loader (person)	kuli	[kuli]

| fashion designer | perancang busana | [pərantʃaŋ busana] |
| model (fem.) | peragawati | [pəragawati] |

112. Occupations. Social status

| schoolboy | siswa | [siswa] |
| student (college ~) | mahasiswa | [mahasiswa] |

philosopher	filsuf	[filsuf]
economist	ahli ekonomi	[ahli ekonomi]
inventor	penemu	[penemu]

unemployed (n)	pengganggur	[peŋgaŋgur]
retiree	pensiunan	[pensiunan]
spy, secret agent	mata-mata	[mata-mata]

prisoner	tahanan	[tahanan]
striker	pemogok	[pemogoʔ]
bureaucrat	birokrat	[birokrat]
traveler (globetrotter)	pelancong	[pelantʃoŋ]

gay, homosexual (n)	homo, homoseksual	[homo], [homoseksual]
hacker	peretas	[pəretas]
hippie	hipi	[hipi]

bandit	bandit	[bandit]
hit man, killer	pembunuh bayaran	[pembunuh bajaran]
drug addict	pecandu narkoba	[petʃandu narkoba]
drug dealer	pengedar narkoba	[peŋedar narkoba]
prostitute (fem.)	pelacur	[pelatʃur]
pimp	germo	[germo]

sorcerer	penyihir lelaki	[penjihir lelaki]
sorceress (evil ~)	penyihir perempuan	[penjihir perempuan]
pirate	bajak laut	[badʒiaʔ laut]
slave	budak	[budaʔ]
samurai	samurai	[samuraj]
savage (primitive)	orang primitif	[oraŋ primitif]

Sports

113. Kinds of sports. Sportspersons

sportsman	olahragawan	[olahragawan]
kind of sports	jenis olahraga	[dʒʲenis olahraga]
basketball	bola basket	[bola basket]
basketball player	pemain bola basket	[pemajn bola basket]
baseball	bisbol	[bisbol]
baseball player	pemain bisbol	[pemajn bisbol]
soccer	sepak bola	[sepaʔ bola]
soccer player	pemain sepak bola	[pemajn sepaʔ bola]
goalkeeper	kiper, penjaga gawang	[kiper], [pendʒʲaga gawaŋ]
hockey	hoki	[hoki]
hockey player	pemain hoki	[pemajn hoki]
volleyball	bola voli	[bola voli]
volleyball player	pemain bola voli	[pemajn bola voli]
boxing	tinju	[tindʒʲu]
boxer	petinju	[petindʒʲu]
wrestling	gulat	[gulat]
wrestler	pegulat	[pegulat]
karate	karate	[karate]
karate fighter	karateka	[karateka]
judo	judo	[dʒʲudo]
judo athlete	pejudo	[pedʒʲudo]
tennis	tenis	[tenis]
tennis player	petenis	[petenis]
swimming	berenang	[bərenaŋ]
swimmer	perenang	[pərenaŋ]
fencing	anggar	[aŋgar]
fencer	pemain anggar	[pemajn aŋgar]
chess	catur	[tʃatur]
chess player	pecatur	[petʃatur]

alpinism	**mendaki gunung**	[məndaki gunuŋ]
alpinist	**pendaki gunung**	[pendaki gunuŋ]
running	**lari**	[lari]
runner	**pelari**	[pelari]
athletics	**atletik**	[atletiʔ]
athlete	**atlet**	[atlet]
horseback riding	**menunggang kuda**	[mənuŋgaŋ kuda]
horse rider	**penunggang kuda**	[penuŋgaŋ kuda]
figure skating	**seluncur indah**	[seluntʃur indah]
figure skater (masc.)	**peseluncur indah**	[peseluntʃur indah]
figure skater (fem.)	**peseluncur indah**	[peseluntʃur indah]
powerlifting	**angkat berat**	[aŋkat bərat]
powerlifter	**atlet angkat berat**	[atlet aŋkat bərat]
car racing	**balapan mobil**	[balapan mobil]
racing driver	**pembalap mobil**	[pembalap mobil]
cycling	**bersepeda**	[bərsepeda]
cyclist	**atlet sepeda**	[atlet sepeda]
broad jump	**lompat jauh**	[lompat dʒʲauh]
pole vault	**lompat galah**	[lompat galah]
jumper	**atlet lompat, pelompat**	[atlet lompat], [pelompat]

114. Kinds of sports. Miscellaneous

football	**futbol**	[futbol]
badminton	**badminton, bulu tangkis**	[badminton], [bulu taŋkis]
biathlon	**biathlon**	[biatlon]
billiards	**biliar**	[biliar]
bobsled	**bobsled**	[bobsled]
bodybuilding	**binaraga**	[binaraga]
water polo	**polo air**	[polo air]
handball	**bola tangan**	[bola taŋan]
golf	**golf**	[golf]
rowing, crew	**mendayung**	[məndajuŋ]
scuba diving	**selam skuba**	[selam skuba]
cross-country skiing	**ski lintas alam**	[ski lintas alam]
table tennis (ping-pong)	**tenis meja**	[tenis medʒʲa]
sailing	**berlayar**	[bərlajar]
rally racing	**balap reli**	[balap reli]
rugby	**rugbi**	[rugbi]

snowboarding   seluncur salju   [sǝluntʃur saldʒu]
archery   memanah   [memanah]

115. Gym

barbell   barbel   [barbel]
dumbbells   dumbel   [dumbel]

training machine   alat senam   [alat senam]
exercise bicycle   sepeda statis   [sepeda statis]
treadmill   treadmill   [tredmil]

horizontal bar   rekstok   [reksto?]
parallel bars   palang sejajar   [palaŋ sedʒʲadʒʲar]
vault (vaulting horse) kuda-kuda   [kuda-kuda]
mat (exercise ~)   matras   [matras]

jump rope   lompat tali   [lompat tali]
aerobics   aerobik   [aerobi?]
yoga   yoga   [yoga]

116. Sports. Miscellaneous

Olympic Games   Olimpiade   [olimpiade]
winner   pemenang   [pemenaŋ]
to be winning   unggul   [uŋgul]
to win (vi)   menang   [menaŋ]

leader   pemimpin   [pemimpin]
to lead (vi)   memimpin   [memimpin]

first place   tempat pertama   [tempat pǝrtama]
second place   tempat kedua   [tempat kedua]
third place   tempat ketiga   [tempat ketiga]

medal   medali   [medali]
trophy   trofi   [trofi]
prize cup (trophy)   piala   [piala]
prize (in game)   hadiah   [hadiah]
main prize   hadiah utama   [hadiah utama]

record   rekor   [rekor]
to set a record   menciptakan rekor   [mǝntʃiptakan rekor]

final   final   [final]
final (adj)   final   [final]
champion   juara   [dʒʲuara]
championship   kejuaraan   [kedʒʲuara?an]

stadium	**stadion**	[stadion]
stand (bleachers)	**tribun**	[tribun]
fan, supporter	**pendukung**	[pendukuŋ]
opponent, rival	**lawan**	[lawan]

| start (start line) | **start** | [start] |
| finish line | **finis** | [finis] |

| defeat | **kekalahan** | [kekalahan] |
| to lose (not win) | **kalah** | [kalah] |

referee	**wasit**	[wasit]
jury (judges)	**juri**	[dʒʲuri]
score	**skor**	[skor]
tie	**seri, hasil imbang**	[seri], [hasil imbaŋ]
to tie (vi)	**bermain seri**	[bərmajn seri]
point	**poin**	[poin]
result (final score)	**skor, hasil akhir**	[skor], [hasil ahir]

| period | **babak** | [babaʔ] |
| half-time | **waktu istirahat** | [waktu istirahat] |

doping	**doping**	[dopiŋ]
to penalize (vt)	**menghukum**	[məŋhukum]
to disqualify (vt)	**mendiskualifikasi**	[məndiskualifikasi]

apparatus	**alat olahraga**	[alat olahraga]
javelin	**lembing**	[lembiŋ]
shot (metal ball)	**peluru**	[peluru]
ball (snooker, etc.)	**bola**	[bola]

aim (target)	**sasaran**	[sasaran]
target	**sasaran**	[sasaran]
to shoot (vi)	**menembak**	[mənembaʔ]
accurate (~ shot)	**akurat**	[akurat]

trainer, coach	**pelatih**	[pelatih]
to train (sb)	**melatih**	[melatih]
to train (vi)	**berlatih**	[bərlatih]
training	**latihan**	[latihan]

gym	**gimnasium**	[gimnasium]
exercise (physical)	**latihan**	[latihan]
warm-up (athlete ~)	**pemanasan**	[pemanasan]

Education

117. School

school	**sekolah**	[sekolah]
principal (headmaster)	**kepala sekolah**	[kepala sekolah]
pupil (boy)	**murid laki-laki**	[murid laki-laki]
pupil (girl)	**murid perempuan**	[murid pərempuan]
schoolboy	**siswa**	[siswa]
schoolgirl	**siswi**	[siswi]
to teach (sb)	**mengajar**	[mənadʒʲar]
to learn (language, etc.)	**belajar**	[beladʒʲar]
to learn by heart	**menghafalkan**	[mənhafalkan]
to learn (~ to count, etc.)	**belajar**	[beladʒʲar]
to be in school	**bersekolah**	[bərsekolah]
to go to school	**ke sekolah**	[ke sekolah]
alphabet	**alfabet, abjad**	[alfabet], [abdʒʲad]
subject (at school)	**subjek,**	[subdʒʲek],
	mata pelajaran	[mata peladʒʲaran]
classroom	**ruang kelas**	[ruaŋ kelas]
lesson	**pelajaran**	[peladʒʲaran]
recess	**waktu istirahat**	[waktu istirahat]
school bell	**lonceng**	[lontʃeŋ]
school desk	**bangku sekolah**	[baŋku sekolah]
chalkboard	**papan tulis hitam**	[papan tulis hitam]
grade	**nilai**	[nilaj]
good grade	**nilai baik**	[nilaj bajʔ]
bad grade	**nilai jelek**	[nilaj dʒʲeleʔ]
to give a grade	**memberikan nilai**	[memberikan nilaj]
mistake, error	**kesalahan**	[kesalahan]
to make mistakes	**melakukan kesalahan**	[melakukan kesalahan]
to correct (an error)	**mengoreksi**	[mənoreksi]
cheat sheet	**contekan**	[tʃontekan]
homework	**pekerjaan rumah**	[pekerdʒʲaʔan rumah]
exercise (in education)	**latihan**	[latihan]
to be present	**hadir**	[hadir]
to be absent	**absen, tidak hadir**	[absen], [tidaʔ hadir]

to miss school	absen dari sekolah	[absen dari sekolah]
to punish (vt)	menghukum	[məŋhukum]
punishment	hukuman	[hukuman]
conduct (behavior)	perilaku	[pərilaku]

report card	rapor	[rapor]
pencil	pensil	[pensil]
eraser	karet penghapus	[karet pəŋhapus]
chalk	kapur	[kapur]
pencil case	kotak pensil	[kotaʔ pensil]

schoolbag	tas sekolah	[tas sekolah]
pen	pen	[pen]
school notebook	buku tulis	[buku tulis]
textbook	buku pelajaran	[buku peladʒʲaran]
compasses	paser, jangka	[paser], [dʒʲaŋka]

| to make technical drawings | menggambar | [məŋgambar] |
| technical drawing | gambar teknik | [gambar tekniʔ] |

poem	puisi, sajak	[puisi], [sadʒʲaʔ]
by heart (adv)	hafal	[hafal]
to learn by heart	menghafalkan	[məŋhafalkan]

school vacation	liburan sekolah	[liburan sekolah]
to be on vacation	berlibur	[bərlibur]
to spend one's vacation	menjalani liburan	[məndʒʲalani liburan]

test (written math ~)	tes, kuis	[tes], [kuis]
essay (composition)	esai, karangan	[esaj], [karaŋan]
dictation	dikte	[dikte]
exam (examination)	ujian	[udʒian]
to take an exam	menempuh ujian	[mənempuh udʒian]
experiment (e.g., chemistry ~)	eksperimen	[eksperimen]

118. College. University

academy	akademi	[akademi]
university	universitas	[universitas]
faculty (e.g., ~ of Medicine)	fakultas	[fakultas]

student (masc.)	mahasiswa	[mahasiswa]
student (fem.)	mahasiswi	[mahasiswi]
lecturer (teacher)	dosen	[dosen]

| lecture hall, room | ruang kuliah | [ruaŋ kuliah] |
| graduate | lulusan | [lulusan] |

| diploma | Ijazah | [idʒʲazah] |
| dissertation | disertasi | [disertasi] |

| study (report) | penelitian | [penelitian] |
| laboratory | laboratorium | [laboratorium] |

lecture	kuliah	[kuliah]
coursemate	rekan sekuliah	[rekan sekuliah]
scholarship	beasiswa	[beasiswa]
academic degree	gelar akademik	[gelar akademiʔ]

119. Sciences. Disciplines

mathematics	matematika	[matematika]
algebra	aljabar	[aldʒʲabar]
geometry	geometri	[geometri]

astronomy	astronomi	[astronomi]
biology	biologi	[biologi]
geography	geografi	[geografi]
geology	geologi	[geologi]
history	sejarah	[sedʒʲarah]

medicine	kedokteran	[kedokteran]
pedagogy	pedagogi	[pedagogi]
law	hukum	[hukum]

physics	fisika	[fisika]
chemistry	kimia	[kimia]
philosophy	filsafat	[filsafat]
psychology	psikologi	[psikologi]

120. Writing system. Orthography

grammar	tatabahasa	[tatabahasa]
vocabulary	kosakata	[kosakata]
phonetics	fonetik	[fonetiʔ]

noun	nomina	[nomina]
adjective	adjektiva	[adʒʲektiva]
verb	verba	[verba]
adverb	adverbia	[adverbia]

pronoun	kata ganti	[kata ganti]
interjection	kata seru	[kata seru]
preposition	preposisi, kata depan	[preposisi], [kata depan]
root	kata dasar	[kata dasar]
ending	akhiran	[ahiran]

prefix	**prefiks, awalan**	[prefiks], [awalan]
syllable	**suku kata**	[suku kata]
suffix	**sufiks, akhiran**	[sufiks], [ahiran]

| stress mark | **tanda tekanan** | [tanda tekanan] |
| apostrophe | **apostrofi** | [apostrofi] |

period, dot	**titik**	[titiʔ]
comma	**koma**	[koma]
semicolon	**titik koma**	[titiʔ koma]
colon	**titik dua**	[titiʔ dua]
ellipsis	**elipsis, lesapan**	[elipsis], [lesapan]

| question mark | **tanda tanya** | [tanda tanja] |
| exclamation point | **tanda seru** | [tanda seru] |

quotation marks	**tanda petik**	[tanda petiʔ]
in quotation marks	**dalam tanda petik**	[dalam tanda petiʔ]
parenthesis	**tanda kurung**	[tanda kuruŋ]
in parenthesis	**dalam tanda kurung**	[dalam tanda kuruŋ]

hyphen	**tanda pisah**	[tanda pisah]
dash	**tanda hubung**	[tanda hubuŋ]
space (between words)	**spasi**	[spasi]

| letter | **huruf** | [huruf] |
| capital letter | **huruf kapital** | [huruf kapital] |

| vowel (n) | **vokal** | [vokal] |
| consonant (n) | **konsonan** | [konsonan] |

sentence	**kalimat**	[kalimat]
subject	**subjek**	[subdʒʲeʔ]
predicate	**predikat**	[predikat]

line	**baris**	[baris]
on a new line	**di baris baru**	[di baris baru]
paragraph	**alinea, paragraf**	[alinea], [paragraf]

word	**kata**	[kata]
group of words	**rangkaian kata**	[raŋkajan kata]
expression	**ungkapan**	[uŋkapan]
synonym	**sinonim**	[sinonim]
antonym	**antonim**	[antonim]

rule	**peraturan**	[peraturan]
exception	**perkecualian**	[perketʃualian]
correct (adj)	**benar, betul**	[benar], [betul]

conjugation	**konjugasi**	[kondʒʲugasi]
declension	**deklinasi**	[deklinasi]
nominal case	**kasus nominal**	[kasus nominal]

question	pertanyaan	[pərtaɲaˈan]
to underline (vt)	**menggaris bawahi**	[məngaris bawahi]
dotted line	**garis bertitik**	[garis bərtitiʔ]

121. Foreign languages

language	**bahasa**	[bahasa]
foreign (adj)	**asing**	[asiŋ]
foreign language	**bahasa asing**	[bahasa asiŋ]
to study (vt)	**mempelajari**	[mempeladʒʲari]
to learn (language, etc.)	**belajar**	[beladʒʲar]

to read (vi, vt)	**membaca**	[membatʃa]
to speak (vi, vt)	**berbicara**	[bərbitʃara]
to understand (vt)	**mengerti**	[məŋerti]
to write (vt)	**menulis**	[mənulis]

fast (adv)	**cepat, fasih**	[tʃepat], [fasih]
slowly (adv)	**perlahan-lahan**	[pərlahan-lahan]
fluently (adv)	**fasih**	[fasih]

rules	**peraturan**	[pəraturan]
grammar	**tatabahasa**	[tatabahasa]
vocabulary	**kosakata**	[kosakata]
phonetics	**fonetik**	[fonetiʔ]

textbook	**buku pelajaran**	[buku peladʒʲaran]
dictionary	**kamus**	[kamus]
teach-yourself book	**buku autodidak**	[buku autodidaʔ]
phrasebook	**panduan percakapan**	[panduan pərtʃakapan]

cassette, tape	**kaset**	[kaset]
videotape	**kaset video**	[kaset video]
CD, compact disc	**cakram kompak**	[tʃakram kompaʔ]
DVD	**cakram DVD**	[tʃakram di-vi-di]

alphabet	**alfabet, abjad**	[alfabet], [abdʒʲad]
to spell (vt)	**mengeja**	[məɲedʒʲa]
pronunciation	**pelafalan**	[pelafalan]

accent	**aksen**	[aksen]
with an accent	**dengan aksen**	[deŋan aksen]
without an accent	**tanpa aksen**	[tanpa aksen]

| word | **kata** | [kata] |
| meaning | **arti** | [arti] |

course (e.g., a French ~)	**kursus**	[kursus]
to sign up	**Mendaftar**	[məndaftar]
teacher	**guru**	[guru]

translation (process)	penerjemahan	[penerdʒˈemahan]
translation (text, etc.)	terjemahan	[tərdʒˈemahan]
translator	penerjemah	[penerdʒˈemah]
interpreter	juru bahasa	[dʒˈuru bahasa]
polyglot	poliglot	[poliglot]
memory	memori, daya ingat	[memori], [daja iŋat]

122. Fairy tale characters

Santa Claus	Sinterklas	[sinterklas]
Cinderella	Cinderella	[tʃinderella]
mermaid	putri duyung	[putri duyuŋ]
Neptune	Neptunus	[neptunus]
magician, wizard	penyihir	[penjihir]
fairy	peri	[peri]
magic (adj)	sihir	[sihir]
magic wand	tongkat sihir	[toŋkat sihir]
fairy tale	dongeng	[doŋeŋ]
miracle	keajaiban	[keadʒˈajban]
dwarf	kerdil, katai	[kerdil], [kataj]
to turn into ...	menjelma menjadi ...	[məndʒˈelma məndʒˈadi ...]
ghost	hantu	[hantu]
phantom	fantom	[fantom]
monster	monster	[monster]
dragon	naga	[naga]
giant	raksasa	[raksasa]

123. Zodiac Signs

Aries	Aries	[aries]
Taurus	Taurus	[taurus]
Gemini	Gemini	[dʒˈemini]
Cancer	Cancer	[kanser]
Leo	Leo	[leo]
Virgo	Virgo	[virgo]
Libra	Libra	[libra]
Scorpio	Scorpio	[skorpio]
Sagittarius	Sagitarius	[sagitarius]
Capricorn	Capricorn	[keprikon]
Aquarius	Aquarius	[akuarius]
Pisces	Pisces	[pistʃes]
character	karakter	[karakter]
character traits	ciri karakter	[tʃiri karakter]

behavior	tingkah laku	[tiŋkah laku]
to tell fortunes	meramal	[meramal]
fortune-teller	peramal	[peramal]
horoscope	horoskop	[horoskop]

Arts

124. Theater

theater	**teater**	[teater]
opera	**opera**	[opera]
operetta	**opereta**	[opereta]
ballet	**balet**	[balet]
theater poster	**poster**	[poster]
troupe (theatrical company)	**rombongan teater**	[romboŋan teater]
tour	**tur, pertunjukan keliling**	[tur], [pərtundʒ ukan keliliŋ]
to be on tour	**mengadakan tur**	[məŋadakan tur]
to rehearse (vi, vt)	**berlatih**	[bərlatih]
rehearsal	**geladi**	[geladi]
repertoire	**repertoar**	[repertoar]
performance	**pertunjukan**	[pərtundʒ ukan]
theatrical show	**pergelaran**	[pərgelaran]
play	**lakon**	[lakon]
ticket	**tiket**	[tiket]
box office (ticket booth)	**loket tiket**	[loket tiket]
lobby, foyer	**lobi, ruang depan**	[lobi], [ruaŋ depan]
coat check (cloakroom)	**tempat penitipan jas**	[tempat penitipan dʒ as]
coat check tag	**nomor penitipan jas**	[nomor penitipan dʒ as]
binoculars	**binokular**	[binokular]
usher	**petugas penyobek tiket**	[petugas penjobeʔ tiket]
orchestra seats	**kursi orkestra**	[kursi orkestra]
balcony	**balkon**	[balkon]
dress circle	**tingkat pertama**	[tiŋkat pərtama]
box	**boks**	[boks]
row	**barisan**	[barisan]
seat	**tempat duduk**	[tempat duduʔ]
audience	**khalayak**	[halajaʔ]
spectator	**penonton**	[penonton]
to clap (vi, vt)	**bertepuk tangan**	[bərtepuʔ taŋan]
applause	**aplaus, tepuk tangan**	[aplaus], [tepuʔ taŋan]
ovation	**ovasi, tepuk tangan**	[ovasi], [tepuʔ taŋan]
stage	**panggung**	[paŋguŋ]
curtain	**tirai**	[tiraj]
scenery	**tata panggung**	[tata paŋguŋ]

backstage	belakang panggung	[belakaŋ pangguŋ]
scene (e.g., the last ~)	adegan	[adegan]
act	babak	[baba']
intermission	waktu istirahat	[waktu istirahat]

125. Cinema

actor	aktor	[aktor]
actress	aktris	[aktris]

movies (industry)	sinematografi, perfilman	[sinematografi], [pərfilman]
movie	film	[film]
episode	episode, seri	[episode], [seri]

detective movie	detektif	[detektif]
action movie	film laga	[film laga]
adventure movie	film petualangan	[film petualaŋan]
science fiction movie	film fiksi ilmiah	[film fiksi ilmiah]
horror movie	film horor	[film horor]

comedy movie	film komedi	[film komedi]
melodrama	melodrama	[melodrama]
drama	drama	[drama]

fictional movie	film fiksi	[film fiksi]
documentary	film dokumenter	[film dokumenter]
cartoon	kartun	[kartun]
silent movies	film bisu	[film bisu]

role (part)	peran	[peran]
leading role	peran utama	[peran utama]
to play (vi, vt)	berperan	[bərperan]

movie star	bintang film	[bintaŋ film]
well-known (adj)	terkenal	[tərkenal]
famous (adj)	terkenal	[tərkenal]
popular (adj)	populer, terkenal	[populer], [tərkenal]

script (screenplay)	skenario	[skenario]
scriptwriter	penulis skenario	[penulis skenario]
movie director	sutradara	[sutradara]
producer	produser	[produser]
assistant	asisten	[asisten]
cameraman	kamerawan	[kamerawan]
stuntman	pemeran pengganti	[pemeran peŋganti]
double (stuntman)	pengganti	[peŋganti]
to shoot a movie	merekam film	[merekam film]
audition, screen test	audisi	[audisi]
shooting	syuting, pengambilan gambar	[ʃyutiŋ], [peɲambilan gambar]

movie crew	rombongan film	[romboŋan film]
movie set	set film	[set film]
camera	kamera	[kamera]

movie theater	bioskop	[bioskop]
screen (e.g., big ~)	layar	[lajar]
to show a movie	menayangkan film	[mənajaŋkan film]

soundtrack	soundtrack, trek suara	[saundtrek], [tre' suara]
special effects	efek khusus	[efe' husus]
subtitles	subjudul, teks film	[subdʒ'udul], [teks film]
credits	ucapan terima kasih	[utʃapan tərima kasih]
translation	terjemahan	[tərdʒ'emahan]

126. Painting

art	seni	[seni]
fine arts	seni rupa	[seni rupa]
art gallery	galeri seni	[galeri seni]
art exhibition	pameran seni	[pameran seni]

painting (art)	seni lukis	[seni lukis]
graphic art	seni grafis	[seni grafis]
abstract art	seni abstrak	[seni abstra']
impressionism	impresionisme	[impresionisme]

picture (painting)	lukisan	[lukisan]
drawing	gambar	[gambar]
poster	poster	[poster]

illustration (picture)	ilustrasi	[ilustrasi]
miniature	miniatur	[miniatur]
copy (of painting, etc.)	salinan	[salinan]
reproduction	reproduksi	[reproduksi]

mosaic	mozaik	[mozaj']
stained glass window	kaca berwarna	[katʃa bərwarna]
fresco	fresko	[fresko]
engraving	gravir	[gravir]

bust (sculpture)	patung sedada	[patuŋ sedada]
sculpture	seni patung	[seni patuŋ]
statue	patung	[patuŋ]
plaster of Paris	gips	[gips]
plaster (as adj)	dari gips	[dari gips]

portrait	potret	[potret]
self-portrait	potret diri	[potret diri]
landscape painting	lukisan lanskap	[lukisan lanskap]
still life	alam benda	[alam benda]

| caricature | karikatur | [karikatur] |
| sketch | sketsa | [sketsa] |

paint	cat	[tʃat]
watercolor paint	cat air	[tʃat air]
oil (paint)	cat minyak	[tʃat minja']
pencil	pensil	[pensil]
India ink	tinta gambar	[tinta gambar]
charcoal	arang	[araŋ]

| to draw (vi, vt) | menggambar | [məŋgambar] |
| to paint (vi, vt) | melukis | [melukis] |

to pose (vi)	berpose	[bərpose]
artist's model (masc.)	model lelaki	[model lelaki]
artist's model (fem.)	model perempuan	[model pərempuan]

artist (painter)	perupa	[pərupa]
work of art	karya seni	[karja seni]
masterpiece	adikarya, mahakarya	[adikarja], [mahakarja]
studio (artist's workroom)	studio seni	[studio seni]

canvas (cloth)	kanvas	[kanvas]
easel	esel, kuda-kuda	[esel], [kuda-kuda]
palette	palet	[palet]

frame (picture ~, etc.)	bingkai	[biŋkaj]
restoration	pemugaran	[pemugaran]
to restore (vt)	memugar	[memugar]

127. Literature & Poetry

literature	sastra, kesusastraan	[sastra], [kesusastra'an]
author (writer)	pengarang	[peŋaraŋ]
pseudonym	pseudonim, nama samaran	[pseudonim], [nama samaran]

book	buku	[buku]
volume	jilid	[dʒilid]
table of contents	daftar isi	[daftar isi]
page	halaman	[halaman]
main character	karakter utama	[karakter utama]
autograph	tanda tangan	[tanda taŋan]

short story	cerpen	[tʃerpen]
story (novella)	novel, cerita	[novel], [tʃerita]
novel	novel	[novel]
work (writing)	karya	[karja]
fable	fabel	[fabel]
detective novel	novel detektif	[novel detektif]

poem (verse)	puisi, sajak	[puisi], [sadʒiaʔ]
poetry	puisi	[puisi]
poem (epic, ballad)	puisi	[puisi]
poet	nenyair	[penjajr]

fiction	fiksi	[fiksi]
science fiction	fiksi ilmiah	[fiksi ilmiah]
adventures	petualangan	[petualaŋan]
educational literature	literatur pendidikan	[literatur pendidikan]
children's literature	sastra kanak-kanak	[sastra kanaʔ-kanaʔ]

128. Circus

circus	sirkus	[sirkus]
traveling circus	sirkus keliling	[sirkus keliliŋ]
program	program	[program]
performance	pertunjukan	[pərtundʒiukan]

| act (circus ~) | aksi | [aksi] |
| circus ring | arena | [arena] |

| pantomime (act) | pantomim | [pantomim] |
| clown | badut | [badut] |

acrobat	pemain akrobat	[pemajn akrobat]
acrobatics	akrobatik	[akrobatiʔ]
gymnast	pesenam	[pesenam]
gymnastics	senam	[senam]
somersault	salto	[salto]
athlete (strongman)	orang kuat	[oraŋ kuat]
tamer (e.g., lion ~)	penjinak hewan	[pendʒinaʔ hewan]
rider (circus horse ~)	penunggang kuda	[penuŋgaŋ kuda]
assistant	asisten	[asisten]

stunt	stunt	[stun]
magic trick	trik sulap	[triʔ sulap]
conjurer, magician	pesulap	[pesulap]

juggler	juggler	[dʒiuggler]
to juggle (vi, vt)	bermain juggling	[bərmajn dʒiuggliŋ]
animal trainer	pelatih binatang	[pelatih binataŋ]
animal training	pelatihan binatang	[pelatihan binataŋ]
to train (animals)	melatih	[melatih]

129. Music. Pop music

| music | musik | [musiʔ] |
| musician | musisi, musikus | [musisi], [musikus] |

musical instrument	alat musik	[alat musiʔ]
to play ...	bermain ...	[bərmajn ...]
guitar	gitar	[gitar]
violin	biola	[biola]
cello	selo	[selo]
double bass	kontrabas	[kontrabas]
harp	harpa	[harpa]
piano	piano	[piano]
grand piano	grand piano	[grand piano]
organ	organ	[organ]
wind instruments	alat musik tiup	[alat musiʔ tiup]
oboe	obo	[obo]
saxophone	saksofon	[saksofon]
clarinet	klarinet	[klarinet]
flute	suling	[suliŋ]
trumpet	trompet	[trompet]
accordion	akordeon	[akordeon]
drum	drum	[drum]
duo	duo, duet	[duo], [duet]
trio	trio	[trio]
quartet	kuartet	[kuartet]
choir	kor	[kor]
orchestra	orkestra	[orkestra]
pop music	musik pop	[musiʔ pop]
rock music	musik rok	[musiʔ roʔ]
rock group	grup musik rok	[grup musiʔ roʔ]
jazz	jaz	[dʒʲaz]
idol	idola	[idola]
admirer, fan	pengagum	[pəŋagum]
concert	konser	[konser]
symphony	simfoni	[simfoni]
composition	komposisi	[komposisi]
to compose (write)	menggubah, mencipta	[məŋgubah], [məntʃipta]
singing (n)	nyanyian	[njanjian]
song	lagu	[lagu]
tune (melody)	nada, melodi	[nada], [melodi]
rhythm	irama	[irama]
blues	musik blues	[musiʔ blus]
sheet music	notasi musik	[notasi musiʔ]
baton	tongkat dirigen	[toŋkat dirigen]
bow	penggesek	[pəŋgeseʔ]
string	tali, senar	[tali], [senar]
case (e.g., guitar ~)	wadah	[wadah]

Rest. Entertainment. Travel

130. Trip. Travel

tourism, travel	**pariwisata**	[pariwisata]
tourist	**turis, wisatawan**	[turis], [wisatawan]
trip, voyage	**pengembaraan**	[peɲembaraʔan]
adventure	**petualangan**	[petualaŋan]
trip, journey	**perjalanan, lawatan**	[pərdʒˈalanan], [lawatan]
vacation	**liburan**	[liburan]
to be on vacation	**berlibur**	[bərlibur]
rest	**istirahat**	[istirahat]
train	**kereta api**	[kereta api]
by train	**naik kereta api**	[naiʔ kereta api]
airplane	**pesawat terbang**	[pesawat tərbaŋ]
by airplane	**naik pesawat terbang**	[naiʔ pesawat tərbaŋ]
by car	**naik mobil**	[naiʔ mobil]
by ship	**naik kapal**	[naiʔ kapal]
luggage	**bagasi**	[bagasi]
suitcase	**koper**	[koper]
luggage cart	**troli bagasi**	[troli bagasi]
passport	**paspor**	[paspor]
visa	**visa**	[visa]
ticket	**tiket**	[tiket]
air ticket	**tiket pesawat terbang**	[tiket pesawat tərbaŋ]
guidebook	**buku pedoman**	[buku pedoman]
map (tourist ~)	**peta**	[peta]
area (rural ~)	**kawasan**	[kawasan]
place, site	**tempat**	[tempat]
exotica (n)	**keeksotisan**	[keeksotisan]
exotic (adj)	**eksotis**	[eksotis]
amazing (adj)	**menakjubkan**	[mənakdʒˈubkan]
group	**kelompok**	[kelompoʔ]
excursion, sightseeing tour	**ekskursi**	[ekskursi]
guide (person)	**pemandu wisata**	[pemandu wisata]

131. Hotel

hotel, inn	**hotel**	[hotel]
motel	**motel**	[motel]
three-star (~ hotel)	**bintang tiga**	[bintaŋ tiga]
five-star	**bintang lima**	[bintaŋ lima]
to stay (in a hotel, etc.)	**menginap**	[məŋinap]
room	**kamar**	[kamar]
single room	**kamar tunggal**	[kamar tuŋgal]
double room	**kamar ganda**	[kamar ganda]
to book a room	**memesan kamar**	[memesan kamar]
half board	**sewa setengah**	[sewa seteŋah]
full board	**sewa penuh**	[sewa penuh]
with bath	**dengan kamar mandi**	[deŋan kamar mandi]
with shower	**dengan pancuran**	[deŋan pantʃuran]
satellite television	**televisi satelit**	[televisi satelit]
air-conditioner	**penyejuk udara**	[penjedʒ'uʔ udara]
towel	**handuk**	[handuʔ]
key	**kunci**	[kuntʃi]
administrator	**administrator**	[administrator]
chambermaid	**pelayan kamar**	[pelajan kamar]
porter, bellboy	**porter**	[porter]
doorman	**pramupintu**	[pramupintu]
restaurant	**restoran**	[restoran]
pub, bar	**bar**	[bar]
breakfast	**makan pagi, sarapan**	[makan pagi], [sarapan]
dinner	**makan malam**	[makan malam]
buffet	**prasmanan**	[prasmanan]
lobby	**lobi**	[lobi]
elevator	**elevator**	[elevator]
DO NOT DISTURB	**JANGAN MENGGANGGU**	[dʒ'aŋan meŋgaŋgu]
NO SMOKING	**DILARANG MEROKOK!**	[dilaraŋ merokoʔ!]

132. Books. Reading

book	**buku**	[buku]
author	**pengarang**	[peŋaraŋ]
writer	**penulis**	[penulis]
to write (~ a book)	**menulis**	[mənulis]
reader	**pembaca**	[pembatʃa]

| to read (vi, vt) | membaca | [membatʃa] |
| reading (activity) | membaca | [membatʃa] |

| silently (to oneself) | dalam hati | [dalam hati] |
| aloud (adv) | dengan keras | [deŋan keras] |

to publish (vt)	menerbitkan	[menerbitkan]
publishing (process)	penerbitan	[penerbitan]
publisher	penerbit	[penerbit]
publishing house	penerbit	[penerbit]

to come out (be released)	terbit	[terbit]
release (of a book)	penerbitan	[penerbitan]
print run	oplah	[oplah]

| bookstore | toko buku | [toko buku] |
| library | perpustakaan | [perpustaka'an] |

story (novella)	novel, cerita	[novel], [tʃerita]
short story	cerpen	[tʃerpen]
novel	novel	[novel]
detective novel	novel detektif	[novel detektif]

memoirs	memoir	[memoir]
legend	legenda	[legenda]
myth	mitos	[mitos]

poetry, poems	puisi	[puisi]
autobiography	autobiografi	[autobiografi]
selected works	karya pilihan	[karja pilihan]
science fiction	fiksi ilmiah	[fiksi ilmiah]

title	judul	[dʒʲudul]
introduction	pendahuluan	[pendahuluan]
title page	halaman judul	[halaman dʒʲudul]

chapter	bab	[bab]
extract	kutipan	[kutipan]
episode	episode	[episode]

plot (storyline)	alur cerita	[alur tʃerita]
contents	daftar isi	[daftar isi]
table of contents	daftar isi	[daftar isi]
main character	karakter utama	[karakter utama]

volume	jilid	[dʒilid]
cover	sampul	[sampul]
binding	penjilidan	[pendʒilidan]
bookmark	pembatas buku	[pembatas buku]

| page | halaman | [halaman] |
| to page through | membolak-balik | [membola'-bali'] |

margins	margin	[margin]
annotation (marginal note, etc.)	anotasi, catatan	[anotasi], [tʃatatan]
footnote	catatan kaki	[tʃatatan kaki]
text	teks	[teks]
type, font	huruf	[huruf]
misprint, typo	salah cetak	[salah tʃeta']
translation	terjemahan	[tərdʒʲemahan]
to translate (vt)	menerjemahkan	[menerdʒʲemahkan]
original (n)	orisinal	[orisinal]
famous (adj)	terkenal	[tərkenal]
unknown (not famous)	tidak dikenali	[tida' dikenali]
interesting (adj)	menarik	[mənari']
bestseller	buku laris	[buku laris]
dictionary	kamus	[kamus]
textbook	buku pelajaran	[buku peladʒʲaran]
encyclopedia	ensiklopedi	[ensiklopedi]

133. Hunting. Fishing

hunting	perburuan	[pərburuan]
to hunt (vi, vt)	berburu	[bərburu]
hunter	pemburu	[pemburu]
to shoot (vi)	menembak	[mənemba']
rifle	senapan	[senapan]
bullet (shell)	peluru, patrun	[peluru], [patrun]
shot (lead balls)	peluru gotri	[peluru gotri]
steel trap	perangkap	[pəraŋkap]
snare (for birds, etc.)	perangkap	[pəraŋkap]
to fall into the steel trap	terperangkap	[tərpəraŋkap]
to lay a steel trap	memasang perangkap	[memasaŋ pəraŋkap]
poacher	pemburu ilegal	[pemburu ilegal]
game (in hunting)	binatang buruan	[binataŋ buruan]
hound dog	anjing pemburu	[andʒiŋ pemburu]
safari	safari	[safari]
mounted animal	patung binatang	[patuŋ binataŋ]
fisherman, angler	nelayan, pemancing	[nelajan], [pemantʃiŋ]
fishing (angling)	memancing	[memantʃiŋ]
to fish (vi)	memancing	[memantʃiŋ]
fishing rod	joran	[dʒoran]
fishing line	tali pancing	[tali pantʃiŋ]

hook	kail	[kail]
float, bobber	pelampung	[pelampuŋ]
bait	umpan	[umpan]

to cast a line	melempar pancing	[melempar pantʃiŋ]
to bite (ab. fish)	memakan umpan	[memakan umpan]
catch (of fish)	tangkapan	[taŋkapan]
ice-hole	lubang es	[lubaŋ es]

fishing net	jala	[dʒʲala]
boat	perahu	[perahu]
to net (to fish with a net)	menjala	[mendʒʲala]
to cast[throw] the net	menabur jala	[menabur dʒʲala]
to haul the net in	menarik jala	[menariʔ dʒʲala]
to fall into the net	tertangkap dalam jala	[tertaŋkap dalam dʒʲala]

whaler (person)	pemburu paus	[pemburu paus]
whaleboat	kapal pemburu paus	[kapal pemburu paus]
harpoon	tempuling	[tempuliŋ]

134. Games. Billiards

billiards	biliar	[biliar]
billiard room, hall	kamar biliar	[kamar biliar]
ball (snooker, etc.)	bola	[bola]

to pocket a ball	memasukkan bola	[memasuʔkan bola]
cue	stik	[stiʔ]
pocket	lubang meja biliar	[lubaŋ medʒʲa biliar]

135. Games. Playing cards

diamonds	wajik	[wadʒiʔ]
spades	sekop	[sekop]
hearts	hati	[hati]
clubs	keriting	[keritiŋ]

ace	as	[as]
king	raja	[radʒʲa]
queen	ratu	[ratu]
jack, knave	jack	[dʒʲeʔ]

playing card	kartu permainan	[kartu permajnan]
cards	kartu	[kartu]
trump	truf	[truf]
deck of cards	pak kartu	[paʔ kartu]
point	poin	[poin]
to deal (vi, vt)	membagikan	[membagikan]

to shuffle (cards)	mengocok	[məŋotʃoʲ]
lead, turn (n)	giliran	[giliran]
cardsharp	pemain kartu curang	[pemajn kartu tʃuraŋ]

136. Rest. Games. Miscellaneous

to stroll (vi, vt)	berjalan-jalan	[bərdʒʲalan-dʒʲalan]
stroll (leisurely walk)	jalan-jalan	[dʒʲalan-dʒʲalan]
car ride	perjalanan	[pərdʒʲalanan]
adventure	petualangan	[petualaŋan]
picnic	piknik	[pikniʔ]

game (chess, etc.)	permainan	[pərmajnan]
player	pemain	[pemajn]
game (one ~ of chess)	partai	[partaj]

collector (e.g., philatelist)	kolektor	[kolektor]
to collect (stamps, etc.)	mengoleksi	[məŋoleksi]
collection	koleksi	[koleksi]

crossword puzzle	teka-teki silang	[teka-teki silaŋ]
racetrack	lapangan pacu	[lapaŋan patʃu]
(horse racing venue)		
disco (discotheque)	diskotik	[diskotiʔ]

| sauna | sauna | [sauna] |
| lottery | lotre | [lotre] |

camping trip	darmawisata	[darmawisata]
camp	perkemahan	[pərkemahan]
tent (for camping)	tenda, kemah	[tenda], [kemah]
compass	kompas	[kompas]
camper	pewisata alam	[pewisata alam]

to watch (movie, etc.)	menonton	[mənonton]
viewer	penonton	[penonton]
TV show (TV program)	acara TV	[atʃara ti-vi]

137. Photography

| camera (photo) | kamera | [kamera] |
| photo, picture | foto | [foto] |

photographer	fotografer	[fotografer]
photo studio	studio foto	[studio foto]
photo album	album foto	[album foto]
camera lens	lensa kamera	[lensa kamera]
telephoto lens	lensa telefoto	[lensa telefoto]

| filter | **filter** | [filter] |
| lens | **lensa** | [lensa] |

optics (high-quality ~)	**alat optik**	[alat optiʔ]
diaphragm (aperture)	**diafragma**	[diafragma]
exposure time (shutter speed)	**kecepatan rana**	[ketʃepatan rana]
viewfinder	**jendela pengamat**	[dʒˈendela peŋamat]

digital camera	**kamera digital**	[kamera digital]
tripod	**kakitiga**	[kakitiga]
flash	**blitz**	[blits]

to photograph (vt)	**memotret**	[memotret]
to take pictures	**memotret**	[memotret]
to have one's picture taken	**berfoto**	[bərfoto]

focus	**fokus**	[fokus]
to focus	**mengatur fokus**	[məŋatur fokus]
sharp, in focus (adj)	**tajam**	[tadʒˈam]
sharpness	**ketajaman**	[ketadʒˈaman]

| contrast | **kekontrasan** | [kekontrasan] |
| contrast (as adj) | **kontras** | [kontras] |

picture (photo)	**gambar foto**	[gambar foto]
negative (n)	**negatif**	[negatif]
film (a roll of ~)	**film**	[film]
frame (still)	**frame, gambar diam**	[frame], [gambar diam]
to print (photos)	**mencetak**	[məntʃetaʔ]

138. Beach. Swimming

beach	**pantai**	[pantaj]
sand	**pasir**	[pasir]
deserted (beach)	**sepi**	[sepi]

suntan	**hitam terbakar matahari**	[hitam tərbakar matahari]
to get a tan	**berjemur di sinar matahari**	[bərdʒˈemur di sinar matahari]
tan (adj)	**hitam terbakar matahari**	[hitam tərbakar matahari]
sunscreen	**tabir surya**	[tabir surja]

bikini	**bikini**	[bikini]
bathing suit	**baju renang**	[badʒˈu renaŋ]
swim trunks	**celana renang**	[tʃelana renaŋ]

| swimming pool | **kolam renang** | [kolam renaŋ] |
| to swim (vi) | **berenang** | [bərenaŋ] |

shower	**pancuran**	[pantʃuran]
to change (one's clothes)	**berganti pakaian**	[bərganti pakajan]
towel	**handuk**	[handuʔ]
boat	**perahu**	[pərahu]
motorboat	**perahu motor**	[pərahu motor]
water ski	**ski air**	[ski air]
paddle boat	**sepeda air**	[sepeda air]
surfing	**berselancar**	[bərselantʃar]
surfer	**peselancar**	[peselantʃar]
scuba set	**alat scuba**	[alat skuba]
flippers (swim fins)	**sirip karet**	[sirip karet]
mask (diving ~)	**masker**	[masker]
diver	**penyelam**	[penjelam]
to dive (vi)	**menyelam**	[mənjelam]
underwater (adv)	**bawah air**	[bawah air]
beach umbrella	**payung**	[pajuŋ]
sunbed (lounger)	**kursi pantai**	[kursi pantaj]
sunglasses	**kacamata hitam**	[katʃamata hitam]
air mattress	**kasur udara**	[kasur udara]
to play (amuse oneself)	**bermain**	[bərmajn]
to go for a swim	**berenang**	[bərenaŋ]
beach ball	**bola pantai**	[bola pantaj]
to inflate (vt)	**meniup**	[məniup]
inflatable, air (adj)	**udara**	[udara]
wave	**gelombang**	[gelombaŋ]
buoy (line of ~s)	**pelampung**	[pelampuŋ]
to drown (ab. person)	**tenggelam**	[teŋgelam]
to save, to rescue	**menyelamatkan**	[mənjelamatkan]
life vest	**jaket pelampung**	[dʒʲaket pelampuŋ]
to observe, to watch	**mengamati**	[məŋamati]
lifeguard	**penyelamat**	[penjelamat]

TECHNICAL EQUIPMENT. TRANSPORTATION

Technical equipment

139. Computer

computer	**komputer**	[komputer]
notebook, laptop	**laptop**	[laptop]
to turn on	**menyalakan**	[mənjalakan]
to turn off	**mematikan**	[mematikan]
keyboard	**keyboard, papan tombol**	[keybor], [papan tombol]
key	**tombol**	[tombol]
mouse	**tetikus**	[tetikus]
mouse pad	**bantal tetikus**	[bantal tetikus]
button	**tombol**	[tombol]
cursor	**kursor**	[kursor]
monitor	**monitor**	[monitor]
screen	**layar**	[lajar]
hard disk	**hard disk, cakram keras**	[hard disk], [t͡ʃakram keras]
hard disk capacity	**kapasitas cakram keras**	[kapasitas t͡ʃakram keras]
memory	**memori**	[memori]
random access memory	**memori akses acak**	[memori akses at͡ʃaʔ]
file	**file, berkas**	[file], [bərkas]
folder	**folder**	[folder]
to open (vt)	**membuka**	[membuka]
to close (vt)	**menutup**	[mənutup]
to save (vt)	**menyimpan**	[mənjimpan]
to delete (vt)	**menghapus**	[mənhapus]
to copy (vt)	**menyalin**	[mənjalin]
to sort (vt)	**menyortir**	[mənjortir]
to transfer (copy)	**mentransfer**	[mentransfer]
program	**program**	[program]
software	**perangkat lunak**	[pəraŋkat lunaʔ]
programmer	**pemrogram**	[pemrogram]
to program (vt)	**memprogram**	[memprogram]
hacker	**peretas**	[peretas]
password	**kata sandi**	[kata sandi]

virus	virus	[virus]
to find, to detect	mendeteksi	[məndeteksi]
byte	bita	[bita]
megabyte	megabita	[megabita]
data	data	[data]
database	basis data, pangkalan data	[basis data], [paŋkalan data]
cable (USB, etc.)	kabel	[kabel]
to disconnect (vt)	melepaskan	[melepaskan]
to connect (sth to sth)	menyambungkan	[mənjambuŋkan]

140. Internet. E-mail

Internet	Internet	[internet]
browser	peramban	[peramban]
search engine	mesin telusur	[mesin telusur]
provider	provider	[provider]
webmaster	webmaster, perancang web	[webmaster], [pərantʃaŋ web]
website	situs web	[situs web]
webpage	halaman web	[halaman web]
address (e-mail ~)	alamat	[alamat]
address book	buku alamat	[buku alamat]
mailbox	kotak surat	[kota' surat]
mail	surat	[surat]
full (adj)	penuh	[penuh]
message	pesan	[pesan]
incoming messages	pesan masuk	[pesan masu']
outgoing messages	pesan keluar	[pesan keluar]
sender	pengirim	[peŋirim]
to send (vt)	mengirim	[məŋirim]
sending (of mail)	pengiriman	[peŋiriman]
receiver	penerima	[penerima]
to receive (vt)	menerima	[menerima]
correspondence	surat-menyurat	[surat-menyurat]
to correspond (vi)	surat-menyurat	[surat-menyurat]
file	file, berkas	[file], [bərkas]
to download (vt)	mengunduh	[məŋunduh]
to create (vt)	membuat	[membuat]

to delete (vt)	menghapus	[məŋhapus]
deleted (adj)	terhapus	[tərhapus]
connection (ADSL, etc.)	koneksi	[koneksi]
speed	kecepatan	[ketʃepatan]
modem	modem	[modem]
access	akses	[akses]
port (e.g., input ~)	porta	[porta]
connection (make a ~)	koneksi	[koneksi]
to connect to ... (vi)	terhubung ke ...	[tərhubuŋ ke ...]
to select (vt)	memilih	[memilih]
to search (for ...)	mencari ...	[məntʃari ...]

Transportation

141. Airplane

airplane	**pesawat terbang**	[pesawat tərbaŋ]
air ticket	**tiket pesawat terbang**	[tiket pesawat tərbaŋ]
airline	**maskapai penerbangan**	[maskapaj penerbaŋan]
airport	**bandara**	[bandara]
supersonic (adj)	**supersonik**	[supersoniʔ]
captain	**kapten**	[kapten]
crew	**awak**	[awaʔ]
pilot	**pilot**	[pilot]
flight attendant (fem.)	**pramugari**	[pramugari]
navigator	**navigator, penavigasi**	[navigator], [penavigasi]
wings	**sayap**	[sajap]
tail	**ekor**	[ekor]
cockpit	**kokpit**	[kokpit]
engine	**mesin**	[mesin]
undercarriage (landing gear)	**roda pendarat**	[roda pendarat]
turbine	**turbin**	[turbin]
propeller	**baling-baling**	[baliŋ-baliŋ]
black box	**kotak hitam**	[kotaʔ hitam]
yoke (control column)	**kemudi**	[kemudi]
fuel	**bahan bakar**	[bahan bakar]
safety card	**instruksi keselamatan**	[instruksi keselamatan]
oxygen mask	**masker oksigen**	[masker oksigen]
uniform	**seragam**	[seragam]
life vest	**jaket pelampung**	[dʒ'aket pelampuŋ]
parachute	**parasut**	[parasut]
takeoff	**lepas landas**	[lepas landas]
to take off (vi)	**bertolak**	[bertolaʔ]
runway	**jalur lepas landas**	[dʒ'alur lepas landas]
visibility	**visibilitas, pandangan**	[visibilitas], [pandaŋan]
flight (act of flying)	**penerbangan**	[penerbaŋan]
altitude	**ketinggian**	[ketiŋgian]
air pocket	**lubang udara**	[lubaŋ udara]
seat	**tempat duduk**	[tempat duduʔ]
headphones	**headphone, fonkepala**	[headphone], [fonkepala]

folding tray (tray table)	**meja lipat**	[medʒʲa lipat]
airplane window	**jendela pesawat**	[dʒʲendela pesawat]
aisle	**lorong**	[loroŋ]

142. Train

train	**kereta api**	[kereta api]
commuter train	**kereta api listrik**	[kereta api listriʔ]
express train	**kereta api cepat**	[kereta api tʃepat]
diesel locomotive	**lokomotif diesel**	[lokomotif disel]
steam locomotive	**lokomotif uap**	[lokomotif uap]

| passenger car | **gerbong penumpang** | [gerboŋ penumpaŋ] |
| dining car | **gerbong makan** | [gerboŋ makan] |

rails	**rel**	[rel]
railroad	**rel kereta api**	[rel kereta api]
railway tie	**bantalan rel**	[bantalan rel]

platform (railway ~)	**platform**	[platform]
track (~ 1, 2, etc.)	**jalur**	[dʒʲalur]
semaphore	**semafor**	[semafor]
station	**stasiun**	[stasiun]

engineer (train driver)	**masinis**	[masinis]
porter (of luggage)	**porter**	[porter]
car attendant	**kondektur**	[kondektur]
passenger	**penumpang**	[penumpaŋ]
conductor (ticket inspector)	**kondektur**	[kondektur]

| corridor (in train) | **koridor** | [koridor] |
| emergency brake | **rem darurat** | [rem darurat] |

compartment	**kabin**	[kabin]
berth	**bangku**	[baŋku]
upper berth	**bangku atas**	[baŋku atas]
lower berth	**bangku bawah**	[baŋku bawah]
bed linen, bedding	**kain kasur**	[kain kasur]

ticket	**tiket**	[tiket]
schedule	**jadwal**	[dʒʲadwal]
information display	**layar informasi**	[lajar informasi]

to leave, to depart	**berangkat**	[beraŋkat]
departure (of train)	**keberangkatan**	[keberaŋkatan]
to arrive (ab. train)	**datang**	[dataŋ]
arrival	**kedatangan**	[kedataŋan]
to arrive by train	**datang naik kereta api**	[dataŋ najʔ kereta api]
to get on the train	**naik ke kereta**	[naiʔ ke kereta]

to get off the train	turun dari kereta	[turun dari kereta]
train wreck	kecelakaan kereta	[ketʃelaka'an kereta]
to derail (vi)	keluar rel	[keluar rel]

steam locomotive	lokomotif uap	[lokomotif uap]
stoker, fireman	juru api	[dʒʲuru api]
firebox	tungku	[tuŋku]
coal	batu bara	[batu bara]

143. Ship

| ship | kapal | [kapal] |
| vessel | kapal | [kapal] |

steamship	kapal uap	[kapal uap]
riverboat	kapal api	[kapal api]
cruise ship	kapal laut	[kapal laut]
cruiser	kapal penjelajah	[kapal pendʒʲeladʒʲah]

yacht	perahu pesiar	[pərahu pesiar]
tugboat	kapal tunda	[kapal tunda]
barge	tongkang	[toŋkaŋ]
ferry	feri	[feri]

| sailing ship | kapal layar | [kapal lajar] |
| brigantine | kapal brigantin | [kapal brigantin] |

| ice breaker | kapal pemecah es | [kapal pemetʃah es] |
| submarine | kapal selam | [kapal selam] |

boat (flat-bottomed ~)	perahu	[pərahu]
dinghy	sekoci	[sekotʃi]
lifeboat	sekoci penyelamat	[sekotʃi penjelamat]
motorboat	perahu motor	[pərahu motor]

captain	kapten	[kapten]
seaman	kelasi	[kelasi]
sailor	pelaut	[pelaut]
crew	awak	[awa']

boatswain	bosman, bosun	[bosman], [bosun]
ship's boy	kadet laut	[kadet laut]
cook	koki	[koki]
ship's doctor	dokter kapal	[dokter kapal]

deck	dek	[de']
mast	tiang	[tiaŋ]
sail	layar	[lajar]
hold	lambung kapal	[lambuŋ kapal]
bow (prow)	haluan	[haluan]

stern	**buritan**	[buritan]
oar	**dayung**	[dajuŋ]
screw propeller	**baling-baling**	[baliŋ-baliŋ]
cabin	**kabin**	[kabin]
wardroom	**ruang rekreasi**	[ruaŋ rekreasi]
engine room	**ruang mesin**	[ruaŋ mesin]
bridge	**anjungan kapal**	[andʒʲuŋan kapal]
radio room	**ruang radio**	[ruaŋ radio]
wave (radio)	**gelombang radio**	[gelombaŋ radio]
logbook	**buku harian kapal**	[buku harian kapal]

spyglass	**teropong**	[təropoŋ]
bell	**lonceng**	[lontʃeŋ]
flag	**bendera**	[bendera]

| hawser (mooring ~) | **tali** | [tali] |
| knot (bowline, etc.) | **simpul** | [simpul] |

| deckrails | **pegangan** | [pegaŋan] |
| gangway | **tangga kapal** | [taŋga kapal] |

anchor	**jangkar**	[dʒʲaŋkar]
to weigh anchor	**mengangkat jangkar**	[mənaŋkat dʒʲaŋkar]
to drop anchor	**menjatuhkan jangkar**	[məndʒʲatuhkan dʒʲaŋkar]
anchor chain	**rantai jangkar**	[rantaj dʒʲaŋkar]

port (harbor)	**pelabuhan**	[pelabuhan]
quay, wharf	**dermaga**	[dermaga]
to berth (moor)	**merapat**	[merapat]
to cast off	**bertolak**	[bərtolaʔ]

trip, voyage	**pengembaraan**	[peɲembaraʔan]
cruise (sea trip)	**pesiar**	[pesiar]
course (route)	**haluan**	[haluan]
route (itinerary)	**rute**	[rute]

| shallows | **beting** | [betiŋ] |
| to run aground | **kandas** | [kandas] |

storm	**badai**	[badaj]
signal	**sinyal**	[sinjal]
to sink (vi)	**tenggelam**	[teŋgelam]
Man overboard!	**Orang hanyut!**	[oraŋ hanyut!]
SOS (distress signal)	**SOS**	[es-o-es]
ring buoy	**pelampung penyelamat**	[pelampuŋ penjelamat]

144. Airport

| airport | **bandara** | [bandara] |
| airplane | **pesawat terbang** | [pesawat tərbaŋ] |

airline	**maskapai penerbangan**	[maskapaj peneɾbaɾjan]
air traffic controller	**pengawas lalu lintas udara**	[peŋawas lalu lintas udara]
departure	**keberangkatan**	[keberaŋkatan]
arrival	**kedatangan**	[kedataŋan]
to arrive (by plane)	**datang**	[dataŋ]
departure time	**waktu keberangkatan**	[waktu keberaŋkatan]
arrival time	**waktu kedatangan**	[waktu kedataŋan]
to be delayed	**terlambat**	[tərlambat]
flight delay	**penundaan penerbangan**	[penunda'an penerbaŋan]
information board	**papan informasi**	[papan informasi]
information	**informasi**	[informasi]
to announce (vt)	**mengumumkan**	[məŋumumkan]
flight (e.g., next ~)	**penerbangan**	[penerbaŋan]
customs	**pabean**	[pabean]
customs officer	**petugas pabean**	[petugas pabean]
customs declaration	**pernyataan pabean**	[pərnjata'an pabean]
to fill out (vt)	**mengisi**	[məŋisi]
to fill out the declaration	**mengisi formulir bea cukai**	[məŋisi formulir bea tʃukaj]
passport control	**pemeriksaan paspor**	[pemeriksa'an paspor]
luggage	**bagasi**	[bagasi]
hand luggage	**jinjingan**	[dʒindʒiŋan]
luggage cart	**troli bagasi**	[troli bagasi]
landing	**pendaratan**	[pendaratan]
landing strip	**jalur pendaratan**	[dʒʲalur pendaratan]
to land (vi)	**mendarat**	[məndarat]
airstairs	**tangga pesawat**	[taŋga pesawat]
check-in	**check-in**	[tʃekin]
check-in counter	**meja check-in**	[medʒʲa tʃekin]
to check-in (vi)	**check-in**	[tʃekin]
boarding pass	**kartu pas**	[kartu pas]
departure gate	**gerbang keberangkatan**	[gerbaŋ keberaŋkatan]
transit	**transit**	[transit]
to wait (vt)	**menunggu**	[mənuŋgu]
departure lounge	**ruang tunggu**	[ruaŋ tuŋgu]
to see off	**mengantar**	[məŋantar]
to say goodbye	**berpamitan**	[bərpamitan]

145. Bicycle. Motorcycle

bicycle	**sepeda**	[sepeda]
scooter	**skuter**	[skuter]
motorcycle, bike	**sepeda motor**	[sepeda motor]
to go by bicycle	**naik sepeda**	[naiʔ sepeda]
handlebars	**kemudi, setang**	[kemudi], [setaŋ]
pedal	**pedal**	[pedal]
brakes	**rem**	[rem]
bicycle seat (saddle)	**sadel**	[sadel]
pump	**pompa**	[pompa]
luggage rack	**boncengan**	[bontʃeŋan]
front lamp	**lampu depan, berko**	[lampu depan], [bərko]
helmet	**helm**	[helm]
wheel	**roda**	[roda]
fender	**sayap roda**	[sajap roda]
rim	**bingkai**	[biŋkaj]
spoke	**jari-jari, ruji**	[dʒˈari-dʒˈari], [rudʒi]

Cars

146. Types of cars

automobile, car	**mobil**	[mobil]
sports car	**mobil sports**	[mobil sports]
limousine	**limusin**	[limusin]
off-road vehicle	**kendaraan lintas medan**	[kendara'an lintas medan]
convertible (n)	**kabriolet**	[kabriolet]
minibus	**minibus**	[minibus]
ambulance	**ambulans**	[ambulans]
snowplow	**truk pembersih salju**	[tru' pembersih saldʒʲu]
truck	**truk**	[tru']
tanker truck	**truk tangki**	[tru' taŋki]
van (small truck)	**mobil van**	[mobil van]
road tractor (trailer truck)	**truk semi trailer**	[tra' semi treyler]
trailer	**trailer**	[treyler]
comfortable (adj)	**nyaman**	[njaman]
used (adj)	**bekas**	[bekas]

147. Cars. Bodywork

hood	**kap**	[kap]
fender	**sepatbor**	[sepatbor]
roof	**atap**	[atap]
windshield	**kaca depan**	[katʃa depan]
rear-view mirror	**spion belakang**	[spion belakaŋ]
windshield washer	**pencuci kaca**	[pentʃutʃi katʃa]
windshield wipers	**karet wiper**	[karet wiper]
side window	**jendela mobil**	[dʒʲendela mobil]
window lift (power window)	**pemutar jendela**	[pemutar dʒʲendela]
antenna	**antena**	[antena]
sunroof	**panel atap**	[panel atap]
bumper	**bumper**	[bumper]
trunk	**bagasi mobil**	[bagasi mobil]
roof luggage rack	**rak bagasi atas**	[ra' bagasi atas]
door	**pintu**	[pintu]

door handle	**gagang pintu**	[gagaŋ pintu]
door lock	**kunci**	[kuntʃi]
license plate	**pelat nomor**	[pelat nomor]
muffler	**peredam suara**	[nərədam suara]
gas tank	**tangki bahan bakar**	[taŋki bahan bakar]
tailpipe	**knalpot**	[knalpot]
gas, accelerator	**gas**	[gas]
pedal	**pedal**	[pedal]
gas pedal	**pedal gas**	[pedal gas]
brake	**rem**	[rem]
brake pedal	**pedal rem**	[pedal rem]
to brake (use the brake)	**mengerem**	[məŋerem]
parking brake	**rem tangan**	[rem taŋan]
clutch	**kopling**	[kopliŋ]
clutch pedal	**pedal kopling**	[pedal kopliŋ]
clutch disc	**pelat kopling**	[pelat kopliŋ]
shock absorber	**peredam kejut**	[pəredam kedʒʲut]
wheel	**roda**	[roda]
spare tire	**ban serep**	[ban serep]
tire	**ban**	[ban]
hubcap	**dop**	[dop]
driving wheels	**roda penggerak**	[roda peŋgeraʔ]
front-wheel drive (as adj)	**penggerak roda depan**	[peŋgeraʔ roda depan]
rear-wheel drive (as adj)	**penggerak roda belakang**	[peŋgeraʔ roda belakaŋ]
all-wheel drive (as adj)	**penggerak roda empat**	[peŋgeraʔ roda empat]
gearbox	**transmisi, girboks**	[transmisi], [girboks]
automatic (adj)	**otomatis**	[otomatis]
mechanical (adj)	**mekanis**	[mekanis]
gear shift	**tuas persneling**	[tuas pərsneliŋ]
headlight	**lampu depan**	[lampu depan]
headlights	**lampu depan**	[lampu depan]
low beam	**lampu dekat**	[lampu dekat]
high beam	**lampu jauh**	[lampu dʒʲauh]
brake light	**lampu rem**	[lampu rem]
parking lights	**lampu kecil**	[lampu ketʃil]
hazard lights	**lampu bahaya**	[lampu bahaja]
fog lights	**lampu kabut**	[lampu kabut]
turn signal	**lampu sein**	[lampu sein]
back-up light	**lampu belakang**	[lampu belakaŋ]

148. Cars. Passenger compartment

car inside (interior)	kabin, interior	[kabin], [interior]
leather (as adj)	kulit	[kulit]
velour (as adj)	velour	[velour]
upholstery	pelapis jok	[pelapis dʒo']
instrument (gage)	alat pengukur	[alat peŋukur]
dashboard	dasbor	[dasbor]
speedometer	spidometer	[spidometer]
needle (pointer)	jarum	[dʒʲarum]
odometer	odometer	[odometer]
indicator (sensor)	indikator, sensor	[indikator], [sensor]
level	level	[level]
warning light	lampu indikator	[lampu indikator]
steering wheel	setir	[setir]
horn	klakson	[klakson]
button	tombol	[tombol]
switch	tuas	[tuas]
seat	jok	[dʒo']
backrest	sandaran	[sandaran]
headrest	sandaran kepala	[sandaran kepala]
seat belt	sabuk pengaman	[sabu' peŋaman]
to fasten the belt	mengencangkan sabuk pengaman	[məŋentʃaŋkan sabu' peŋaman]
adjustment (of seats)	penyetelan	[penjetelan]
airbag	bantal udara	[bantal udara]
air-conditioner	penyejuk udara	[penjedʒʲu' udara]
radio	radio	[radio]
CD player	pemutar CD	[pemutar si-di]
to turn on	menyalakan	[mənjalakan]
antenna	antena	[antena]
glove box	laci depan	[latʃi depan]
ashtray	asbak	[asba']

149. Cars. Engine

engine	mesin	[mesin]
motor	motor	[motor]
diesel (as adj)	diesel	[disel]
gasoline (as adj)	bensin	[bensin]
engine volume	kapasitas mesin	[kapasitas mesin]
power	daya, tenaga	[daja], [tenaga]

horsepower	tenaga kuda	[tenaga kuda]
piston	piston	[piston]
cylinder	silinder	[silinder]
valve	katup	[katup]

injector	injektor	[indʒʲektor]
generator (alternator)	generator	[generator]
carburetor	karburator	[karburator]
motor oil	oli	[oli]

radiator	radiator	[radiator]
coolant	cairan pendingin	[tʃajran pendiŋin]
cooling fan	kipas angin	[kipas aŋin]

battery (accumulator)	aki	[aki]
starter	starter	[starter]
ignition	pengapian	[peŋapian]
spark plug	busi	[busi]

terminal (of battery)	elektroda	[elektroda]
positive terminal	terminal positif	[terminal positif]
negative terminal	terminal negatif	[terminal negatif]
fuse	sekering	[sekeriŋ]

air filter	filter udara	[filter udara]
oil filter	filter oli	[filter oli]
fuel filter	filter bahan bakar	[filter bahan bakar]

150. Cars. Crash. Repair

car crash	kecelakaan mobil	[ketʃelakaʔan mobil]
traffic accident	kecelakaan jalan raya	[ketʃelakaʔan dʒʲalan raja]
to crash (into the wall, etc.)	menabrak	[menabraʔ]
to get smashed up	mengalami kecelakaan	[meŋalami ketʃelakaʔan]
damage	kerusakan	[kerusakan]
intact (unscathed)	tidak tersentuh	[tidaʔ tersentuh]

breakdown	kerusakan	[kerusakan]
to break down (vi)	rusak	[rusaʔ]
towrope	tali penyeret	[tali penjeret]

puncture	ban bocor	[ban botʃor]
to be flat	kempes	[kempes]
to pump up	memompa	[memompa]
pressure	tekanan	[tekanan]
to check (to examine)	memeriksa	[memeriksa]

| repair | reparasi | [reparasi] |
| auto repair shop | bengkel mobil | [beŋkel mobil] |

spare part	onderdil, suku cadang	[onderdil], [suku ʃadaij]
part	komponen	[komponen]
bolt (with nut)	baut	[baut]
screw (fastener)	sekrup	[sekrup]
nut	mur	[mur]
washer	ring	[riŋ]
bearing	bantalan luncur	[bantalan lunʧur]
tube	pipa	[pipa]
gasket (head ~)	gasket	[gasket]
cable, wire	kabel, kawat	[kabel], [kawat]
jack	dongkrak	[doŋkraʔ]
wrench	kunci pas	[kunʧi pas]
hammer	martil, palu	[martil], [palu]
pump	pompa	[pompa]
screwdriver	obeng	[obeŋ]
fire extinguisher	pemadam api	[pemadam api]
warning triangle	segi tiga pengaman	[segi tiga peŋaman]
to stall (vi)	mogok	[mogoʔ]
stall (n)	mogok	[mogoʔ]
to be broken	rusak	[rusaʔ]
to overheat (vi)	kepanasan	[kepanasan]
to be clogged up	tersumbat	[tersumbat]
to freeze up (pipes, etc.)	membeku	[membeku]
to burst (vi, ab. tube)	pecah	[peʧah]
pressure	tekanan	[tekanan]
level	level	[level]
slack (~ belt)	longgar	[loŋgar]
dent	penyok	[penjoʔ]
knocking noise (engine)	ketukan	[ketukan]
crack	retak	[retaʔ]
scratch	gores	[gores]

151. Cars. Road

road	jalan	[ʤʲalan]
highway	jalan raya	[ʤʲalan raja]
freeway	jalan raya	[ʤʲalan raja]
direction (way)	arah	[arah]
distance	jarak	[ʤʲaraʔ]
bridge	jembatan	[ʤʲembatan]
parking lot	tempat parkir	[tempat parkir]

square	**lapangan**	[lapaŋan]
interchange	**jembatan simpang susun**	[dʒʲembatan simpaŋ susun]
tunnel	**terowongan**	[tərowoŋan]
gas station	**SPBU, stasiun bensin**	[es-pe-be-u], [stasjun bensin]
parking lot	**tempat parkir**	[tempat parkir]
gas pump (fuel dispenser)	**stasiun bahan bakar**	[stasiun bahan bakar]
auto repair shop	**bengkel mobil**	[beŋkel mobil]
to get gas (to fill up)	**mengisi bahan bakar**	[məŋisi bahan bakar]
fuel	**bahan bakar**	[bahan bakar]
jerrycan	**jeriken**	[dʒʲeriken]
asphalt	**aspal**	[aspal]
road markings	**penandaan jalan**	[penanda'an dʒʲalan]
curb	**kerb jalan**	[kerb dʒʲalan]
guardrail	**pagar pematas**	[pagar pematas]
ditch	**parit**	[parit]
roadside (shoulder)	**bahu jalan**	[bahu dʒʲalan]
lamppost	**tiang lampu**	[tiaŋ lampu]
to drive (a car)	**menyetir**	[mənjetir]
to turn (e.g., ~ left)	**membelok**	[membeloʔ]
to make a U-turn	**memutar arah**	[memutar arah]
reverse (~ gear)	**mundur**	[mundur]
to honk (vi)	**membunyikan klakson**	[membunjikan klakson]
honk (sound)	**suara klakson**	[suara klakson]
to get stuck (in the mud, etc.)	**terjebak**	[tərdʒʲebaʔ]
to spin the wheels	**terjebak**	[tərdʒʲebaʔ]
to cut, to turn off (vt)	**mematikan**	[mematikan]
speed	**kecepatan**	[ketʃepatan]
to exceed the speed limit	**melebihi batas kecepatan**	[melebihi batas ketʃepatan]
to give a ticket	**memberikan surat tilang**	[memberikan surat tilaŋ]
traffic lights	**lampu lalu lintas**	[lampu lalu lintas]
driver's license	**Surat Izin Mengemudi, SIM**	[surat izin məŋemudi], [sim]
grade crossing	**lintasan**	[lintasan]
intersection	**persimpangan**	[pərsimpaŋan]
crosswalk	**penyeberangan**	[penjeberaŋan]
bend, curve	**tikungan**	[tikuŋan]
pedestrian zone	**kawasan pejalan kaki**	[kawasan pedʒʲalan kaki]

PEOPLE. LIFE EVENTS

Life events

152. Holidays. Event

celebration, holiday	**perayaan**	[pəraja'an]
national day	**hari besar nasional**	[hari besar nasional]
public holiday	**hari libur**	[hari libur]
to commemorate (vt)	**merayakan**	[merajakan]
event (happening)	**peristiwa, kejadian**	[pəristiwa], [kedʒˈadian]
event (organized activity)	**acara**	[atʃara]
banquet (party)	**banket**	[banket]
reception (formal party)	**resepsi**	[resepsi]
feast	**pesta**	[pesta]
anniversary	**hari jadi, HUT**	[hari dʒˈadi], [ha-u-te]
jubilee	**yubileum**	[yubileum]
to celebrate (vt)	**merayakan**	[merajakan]
New Year	**Tahun Baru**	[tahun baru]
Happy New Year!	**Selamat Tahun Baru!**	[selamat tahun baru!]
Santa Claus	**Sinterklas**	[sinterklas]
Christmas	**Natal**	[natal]
Merry Christmas!	**Selamat Hari Natal!**	[selamat hari natal!]
Christmas tree	**pohon Natal**	[pohon natal]
fireworks (fireworks show)	**kembang api**	[kembaŋ api]
wedding	**pernikahan**	[pərnikahan]
groom	**mempelai lelaki**	[mempelaj lelaki]
bride	**mempelai perempuan**	[mempelaj perempuan]
to invite (vt)	**mengundang**	[məŋundaŋ]
invitation card	**kartu undangan**	[kartu undaŋan]
guest	**tamu**	[tamu]
to visit	**mengunjungi**	[məŋundʒˈuŋi]
(~ your parents, etc.)		
to meet the guests	**menyambut tamu**	[mənjambut tamu]
gift, present	**hadiah**	[hadiah]
to give (sth as present)	**memberi**	[memberi]
to receive gifts	**menerima hadiah**	[mənerima hadiah]

bouquet (of flowers)	**buket**	[buket]
congratulations	**ucapan selamat**	[utʃapan selamat]
to congratulate (vt)	**mengucapkan selamat**	[mənutʃapkan selamat]
greeting card	**kartu ucapan selamat**	[kartu utʃapan selamat]
to send a postcard	**mengirim kartu pos**	[məŋirim kartu pos]
to get a postcard	**menerima kartu pos**	[mənerima kartu pos]
toast	**toas**	[toas]
to offer (a drink, etc.)	**menawari**	[mənawari]
champagne	**sampanye**	[sampanje]
to enjoy oneself	**bersukaria**	[bərsukaria]
merriment (gaiety)	**keriangan, kegembiraan**	[kerianan], [kegembira'an]
joy (emotion)	**kegembiraan**	[kegembira'an]
dance	**dansa, tari**	[dansa], [tari]
to dance (vi, vt)	**berdansa, menari**	[bərdansa], [menari]
waltz	**wals**	[wals]
tango	**tango**	[taŋo]

153. Funerals. Burial

cemetery	**pemakaman**	[pemakaman]
grave, tomb	**makam**	[makam]
cross	**salib**	[salib]
gravestone	**batu nisan**	[batu nisan]
fence	**pagar**	[pagar]
chapel	**kapel**	[kapel]
death	**kematian**	[kematian]
to die (vi)	**mati, meninggal**	[mati], [meninggal]
the deceased	**almarhum**	[almarhum]
mourning	**perkabungan**	[pərkabunan]
to bury (vt)	**memakamkan**	[memakamkan]
funeral home	**rumah duka**	[rumah duka]
funeral	**pemakaman**	[pemakaman]
wreath	**karangan bunga**	[karanan buna]
casket, coffin	**keranda**	[keranda]
hearse	**mobil jenazah**	[mobil dʒienazah]
shroud	**kain kafan**	[kain kafan]
funeral procession	**prosesi pemakaman**	[prosesi pemakaman]
funerary urn	**guci abu jenazah**	[gutʃi abu dʒienazah]
crematory	**krematorium**	[krematorium]
obituary	**obituarium**	[obituarium]
to cry (weep)	**menangis**	[mənanis]
to sob (vi)	**meratap**	[meratap]

154. War. Soldiers

platoon	**peleton**	[peleton]
company	**kompi**	[kompi]
regiment	**resimen**	[resimen]
army	**tentara**	[tentara]
division	**divisi**	[divisi]
section, squad	**pasukan**	[pasukan]
host (army)	**tentara**	[tentara]
soldier	**tentara, serdadu**	[tentara], [serdadu]
officer	**perwira**	[pərwira]
private	**prajurit**	[pradʒˈurit]
sergeant	**sersan**	[sersan]
lieutenant	**letnan**	[letnan]
captain	**kapten**	[kapten]
major	**mayor**	[major]
colonel	**kolonel**	[kolonel]
general	**jenderal**	[dʒˈenderal]
sailor	**pelaut**	[pelaut]
captain	**kapten**	[kapten]
boatswain	**bosman, bosun**	[bosman], [bosun]
artilleryman	**tentara artileri**	[tentara artileri]
paratrooper	**pasukan penerjun**	[pasukan penerdʒˈun]
pilot	**pilot**	[pilot]
navigator	**navigator, penavigasi**	[navigator], [penavigasi]
mechanic	**mekanik**	[mekaniʔ]
pioneer (sapper)	**pencari ranjau**	[pentʃari randʒˈau]
parachutist	**parasutis**	[parasutis]
reconnaissance scout	**pengintai**	[peɲintaj]
sniper	**penembak jitu**	[penembaʔ dʒitu]
patrol (group)	**patroli**	[patroli]
to patrol (vt)	**berpatroli**	[bərpatroli]
sentry, guard	**pengawal**	[peɲawal]
warrior	**prajurit**	[pradʒˈurit]
hero	**pahlawan**	[pahlawan]
heroine	**pahlawan wanita**	[pahlawan wanita]
patriot	**patriot**	[patriot]
traitor	**pengkhianat**	[peɲhianat]
to betray (vt)	**mengkhianati**	[məɲhianati]
deserter	**desertir**	[desertir]
to desert (vi)	**melakukan desersi**	[melakukan desersi]

mercenary	**tentara bayaran**	[tentara bajaran]
recruit	**rekrut, calon tentara**	[rekrut], [tʃalon tentara]
volunteer	**sukarelawan**	[sukarelawan]

dead (n)	**korban meninggal**	[korban menɪŋgal]
wounded (n)	**korban luka**	[korban luka]
prisoner of war	**tawanan perang**	[tawanan pəraŋ]

155. War. Military actions. Part 1

war	**perang**	[peraŋ]
to be at war	**berperang**	[bərperaŋ]
civil war	**perang saudara**	[peraŋ saudara]

treacherously (adv)	**secara curang**	[setʃara tʃuraŋ]
declaration of war	**pernyataan perang**	[pərnjata'an peraŋ]
to declare (~ war)	**menyatakan perang**	[mənjatakan peraŋ]
aggression	**agresi**	[agresi]
to attack (invade)	**menyerang**	[mənjeraŋ]

to invade (vt)	**menduduki**	[mənduduki]
invader	**penduduk**	[pendudu']
conqueror	**penakluk**	[penaklu']

defense	**pertahanan**	[pertahanan]
to defend (a country, etc.)	**mempertahankan**	[mempertahankan]
to defend (against ...)	**bertahan ...**	[bərtahan ...]

enemy	**musuh**	[musuh]
foe, adversary	**lawan**	[lawan]
enemy (as adj)	**musuh**	[musuh]

| strategy | **strategi** | [strategi] |
| tactics | **taktik** | [takti'] |

order	**perintah**	[pərintah]
command (order)	**perintah**	[pərintah]
to order (vt)	**memerintahkan**	[memerintahkan]
mission	**tugas**	[tugas]
secret (adj)	**rahasia**	[rahasia]

| battle | **pertempuran** | [pertempuran] |
| combat | **pertempuran** | [pertempuran] |

attack	**serangan**	[seraŋan]
charge (assault)	**serbuan**	[serbuan]
to storm (vt)	**menyerbu**	[mənjerbu]
siege (to be under ~)	**kepungan**	[kepuŋan]
offensive (n)	**serangan**	[seraŋan]
to go on the offensive	**menyerang**	[mənjeraŋ]

retreat
to retreat (vi)

pengunduran
mundur

[pəŋunduran]
[mundur]

encirclement
to encircle (vt)

pengepungan
mengepung

[peŋepuŋan]
[məŋepuŋ]

bombing (by aircraft)
to drop a bomb
to bomb (vt)
explosion

pengeboman
menjatuhkan bom
mengebom
ledakan

[peŋeboman]
[məndʒatuhkan bom]
[məŋebom]
[ledakan]

shot
to fire (~ a shot)
firing (burst of ~)

tembakan
melepaskan
penembakan

[tembakan]
[melepaskan]
[penembakan]

to aim (to point a weapon)
to point (a gun)
to hit (the target)

membidik
mengarahkan
mengenai

[membidiʔ]
[məŋarahkan]
[məŋenaj]

to sink (~ a ship)
hole (in a ship)
to founder, to sink (vi)

menenggelamkan
lubang
karam

[mənəŋgelamkan]
[lubaŋ]
[karam]

front (war ~)
evacuation
to evacuate (vt)

garis depan
evakuasi
mengevakuasi

[garis depan]
[evakuasi]
[məŋevakuasi]

trench
barbwire
barrier (anti tank ~)
watchtower

parit perlindungan
kawat berduri
rintangan
menara

[parit pərlinduŋan]
[kawat bərduri]
[rintaŋan]
[mənara]

military hospital
to wound (vt)
wound
wounded (n)
to be wounded
serious (wound)

rumah sakit militer
melukai
luka
korban luka
terluka
parah

[rumah sakit militer]
[melukaj]
[luka]
[korban luka]
[tərluka]
[parah]

156. Weapons

weapons
firearms
cold weapons
(knives, etc.)

senjata
senjata api
sejata tajam

[sendʒ'ata]
[sendʒ'ata api]
[sedʒ'ata tadʒ'am]

chemical weapons
nuclear (adj)
nuclear weapons
bomb

senjata kimia
nuklir
senjata nuklir
bom

[sendʒ'ata kimia]
[nuklir]
[sendʒ'ata nuklir]
[bom]

atomic bomb	**bom atom**	[bom atom]
pistol (gun)	**pistol**	[pistol]
rifle	**senapan**	[senapan]
submachine gun	**senapan otomatis**	[senapan otomatis]
machine gun	**senapan mesin**	[senapan mesin]
muzzle	**moncong**	[montʃoŋ]
barrel	**laras**	[laras]
caliber	**kaliber**	[kaliber]
trigger	**pelatuk**	[pelatuʔ]
sight (aiming device)	**pembidik**	[pembidiʔ]
magazine	**magasin**	[magasin]
butt (shoulder stock)	**pantat senapan**	[pantat senapan]
hand grenade	**granat tangan**	[granat taŋan]
explosive	**bahan peledak**	[bahan peledaʔ]
bullet	**peluru**	[peluru]
cartridge	**patrun**	[patrun]
charge	**isian**	[isian]
ammunition	**amunisi**	[amunisi]
bomber (aircraft)	**pesawat pengebom**	[pesawat peŋebom]
fighter	**pesawat pemburu**	[pesawat pemburu]
helicopter	**helikopter**	[helikopter]
anti-aircraft gun	**meriam penangkis serangan udara**	[meriam penaŋkis seraŋan udara]
tank	**tank**	[tanʔ]
tank gun	**meriam tank**	[meriam tanʔ]
artillery	**artileri**	[artileri]
gun (cannon, howitzer)	**meriam**	[meriam]
to lay (a gun)	**mengarahkan**	[meŋarahkan]
shell (projectile)	**peluru**	[peluru]
mortar bomb	**peluru mortir**	[peluru mortir]
mortar	**mortir**	[mortir]
splinter (shell fragment)	**serpihan**	[serpihan]
submarine	**kapal selam**	[kapal selam]
torpedo	**torpedo**	[torpedo]
missile	**rudal**	[rudal]
to load (gun)	**mengisi**	[meŋisi]
to shoot (vi)	**menembak**	[menembaʔ]
to point at (the cannon)	**membidik**	[membidiʔ]
bayonet	**bayonet**	[bajonet]
rapier	**pedang rapier**	[pedaŋ rapier]
saber (e.g., cavalry ~)	**pedang saber**	[pedaŋ saber]

spear (weapon)	**lembing**	[lembliŋ]
bow	**busur panah**	[busur panah]
arrow	**anak panah**	[anaʔ panah]
musket	**senapan lantak**	[senapan lantaʔ]
crossbow	**busur silang**	[busur silaŋ]

157. Ancient people

primitive (prehistoric)	**primitif**	[primitif]
prehistoric (adj)	**prasejarah**	[prasedʒّarah]
ancient (~ civilization)	**kuno**	[kuno]

Stone Age	**Zaman Batu**	[zaman batu]
Bronze Age	**Zaman Perunggu**	[zaman peruŋgu]
Ice Age	**Zaman Es**	[zaman es]

tribe	**suku**	[suku]
cannibal	**kanibal**	[kanibal]
hunter	**pemburu**	[pemburu]
to hunt (vi, vt)	**berburu**	[berburu]
mammoth	**mamut**	[mamut]

cave	**gua**	[gua]
fire	**api**	[api]
campfire	**api unggun**	[api uŋgun]
cave painting	**lukisan gua**	[lukisan gua]
tool (e.g., stone ax)	**alat kerja**	[alat kerdʒّa]
spear	**tombak**	[tombaʔ]
stone ax	**kapak batu**	[kapaʔ batu]
to be at war	**berperang**	[berperaŋ]
to domesticate (vt)	**menjinakkan**	[mendʒina'kan]

idol	**berhala**	[berhala]
to worship (vt)	**memuja**	[memudʒّa]
superstition	**takhayul**	[tahajul]
rite	**upacara**	[upatʃara]

evolution	**evolusi**	[evolusi]
development	**perkembangan**	[perkembaŋan]
disappearance (extinction)	**kehilangan**	[kehilaŋan]
to adapt oneself	**menyesuaikan diri**	[menjesuajkan diri]

archeology	**arkeologi**	[arkeologi]
archeologist	**arkeolog**	[arkeolog]
archeological (adj)	**arkeologis**	[arkeologis]

excavation site	**situs ekskavasi**	[situs ekskavasi]
excavations	**ekskavasi**	[ekskavasi]
find (object)	**penemuan**	[penemuan]
fragment	**fragmen**	[fragmen]

158. Middle Ages

people (ethnic group)	rakyat	[raljat]
peoples	bangsa-bangsa	[baŋsa-baŋsa]
tribe	suku	[suku]
tribes	suku-suku	[suku-suku]
barbarians	kaum barbar	[kaum barbar]
Gauls	kaum Gaul	[kaum gaul]
Goths	kaum Goth	[kaum got]
Slavs	kaum Slavia	[kaum slavia]
Vikings	kaum Viking	[kaum vikiŋ]
Romans	kaum Roma	[kaum roma]
Roman (adj)	Romawi	[romawi]
Byzantines	kaum Byzantium	[kaum bizantium]
Byzantium	Byzantium	[bizantium]
Byzantine (adj)	Byzantium	[bizantium]
emperor	kaisar	[kajsar]
leader, chief (tribal ~)	pemimpin	[pemimpin]
powerful (~ king)	adikuasa, berkuasa	[adikuasa], [bərkuasa]
king	raja	[radʒʲa]
ruler (sovereign)	penguasa	[peŋuasa]
knight	ksatria	[ksatria]
feudal lord	tuan	[tuan]
feudal (adj)	feodal	[feodal]
vassal	vasal	[vasal]
duke	duke	[duke]
earl	earl	[earl]
baron	baron	[baron]
bishop	uskup	[uskup]
armor	baju besi	[badʒʲu besi]
shield	perisai	[pərisaj]
sword	pedang	[pedaŋ]
visor	visor, topeng besi	[visor], [topeŋ besi]
chainmail	baju zirah	[badʒʲu zirah]
Crusade	Perang Salib	[pəraŋ salib]
crusader	kaum salib	[kaum salib]
territory	wilayah	[wilajah]
to attack (invade)	menyerang	[mənjeraŋ]
to conquer (vt)	menaklukkan	[mənakluʔkan]
to occupy (invade)	menduduki	[mənduduki]
siege (to be under ~)	kepungan	[kepuŋan]
besieged (adj)	terkepung	[tərkepuŋ]

to besiege (vt)	mengepung	[məɲəpuŋ]
inquisition	inkuisisi	[inkuisisi]
inquisitor	inkuisitor	[inkuisitor]
torture	siksaan	[siksa'an]
cruel (adj)	kejam	[kedʒʲam]
heretic	penganut bidah	[peɲanut bidah]
heresy	bidah	[bidah]
seafaring	pelayaran laut	[pelajaran laut]
pirate	bajak laut	[badʒʲa' laut]
piracy	pembajakan	[pembadʒʲakan]
boarding (attack)	serangan terhadap kapal dari dekat	[seraŋan tərhadap kapal dari dekat]
loot, booty	rampasan	[rampasan]
treasures	harta karun	[harta karun]
discovery	penemuan	[penemuan]
to discover (new land, etc.)	menemukan	[mənemukan]
expedition	ekspedisi	[ekspedisi]
musketeer	musketir	[musketir]
cardinal	kardinal	[kardinal]
heraldry	heraldik	[heraldi']
heraldic (adj)	heraldik	[heraldi']

159. Leader. Chief. Authorities

king	raja	[radʒʲa]
queen	ratu	[ratu]
royal (adj)	kerajaan, raja	[keradʒʲa'an], [radʒʲa]
kingdom	kerajaan	[keradʒʲa'an]
prince	pangeran	[paŋeran]
princess	putri	[putri]
president	presiden	[presiden]
vice-president	wakil presiden	[wakil presiden]
senator	senator	[senator]
monarch	monark	[monar']
ruler (sovereign)	penguasa	[peŋuasa]
dictator	diktator	[diktator]
tyrant	tiran	[tiran]
magnate	magnat	[magnat]
director	direktur	[direktur]
chief	atasan	[atasan]
manager (director)	manajer	[manadʒʲer]
boss	bos	[bos]
owner	pemilik	[pemili']

leader	pemimpin	[pemimpin]
head (~ of delegation)	kepala	[kepala]
authorities	pihak berwenang	[piha' bərwenaŋ]
superiors	atasan	[atasan]

governor	gabernur	[gabernur]
consul	konsul	[konsul]
diplomat	diplomat	[diplomat]
mayor	walikota	[walikota]
sheriff	sheriff	[ʃeriff]

emperor	kaisar	[kajsar]
tsar, czar	tsar, raja	[tsar], [radʒ'a]
pharaoh	firaun	[firaun]
khan	khan	[han]

160. Breaking the law. Criminals. Part 1

bandit	bandit	[bandit]
crime	kejahatan	[kedʒ'ahatan]
criminal (person)	penjahat	[pendʒ'ahat]

thief	pencuri	[pentʃuri]
to steal (vi, vt)	mencuri	[məntʃuri]
stealing, theft	pencurian	[pentʃurian]

to kidnap (vt)	menculik	[məntʃuli']
kidnapping	penculikan	[pentʃulikan]
kidnapper	penculik	[pentʃuli']

| ransom | uang tebusan | [uaŋ tebusan] |
| to demand ransom | menuntut uang tebusan | [mənuntut uaŋ tebusan] |

to rob (vt)	merampok	[merampo']
robbery	perampokan	[pərampokan]
robber	perampok	[pərampo']

to extort (vt)	memeras	[memeras]
extortionist	pemeras	[pemeras]
extortion	pemerasan	[pemerasan]

to murder, to kill	membunuh	[membunuh]
murder	pembunuhan	[pembunuhan]
murderer	pembunuh	[pembunuh]

gunshot	tembakan	[tembakan]
to fire (~ a shot)	melepaskan	[melepaskan]
to shoot to death	menembak mati	[mənemba' mati]
to shoot (vi)	menembak	[mənemba']
shooting	penembakan	[penembakan]

incident (fight, etc.)	insiden, kejadian	[insiden], [kedʒadian]
fight, brawl	perkelahian	[pərkelahian]
Help!	Tolong!	[toloŋ!]
victim	korban	[korban]
to damage (vt)	merusak	[merusaʔ]
damage	kerusakan	[kerusakan]
dead body, corpse	jenazah, mayat	[dʒenazah], [majat]
grave (~ crime)	berat	[berat]
to attack (vt)	menyerang	[mənjeraŋ]
to beat (to hit)	memukul	[memukul]
to beat up	memukuli	[memukuli]
to take (rob of sth)	merebut	[merebut]
to stab to death	menikam mati	[menikam mati]
to maim (vt)	mencederai	[məntʃederaj]
to wound (vt)	melukai	[melukaj]
blackmail	pemerasan	[pemerasan]
to blackmail (vt)	memeras	[memeras]
blackmailer	pemeras	[pemeras]
protection racket	pemerasan	[pemerasan]
racketeer	pemeras	[pemeras]
gangster	gangster, preman	[gaŋster], [preman]
mafia, Mob	mafia	[mafia]
pickpocket	pencopet	[pentʃopet]
burglar	perampok	[perampoʔ]
smuggling	penyelundupan	[penjelundupan]
smuggler	penyelundup	[penjelundup]
forgery	pemalsuan	[pemalsuan]
to forge (counterfeit)	memalsukan	[memalsukan]
fake (forged)	palsu	[palsu]

161. Breaking the law. Criminals. Part 2

rape	pemerkosaan	[pemerkosa'an]
to rape (vt)	memerkosa	[memerkosa]
rapist	pemerkosa	[pemerkosa]
maniac	maniak	[maniaʔ]
prostitute (fem.)	pelacur	[pelatʃur]
prostitution	pelacuran	[pelatʃuran]
pimp	germo	[germo]
drug addict	pecandu narkoba	[petʃandu narkoba]
drug dealer	pengedar narkoba	[peŋedar narkoba]
to blow up (bomb)	meledakkan	[meleda'kan]

explosion	**ledakan**	[ledakan]
to set fire	**membakar**	[membakar]
arsonist	**pelaku pembakaran**	[pelaku pembakaran]
terrorism	**terorisme**	[tərorisme]
terrorist	**teroris**	[təroris]
hostage	**sandera**	[sandera]
to swindle (deceive)	**menipu**	[mənipu]
swindle, deception	**penipuan**	[penipuan]
swindler	**penipu**	[penipu]
to bribe (vt)	**menyuap**	[mənyuap]
bribery	**penyuapan**	[penyuapan]
bribe	**uang suap, suapan**	[uaŋ suap], [suapan]
poison	**racun**	[ratʃun]
to poison (vt)	**meracuni**	[meratʃuni]
to poison oneself	**meracuni diri sendiri**	[meratʃuni diri sendiri]
suicide (act)	**bunuh diri**	[bunuh diri]
suicide (person)	**pelaku bunuh diri**	[pelaku bunuh diri]
to threaten (vt)	**mengancam**	[məŋantʃam]
threat	**ancaman**	[antʃaman]
to make an attempt	**melakukan percobaan pembunuhan**	[melakukan pərtʃoba'an pembunuhan]
attempt (attack)	**percobaan pembunuhan**	[pərtʃoba'an pembunuhan]
to steal (a car)	**mencuri**	[məntʃuri]
to hijack (a plane)	**membajak**	[membadʒ'a']
revenge	**dendam**	[dendam]
to avenge (get revenge)	**membalas dendam**	[membalas dendam]
to torture (vt)	**menyiksa**	[mənjiksa]
torture	**siksaan**	[siksa'an]
to torment (vt)	**menyiksa**	[mənjiksa]
pirate	**bajak laut**	[badʒ'a' laut]
hooligan	**berandal**	[berandal]
armed (adj)	**bersenjata**	[bərsendʒ'ata]
violence	**kekerasan**	[kekerasan]
illegal (unlawful)	**ilegal**	[ilegal]
spying (espionage)	**spionase**	[spionase]
to spy (vi)	**memata-matai**	[memata-mataj]

162. Police. Law. Part 1

justice	**keadilan**	[keadilan]
court (see you in ~)	**pengadilan**	[peŋadilan]

judge	hakım	[hakim]
jurors	anggota juri	[aŋgota dʒʲuri]
jury trial	pengadilan juri	[peŋadilan dʒʲuri]
to judge (vt)	mengadili	[məŋadili]

lawyer, attorney	advokat, pengacara	[advokat], [peŋatʃara]
defendant	terdakwa	[tərdakwa]
dock	bangku terdakwa	[baŋku tərdakwa]

| charge | tuduhan | [tuduhan] |
| accused | terdakwa | [tərdakwa] |

| sentence | hukuman | [hukuman] |
| to sentence (vt) | menjatuhkan hukuman | [məndʒʲatuhkan hukuman] |

guilty (culprit)	bersalah	[bərsalah]
to punish (vt)	menghukum	[məŋhukum]
punishment	hukuman	[hukuman]

fine (penalty)	denda	[denda]
life imprisonment	penjara seumur hidup	[pendʒʲara seumur hidup]
death penalty	hukuman mati	[hukuman mati]
electric chair	kursi listrik	[kursi listriʔ]
gallows	tiang gantungan	[tiaŋ gantuŋan]

| to execute (vt) | menjalankan hukuman mati | [məndʒʲalankan hukuman mati] |
| execution | hukuman mati | [hukuman mati] |

| prison, jail | penjara | [pendʒʲara] |
| cell | sel | [sel] |

escort	pengawal	[peŋawal]
prison guard	sipir, penjaga penjara	[sipir], [pendʒʲaga pendʒʲara]
prisoner	tahanan	[tahanan]

| handcuffs | borgol | [borgol] |
| to handcuff (vt) | memborgol | [memborgol] |

prison break	pelarian	[pelarian]
to break out (vi)	melarikan diri	[melarikan diri]
to disappear (vi)	menghilang	[məŋhilaŋ]
to release (from prison)	membebaskan	[membebaskan]
amnesty	amnesti	[amnesti]

police	polisi, kepolisian	[polisi], [kepolisian]
police officer	polisi	[polisi]
police station	kantor polisi	[kantor polisi]
billy club	pentungan karet	[pentuŋan karet]
bullhorn	pengeras suara	[peŋeras suara]
patrol car	mobil patroli	[mobil patroli]

siren	**sirene**	[sirene]
to turn on the siren	**membunyikan sirene**	[membunjikan sirene]
siren call	**suara sirene**	[suara sirene]
crime scene	**tempat kejadian perkara**	[tempat kedʒˈadian pərkara]
witness	**saksi**	[saksi]
freedom	**kebebasan**	[kebebasan]
accomplice	**kaki tangan**	[kaki taŋan]
to flee (vi)	**melarikan diri**	[melarikan diri]
trace (to leave a ~)	**jejak**	[dʒˈedʒˈaʔ]

163. Police. Law. Part 2

search (investigation)	**pencarian**	[pentʃarian]
to look for ...	**mencari ...**	[məntʃari ...]
suspicion	**kecurigaan**	[ketʃurigaʔan]
suspicious (e.g., ~ vehicle)	**mencurigakan**	[məntʃurigakan]
to stop (cause to halt)	**menghentikan**	[məŋhentikan]
to detain (keep in custody)	**menahan**	[mənahan]
case (lawsuit)	**kasus, perkara**	[kasus], [pərkara]
investigation	**investigasi, penyidikan**	[investigasi], [penjidikan]
detective	**detektif**	[detektif]
investigator	**penyidik**	[penjidiʔ]
hypothesis	**hipotesis**	[hipotesis]
motive	**motif**	[motif]
interrogation	**interogasi**	[interogasi]
to interrogate (vt)	**menginterogasi**	[məŋinterogasi]
to question (~ neighbors, etc.)	**menanyai**	[mənanjaj]
check (identity ~)	**pemeriksaan**	[pemeriksaʔan]
round-up	**razia**	[razia]
search (~ warrant)	**penggeledahan**	[peŋgeledahan]
chase (pursuit)	**pengejaran, perburuan**	[peŋedʒˈaran], [pərburuan]
to pursue, to chase	**mengejar**	[məŋedʒˈar]
to track (a criminal)	**melacak**	[melatʃaʔ]
arrest	**penahanan**	[penahanan]
to arrest (sb)	**menahan**	[mənahan]
to catch (thief, etc.)	**menangkap**	[mənaŋkap]
capture	**penangkapan**	[penaŋkapan]
document	**dokumen**	[dokumen]
proof (evidence)	**bukti**	[bukti]
to prove (vt)	**membuktikan**	[membuktikan]
footprint	**jejak**	[dʒˈedʒˈaʔ]
fingerprints	**sidik jari**	[sidiʔ dʒˈari]

piece of evidence	**barang bukti**	[baraŋ bukti]
alibi	**alibi**	[alibi]
innocent (not guilty)	**tidak bersalah**	[tida' bərsalah]
injustice	**ketidakadilan**	[ketidakadilan]
unjust, unfair (adj)	**tidak adil**	[tida' adil]
criminal (adj)	**pidana**	[pidana]
to confiscate (vt)	**menyita**	[mənjita]
drug (illegal substance)	**narkoba**	[narkoba]
weapon, gun	**senjata**	[sendʒ'ata]
to disarm (vt)	**melucuti**	[meluʧuti]
to order (command)	**memerintahkan**	[memerintahkan]
to disappear (vi)	**menghilang**	[mənhilaŋ]
law	**hukum**	[hukum]
legal, lawful (adj)	**sah**	[sah]
illegal, illicit (adj)	**tidak sah**	[tida' sah]
responsibility (blame)	**tanggung jawab**	[taŋguŋ dʒ'awab]
responsible (adj)	**bertanggung jawab**	[bərtaŋguŋ dʒ'awab]

NATURE

The Earth. Part 1

164. Outer space

space	angkasa	[aŋkasa]
space (as adj)	angkasa	[aŋkasa]
outer space	ruang angkasa	[ruaŋ aŋkasa]
world	dunia	[dunia]
universe	jagat raya	[dʒ'agat raja]
galaxy	galaksi	[galaksi]
star	bintang	[bintaŋ]
constellation	gugusan bintang	[gugusan bintaŋ]
planet	planet	[planet]
satellite	satelit	[satelit]
meteorite	meteorit	[meteorit]
comet	komet	[komet]
asteroid	asteroid	[asteroid]
orbit	orbit	[orbit]
to revolve (~ around the Earth)	berputar	[bərputar]
atmosphere	atmosfer	[atmosfer]
the Sun	matahari	[matahari]
solar system	tata surya	[tata surja]
solar eclipse	gerhana matahari	[gerhana matahari]
the Earth	Bumi	[bumi]
the Moon	Bulan	[bulan]
Mars	Mars	[mars]
Venus	Venus	[venus]
Jupiter	Yupiter	[yupiter]
Saturn	Saturnus	[saturnus]
Mercury	Merkurius	[merkurius]
Uranus	Uranus	[uranus]
Neptune	Neptunus	[neptunus]
Pluto	Pluto	[pluto]
Milky Way	Bimasakti	[bimasakti]
Great Bear (Ursa Major)	Ursa Major	[ursa madʒor]

North Star	Bintang Utara	[bɪntaŋ utara]
Martian	makhluk Mars	[mahluʔ mars]
extraterrestrial (n)	makhluk ruang angkasa	[mahluʔ ruaŋ aŋkasa]
alien	alien, makhluk asing	[alien], [mahluʔ asiŋ]
flying saucer	piring terbang	[pirɪŋ tərbaŋ]
spaceship	kapal antariksa	[kapal antariksa]
space station	stasiun antariksa	[stasiun antariksa]
blast-off	peluncuran	[peluntʃuran]
engine	mesin	[mesin]
nozzle	nosel	[nosel]
fuel	bahan bakar	[bahan bakar]
cockpit, flight deck	kokpit	[kokpit]
antenna	antena	[antena]
porthole	jendela	[dʒʲendela]
solar panel	sel surya	[sel surja]
spacesuit	pakaian antariksa	[pakajan antariksa]
weightlessness	keadaan tanpa bobot	[keadaʔan tanpa bobot]
oxygen	oksigen	[oksigen]
docking (in space)	penggabungan	[peŋgabuŋan]
to dock (vi, vt)	bergabung	[bərgabuŋ]
observatory	observatorium	[observatorium]
telescope	teleskop	[teleskop]
to observe (vt)	mengamati	[məŋamati]
to explore (vt)	mengeksplorasi	[məŋeksplorasi]

165. The Earth

the Earth	Bumi	[bumi]
the globe (the Earth)	bola Bumi	[bola bumi]
planet	planet	[planet]
atmosphere	atmosfer	[atmosfer]
geography	geografi	[geografi]
nature	alam	[alam]
globe (table ~)	globe	[globe]
map	peta	[peta]
atlas	atlas	[atlas]
Europe	Eropa	[eropa]
Asia	Asia	[asia]
Africa	Afrika	[afrika]
Australia	Australia	[australia]
America	Amerika	[amerika]

North America	**Amerika Utara**	[amerika utara]
South America	**Amerika Selatan**	[amerika selatan]
Antarctica	**Antartika**	[antartika]
the Arctic	**Arktika**	[arktika]

166. Cardinal directions

north	**utara**	[utara]
to the north	**ke utara**	[ke utara]
in the north	**di utara**	[di utara]
northern (adj)	**utara**	[utara]
south	**selatan**	[selatan]
to the south	**ke selatan**	[ke selatan]
in the south	**di selatan**	[di selatan]
southern (adj)	**selatan**	[selatan]
west	**barat**	[barat]
to the west	**ke barat**	[ke barat]
in the west	**di barat**	[di barat]
western (adj)	**barat**	[barat]
east	**timur**	[timur]
to the east	**ke timur**	[ke timur]
in the east	**di timur**	[di timur]
eastern (adj)	**timur**	[timur]

167. Sea. Ocean

sea	**laut**	[laut]
ocean	**samudra**	[samudra]
gulf (bay)	**teluk**	[teluˀ]
straits	**selat**	[selat]
land (solid ground)	**daratan**	[daratan]
continent (mainland)	**benua**	[benua]
island	**pulau**	[pulau]
peninsula	**semenanjung, jazirah**	[semenandʒˈuŋ], [dʒˈazirah]
archipelago	**kepulauan**	[kepulauan]
bay, cove	**teluk**	[teluˀ]
harbor	**pelabuhan**	[pelabuhan]
lagoon	**laguna**	[laguna]
cape	**tanjung**	[tandʒˈuŋ]
atoll	**pulau karang**	[pulau karaŋ]
reef	**terumbu**	[tərumbu]

coral	**karang**	[karaŋ]
coral reef	**terumbu karang**	[tərumbu karaŋ]
deep (adj)	**dalam**	[dalam]
depth (deep water)	**kedalaman**	[kedalaman]
abyss	**jurang**	[dʒʲuraŋ]
trench (e.g., Mariana ~)	**palung**	[paluŋ]
current (Ocean ~)	**arus**	[arus]
to surround (bathe)	**berbatasan dengan**	[bərbatasan deŋan]
shore	**pantai**	[pantaj]
coast	**pantai**	[pantaj]
flow (flood tide)	**air pasang**	[air pasaŋ]
ebb (ebb tide)	**air surut**	[air surut]
shoal	**beting**	[betiŋ]
bottom (~ of the sea)	**dasar**	[dasar]
wave	**gelombang**	[gelombaŋ]
crest (~ of a wave)	**puncak gelombang**	[puntʃaʔ gelombaŋ]
spume (sea foam)	**busa, buih**	[busa], [buih]
storm (sea storm)	**badai**	[badaj]
hurricane	**topan**	[topan]
tsunami	**tsunami**	[tsunami]
calm (dead ~)	**angin tenang**	[aŋin tenaŋ]
quiet, calm (adj)	**tenang**	[tenaŋ]
pole	**kutub**	[kutub]
polar (adj)	**kutub**	[kutub]
latitude	**lintang**	[lintaŋ]
longitude	**garis bujur**	[garis budʒʲur]
parallel	**sejajar**	[sedʒʲadʒʲar]
equator	**khatulistiwa**	[hatulistiwa]
sky	**langit**	[laŋit]
horizon	**horizon**	[horizon]
air	**udara**	[udara]
lighthouse	**mercusuar**	[mertʃusuar]
to dive (vi)	**menyelam**	[mənjelam]
to sink (ab. boat)	**karam**	[karam]
treasures	**harta karun**	[harta karun]

168. Mountains

mountain	**gunung**	[gunuŋ]
mountain range	**jajaran gunung**	[dʒʲadʒʲaran gunuŋ]

mountain ridge	**sisir gunung**	[sisir gunuŋ]
summit, top	**puncak**	[puntʃaʔ]
peak	**puncak**	[puntʃaʔ]
foot (~ of the mountain)	**kaki**	[kaki]
slope (mountainside)	**lereng**	[lereŋ]

volcano	**gunung api**	[gunuŋ api]
active volcano	**gunung api yang aktif**	[gunuŋ api yaŋ aktif]
dormant volcano	**gunung api yang tidak aktif**	[gunuŋ api yaŋ tidaʔ aktif]

eruption	**erupsi, letusan**	[erupsi], [letusan]
crater	**kawah**	[kawah]
magma	**magma**	[magma]
lava	**lava, lahar**	[lava], [lahar]
molten (~ lava)	**pijar**	[pidʒar]

canyon	**kanyon**	[kanjon]
gorge	**jurang**	[dʒuraŋ]
crevice	**celah**	[tʃelah]
abyss (chasm)	**jurang**	[dʒuraŋ]

pass, col	**pass, celah**	[pass], [tʃelah]
plateau	**plato, dataran tinggi**	[plato], [dataran tiŋgi]
cliff	**tebing**	[tebiŋ]
hill	**bukit**	[bukit]

glacier	**gletser**	[gletser]
waterfall	**air terjun**	[air tərdʒun]
geyser	**geiser**	[geyser]
lake	**danau**	[danau]

plain	**dataran**	[dataran]
landscape	**landskap**	[landskap]
echo	**gema**	[gema]

alpinist	**pendaki gunung**	[pendaki gunuŋ]
rock climber	**pemanjat tebing**	[pemandʒat tebiŋ]
to conquer (in climbing)	**menaklukkan**	[mənakluʔkan]
climb (an easy ~)	**pendakian**	[pendakian]

169. Rivers

river	**sungai**	[suŋaj]
spring (natural source)	**mata air**	[mata air]
riverbed (river channel)	**badan sungai**	[badan suŋaj]
basin (river valley)	**basin**	[basin]
to flow into …	**mengalir ke …**	[məŋalir ke …]
tributary	**anak sungai**	[anaʔ suŋaj]
bank (of river)	**tebing sungai**	[tebiŋ suŋaj]

current (stream)	arus	[arus]
downstream (adv)	ke hilir	[ke hilir]
upstream (adv)	ke hulu	[ke hulu]

inundation	banjir	[bandʒir]
flooding	banjir	[bandʒir]
to overflow (vi)	membanjiri	[membandʒiri]
to flood (vt)	membanjiri	[membandʒiri]

| shallow (shoal) | beting | [betiŋ] |
| rapids | jeram | [dʒⁱeram] |

dam	dam, bendungan	[dam], [benduŋan]
canal	kanal, terusan	[kanal], [tərusan]
reservoir (artificial lake)	waduk	[waduʔ]
sluice, lock	pintu air	[pintu air]

water body (pond, etc.)	kolam	[kolam]
swamp (marshland)	rawa	[rawa]
bog, marsh	bencah, paya	[bentʃah], [paja]
whirlpool	pusaran air	[pusaran air]

stream (brook)	selokan	[selokan]
drinking (ab. water)	minum	[minum]
fresh (~ water)	tawar	[tawar]

| ice | es | [es] |
| to freeze over (ab. river, etc.) | membeku | [membeku] |

170. Forest

| forest, wood | hutan | [hutan] |
| forest (as adj) | hutan | [hutan] |

thick forest	hutan lebat	[hutan lebat]
grove	hutan kecil	[hutan ketʃil]
forest clearing	pembukaan hutan	[pembukaʔan hutan]

| thicket | semak belukar | [semaʔ belukar] |
| scrubland | belukar | [belukar] |

| footpath (troddenpath) | jalan setapak | [dʒⁱalan setapaʔ] |
| gully | parit | [parit] |

tree	pohon	[pohon]
leaf	daun	[daun]
leaves (foliage)	daun-daunan	[daun-daunan]
fall of leaves	daun berguguran	[daun bərguguran]
to fall (ab. leaves)	luruh	[luruh]

top (of the tree)	puncak	[puntʃaʔ]
branch	cabang	[tʃabaŋ]
bough	dahan	[dahan]
bud (on shrub, tree)	tunas	[tunas]
needle (of pine tree)	daun jarum	[daun dʒarum]
pine cone	buah pinus	[buah pinus]

hollow (in a tree)	lubang pohon	[lubaŋ pohon]
nest	sarang	[saraŋ]
burrow (animal hole)	lubang	[lubaŋ]

trunk	batang	[bataŋ]
root	akar	[akar]
bark	kulit	[kulit]
moss	lumut	[lumut]

to uproot (remove trees or tree stumps)	mencabut	[məntʃabut]
to chop down	menebang	[mənebaŋ]
to deforest (vt)	deforestasi, penggundulan hutan	[deforestasi], [pəŋgundulan hutan]
tree stump	tunggul	[tuŋgul]

campfire	api unggun	[api uŋgun]
forest fire	kebakaran hutan	[kebakaran hutan]
to extinguish (vt)	memadamkan	[memadamkan]

forest ranger	penjaga hutan	[pendʒaga hutan]
protection	perlindungan	[pərlinduŋan]
to protect (~ nature)	melindungi	[melinduŋi]
poacher	pemburu ilegal	[pemburu ilegal]
steel trap	perangkap	[pəraŋkap]

| to gather, to pick (vt) | memetik | [memetiʔ] |
| to lose one's way | tersesat | [tərsesat] |

171. Natural resources

natural resources	sumber daya alam	[sumber daja alam]
minerals	bahan tambang	[bahan tambaŋ]
deposits	endapan	[endapan]
field (e.g., oilfield)	ladang	[ladaŋ]

to mine (extract)	menambang	[mənambaŋ]
mining (extraction)	pertambangan	[pərtambaŋan]
ore	bijih	[bidʒih]
mine (e.g., for coal)	tambang	[tambaŋ]
shaft (mine ~)	sumur tambang	[sumur tambaŋ]
miner	penambang	[penambaŋ]
gas (natural ~)	gas	[gas]

gas pipeline	pipa saluran gas	[pipa saluran gas]
oil (petroleum)	petroleum, minyak	[petroleum], [minja']
oil pipeline	pipa saluran minyak	[pipa saluran minja']
oil well	sumur minyak	[sumur minja']
derrick (tower)	menara bor minyak	[mənara bor minja']
tanker	kapal tangki	[kapal taŋki]

sand	pasir	[pasir]
limestone	batu kapur	[batu kapur]
gravel	kerikil	[kerikil]
peat	gambut	[gambut]
clay	tanah liat	[tanah liat]
coal	arang	[araŋ]

iron (ore)	besi	[besi]
gold	emas	[emas]
silver	perak	[pera']
nickel	nikel	[nikel]
copper	tembaga	[tembaga]

zinc	seng	[seŋ]
manganese	mangan	[maŋan]
mercury	air raksa	[air raksa]
lead	timbal	[timbal]

mineral	mineral	[mineral]
crystal	kristal, hablur	[kristal], [hablur]
marble	marmer	[marmer]
uranium	uranium	[uranium]

The Earth. Part 2

172. Weather

weather	**cuaca**	[ʧuatʃa]
weather forecast	**prakiraan cuaca**	[prakiraʔan ʧuatʃa]
temperature	**temperatur, suhu**	[temperatur], [suhu]
thermometer	**termometer**	[tərmometər]
barometer	**barometer**	[barometer]
humid (adj)	**lembap**	[lembap]
humidity	**kelembapan**	[kelembapan]
heat (extreme ~)	**panas, gerah**	[panas], [gerah]
hot (torrid)	**panas terik**	[panas təriʔ]
it's hot	**panas**	[panas]
it's warm	**hangat**	[haŋat]
warm (moderately hot)	**hangat**	[haŋat]
it's cold	**dingin**	[diŋin]
cold (adj)	**dingin**	[diŋin]
sun	**matahari**	[matahari]
to shine (vi)	**bersinar**	[bərsinar]
sunny (day)	**cerah**	[ʧerah]
to come up (vi)	**terbit**	[terbit]
to set (vi)	**terbenam**	[tərbenam]
cloud	**awan**	[awan]
cloudy (adj)	**berawan**	[bərawan]
rain cloud	**awan mendung**	[awan menduŋ]
somber (gloomy)	**mendung**	[menduŋ]
rain	**hujan**	[huʤian]
it's raining	**hujan turun**	[huʤian turun]
rainy (~ day, weather)	**hujan**	[huʤian]
to drizzle (vi)	**gerimis**	[gerimis]
pouring rain	**hujan lebat**	[huʤian lebat]
downpour	**hujan lebat**	[huʤian lebat]
heavy (e.g., ~ rain)	**lebat**	[lebat]
puddle	**kubangan**	[kubaŋan]
to get wet (in rain)	**kehujanan**	[kehuʤianan]
fog (mist)	**kabut**	[kabut]
foggy	**berkabut**	[bərkabut]

| snow | salju | [saldʒu] |
| it's snowing | turun salju | [turun saldʒu] |

173. Severe weather. Natural disasters

thunderstorm	hujan badai	[hudʒan badaj]
lightning (~ strike)	kilat	[kilat]
to flash (vi)	berkilau	[bərkilau]

thunder	petir	[petir]
to thunder (vi)	bergemuruh	[bərgemuruh]
it's thundering	bergemuruh	[bərgemuruh]

| hail | hujan es | [hudʒan es] |
| it's hailing | hujan es | [hudʒan es] |

| to flood (vt) | membanjiri | [membandʒiri] |
| flood, inundation | banjir | [bandʒir] |

earthquake	gempa bumi	[gempa bumi]
tremor, quake	gempa	[gempa]
epicenter	episentrum	[episentrum]

| eruption | erupsi, letusan | [erupsi], [letusan] |
| lava | lava, lahar | [lava], [lahar] |

twister	puting beliung	[putiŋ beliuŋ]
tornado	tornado	[tornado]
typhoon	topan	[topan]

hurricane	topan	[topan]
storm	badai	[badaj]
tsunami	tsunami	[tsunami]

cyclone	siklon	[siklon]
bad weather	cuaca buruk	[tʃuatʃa buruʔ]
fire (accident)	kebakaran	[kebakaran]
disaster	bencana	[bentʃana]
meteorite	meteorit	[meteorit]

avalanche	longsor	[loŋsor]
snowslide	salju longsor	[saldʒu loŋsor]
blizzard	badai salju	[badaj saldʒu]
snowstorm	badai salju	[badaj saldʒu]

Fauna

174. Mammals. Predators

predator	**predator, pemangsa**	[predator], [pemaŋsa]
tiger	**harimau**	[harimau]
lion	**singa**	[siŋa]
wolf	**serigala**	[serigala]
fox	**rubah**	[rubah]
jaguar	**jaguar**	[dʒˈaguar]
leopard	**leopard, macan tutul**	[leopard], [matʃan tutul]
cheetah	**cheetah**	[tʃeetah]
black panther	**harimau kumbang**	[harimau kumbaŋ]
puma	**singa gunung**	[siŋa gunuŋ]
snow leopard	**harimau bintang salju**	[harimau bintaŋ saldʒˈu]
lynx	**lynx**	[links]
coyote	**koyote**	[koyot]
jackal	**jakal**	[dʒˈakal]
hyena	**hiena**	[hiena]

175. Wild animals

animal	**binatang**	[binataŋ]
beast (animal)	**binatang buas**	[binataŋ buas]
squirrel	**bajing**	[badʒiŋ]
hedgehog	**landak susu**	[landa' susu]
hare	**terwelu**	[tərwelu]
rabbit	**kelinci**	[kelintʃi]
badger	**luak**	[lua']
raccoon	**rakun**	[rakun]
hamster	**hamster**	[hamster]
marmot	**marmut**	[marmut]
mole	**tikus mondok**	[tikus mondo']
mouse	**tikus**	[tikus]
rat	**tikus besar**	[tikus besar]
bat	**kelelawar**	[kelelawar]
ermine	**ermin**	[ermin]
sable	**sabel**	[sabel]

marten	**marten**	[marten]
weasel	**musang**	[musaŋ]
mink	**cerpelai**	[ʧerpelaj]
beaver	**beaver**	[beaver]
otter	**berang-berang**	[bəraŋ-bəraŋ]
horse	**kuda**	[kuda]
moose	**rusa besar**	[rusa besar]
deer	**rusa**	[rusa]
camel	**unta**	[unta]
bison	**bison**	[bison]
aurochs	**aurochs**	[oroks]
buffalo	**kerbau**	[kerbau]
zebra	**kuda belang**	[kuda belaŋ]
antelope	**antelop**	[antelop]
roe deer	**kijang**	[kidʒʲaŋ]
fallow deer	**rusa**	[rusa]
chamois	**chamois**	[ʃemva]
wild boar	**babi hutan jantan**	[babi hutan dʒʲantan]
whale	**ikan paus**	[ikan paus]
seal	**anjing laut**	[andʒiŋ laut]
walrus	**walrus**	[walrus]
fur seal	**anjing laut berbulu**	[andʒiŋ laut bərbulu]
dolphin	**lumba-lumba**	[lumba-lumba]
bear	**beruang**	[bəruaŋ]
polar bear	**beruang kutub**	[bəruaŋ kutub]
panda	**panda**	[panda]
monkey	**monyet**	[monjet]
chimpanzee	**simpanse**	[simpanse]
orangutan	**orang utan**	[oraŋ utan]
gorilla	**gorila**	[gorila]
macaque	**kera**	[kera]
gibbon	**siamang, ungka**	[siamaŋ], [uŋka]
elephant	**gajah**	[gadʒʲah]
rhinoceros	**badak**	[badaʔ]
giraffe	**jerapah**	[dʒʲerapah]
hippopotamus	**kuda nil**	[kuda nil]
kangaroo	**kanguru**	[kaŋuru]
koala (bear)	**koala**	[koala]
mongoose	**garangan**	[garaŋan]
chinchilla	**chinchilla**	[ʧinʧilla]
skunk	**sigung**	[siguŋ]
porcupine	**landak**	[landaʔ]

176. Domestic animals

cat	kucing betina	[kutʃiŋ betina]
tomcat	kucing jantan	[kutʃiŋ dʒʲantan]
dog	anjing	[andʒiŋ]

horse	kuda	[kuda]
stallion (male horse)	kuda jantan	[kuda dʒʲantan]
mare	kuda betina	[kuda betina]

cow	sapi	[sapi]
bull	sapi jantan	[sapi dʒʲantan]
ox	lembu jantan	[lembu dʒʲantan]

sheep (ewe)	domba	[domba]
ram	domba jantan	[domba dʒʲantan]
goat	kambing betina	[kambiŋ betina]
billy goat, he-goat	kambing jantan	[kambiŋ dʒʲantan]

| donkey | keledai | [keledaj] |
| mule | bagal | [bagal] |

pig, hog	babi	[babi]
piglet	anak babi	[ana' babi]
rabbit	kelinci	[kelintʃi]

| hen (chicken) | ayam betina | [ajam betina] |
| rooster | ayam jago | [ajam dʒʲago] |

duck	bebek	[bebe']
drake	bebek jantan	[bebe' dʒʲantan]
goose	angsa	[aŋsa]

| tom turkey, gobbler | kalkun jantan | [kalkun dʒʲantan] |
| turkey (hen) | kalkun betina | [kalkun betina] |

domestic animals	binatang piaraan	[binataŋ piara'an]
tame (e.g., ~ hamster)	jinak	[dʒina']
to tame (vt)	menjinakkan	[mendʒina'kan]
to breed (vt)	membiakkan	[membia'kan]

farm	peternakan	[peternakan]
poultry	unggas	[uŋgas]
cattle	ternak	[terna']
herd (cattle)	kawanan	[kawanan]

stable	kandang kuda	[kandaŋ kuda]
pigpen	kandang babi	[kandaŋ babi]
cowshed	kandang sapi	[kandaŋ sapi]
rabbit hutch	sangkar kelinci	[saŋkar kelintʃi]
hen house	kandang ayam	[kandaŋ ajam]

177. Dogs. Dog breeds

dog	**anjing**	[andʒiŋ]
sheepdog	**anjing gembala**	[andʒiŋ gembala]
German shepherd	**anjing gembala jerman**	[andʒiŋ gembala dʒ'erman]
poodle	**pudel**	[pudel]
dachshund	**anjing tekel**	[andʒiŋ tekel]
bulldog	**buldog**	[buldog]
boxer	**boxer**	[bokser]
mastiff	**Mastiff**	[mastiff]
Rottweiler	**Rottweiler**	[rotweyler]
Doberman	**Doberman**	[doberman]
basset	**Basset**	[basset]
bobtail	**bobtail**	[bobteyl]
Dalmatian	**Dalmatian**	[dalmatian]
cocker spaniel	**Cocker Spaniel**	[koker spaniel]
Newfoundland	**Newfoundland**	[njufaundland]
Saint Bernard	**Saint Bernard**	[sen bərnar]
husky	**Husky**	[haski]
Chow Chow	**Chow Chow**	[tʃau tʃau]
spitz	**Spitz**	[spits]
pug	**Pug**	[pag]

178. Sounds made by animals

barking (n)	**salak**	[salaʔ]
to bark (vi)	**menyalak**	[mənjalaʔ]
to meow (vi)	**mengeong**	[məŋeoŋ]
to purr (vi)	**mendengkur**	[məndeŋkur]
to moo (vi)	**melenguh**	[meleŋuh]
to bellow (bull)	**menguak**	[meŋuaʔ]
to growl (vi)	**menggeram**	[məŋgeram]
howl (n)	**auman**	[auman]
to howl (vi)	**mengaum**	[məŋaum]
to whine (vi)	**merengek**	[mereŋeʔ]
to bleat (sheep)	**mengembik**	[məŋembiʔ]
to oink, to grunt (pig)	**menguik**	[meŋuiʔ]
to squeal (vi)	**memekik**	[memekiʔ]
to croak (vi)	**berdengkang**	[bərdeŋkaŋ]
to buzz (insect)	**mendengung**	[məndeŋuŋ]
to chirp (crickets, grasshopper)	**mencicit**	[məntʃitʃit]

179. Birds

bird	burung	[buruŋ]
pigeon	burung dara	[buruŋ dara]
sparrow	burung gereja	[buruŋ geredʒʲa]
tit (great tit)	burung tit	[buruŋ tit]
magpie	burung murai	[buruŋ muraj]
raven	burung raven	[buruŋ raven]
crow	burung gagak	[buruŋ gagaʔ]
jackdaw	burung gagak kecil	[buruŋ gagaʔ ketʃil]
rook	burung rook	[buruŋ rooʔ]
duck	bebek	[bebeʔ]
goose	angsa	[aŋsa]
pheasant	burung kuau	[buruŋ kuau]
eagle	rajawali	[radʒʲawali]
hawk	elang	[elaŋ]
falcon	alap-alap	[alap-alap]
vulture	hering	[heriŋ]
condor (Andean ~)	kondor	[kondor]
swan	angsa	[aŋsa]
crane	burung jenjang	[buruŋ dʒʲendʒʲaŋ]
stork	bangau	[baŋau]
parrot	burung nuri	[buruŋ nuri]
hummingbird	burung kolibri	[buruŋ kolibri]
peacock	burung merak	[buruŋ meraʔ]
ostrich	burung unta	[buruŋ unta]
heron	kuntul	[kuntul]
flamingo	burung flamingo	[buruŋ flamiŋo]
pelican	pelikan	[pelikan]
nightingale	burung bulbul	[buruŋ bulbul]
swallow	burung walet	[buruŋ walet]
thrush	burung jalak	[buruŋ dʒʲalaʔ]
song thrush	burung jalak suren	[buruŋ dʒʲalaʔ suren]
blackbird	burung jalak hitam	[buruŋ dʒʲalaʔ hitam]
swift	burung apus-apus	[buruŋ apus-apus]
lark	burung lark	[buruŋ larʔ]
quail	burung puyuh	[buruŋ puyuh]
woodpecker	burung pelatuk	[buruŋ pelatuʔ]
cuckoo	burung kukuk	[buruŋ kukuʔ]
owl	burung hantu	[buruŋ hantu]
eagle owl	burung hantu bertanduk	[buruŋ hantu bərtanduʔ]

wood grouse	burung murai kayu	[buruŋ muraj kaju]
black grouse	burung belibis hitam	[buruŋ belibis hitam]
partridge	ayam hutan	[ajam hutan]

starling	burung starling	[buruŋ starliŋ]
canary	burung kenari	[buruŋ kenari]
hazel grouse	ayam hutan hazel	[ajam hutan hazel]
chaffinch	burung chaffinch	[buruŋ tʃaffintʃ]
bullfinch	burung bullfinch	[buruŋ bullfintʃ]

seagull	burung camar	[buruŋ tʃamar]
albatross	albatros	[albatros]
penguin	penguin	[peŋuin]

180. Birds. Singing and sounds

to sing (vi)	menyanyi	[mənjanji]
to call (animal, bird)	berteriak	[bərteriaʔ]
to crow (rooster)	berkokok	[bərkokoʔ]
cock-a-doodle-doo	kukuruyuk	[kukuruyuʔ]

to cluck (hen)	berkotek	[bərkoteʔ]
to caw (vi)	berkaok-kaok	[berkaoʔ-kaoʔ]
to quack (duck)	meleter	[meleter]
to cheep (vi)	berdecit	[bərdetʃit]
to chirp, to twitter	berkicau	[bərkitʃau]

181. Fish. Marine animals

bream	ikan bream	[ikan bream]
carp	ikan karper	[ikan karper]
perch	ikan tilapia	[ikan tilapia]
catfish	lais junggang	[lajs dʒʲuŋgaŋ]
pike	ikan pike	[ikan paik]

| salmon | salmon | [salmon] |
| sturgeon | ikan sturgeon | [ikan sturdʒʲen] |

herring	ikan haring	[ikan hariŋ]
Atlantic salmon	ikan salem	[ikan salem]
mackerel	ikan kembung	[ikan kembuŋ]
flatfish	ikan sebelah	[ikan sebelah]

zander, pike perch	ikan seligi tenggeran	[ikan seligi teŋeran]
cod	ikan kod	[ikan kod]
tuna	tuna	[tuna]
trout	ikan forel	[ikan forel]
eel	belut	[belut]

electric ray	ikan pari listrik	[ikan pari listriʔ]
moray eel	belut moray	[belut morey]
piranha	ikan piranha	[ikan piranha]

shark	ikan hiu	[ikan hiu]
dolphin	lumba-lumba	[lumba-lumba]
whale	ikan paus	[ikan paus]

crab	kepiting	[kepitiŋ]
jellyfish	ubur-ubur	[ubur-ubur]
octopus	gurita	[gurita]

starfish	bintang laut	[bintaŋ laut]
sea urchin	landak laut	[landaʔ laut]
seahorse	kuda laut	[kuda laut]

oyster	tiram	[tiram]
shrimp	udang	[udaŋ]
lobster	udang karang	[udaŋ karaŋ]
spiny lobster	lobster berduri	[lobster bərduri]

182. Amphibians. Reptiles

| snake | ular | [ular] |
| venomous (snake) | berbisa | [bərbisa] |

| viper | ular viper | [ular viper] |
| cobra | kobra | [kobra] |

| python | ular sanca | [ular santʃa] |
| boa | ular boa | [ular boa] |

grass snake	ular tanah	[ular tanah]
rattle snake	ular derik	[ular deriʔ]
anaconda	ular anakonda	[ular anakonda]

| lizard | kadal | [kadal] |
| iguana | iguana | [iguana] |

| monitor lizard | biawak | [biawaʔ] |
| salamander | salamander | [salamander] |

| chameleon | bunglon | [buŋlon] |
| scorpion | kalajengking | [kaladʒ'eŋkiŋ] |

| turtle | kura-kura | [kura-kura] |
| frog | katak | [kataʔ] |

| toad | kodok | [kodoʔ] |
| crocodile | buaya | [buaja] |

183. Insects

insect, bug	**serangga**	[seraŋga]
butterfly	**kupu-kupu**	[kupu-kupu]
ant	**semut**	[semut]
fly	**lalat**	[lalat]
mosquito	**nyamuk**	[njamuʔ]
beetle	**kumbang**	[kumbaŋ]
wasp	**tawon**	[tawon]
bee	**lebah**	[lebah]
bumblebee	**kumbang**	[kumbaŋ]
gadfly (botfly)	**lalat kerbau**	[lalat kerbau]
spider	**laba-laba**	[laba-laba]
spiderweb	**sarang laba-laba**	[saraŋ laba-laba]
dragonfly	**capung**	[ʧapuŋ]
grasshopper	**belalang**	[belalaŋ]
moth (night butterfly)	**ngengat**	[ŋeŋat]
cockroach	**kecoa**	[keʧoa]
tick	**kutu**	[kutu]
flea	**kutu loncat**	[kutu lonʧat]
midge	**agas**	[agas]
locust	**belalang**	[belalaŋ]
snail	**siput**	[siput]
cricket	**jangkrik**	[dʒiaŋkriʔ]
lightning bug	**kunang-kunang**	[kunaŋ-kunaŋ]
ladybug	**kumbang koksi**	[kumbaŋ koksi]
cockchafer	**kumbang Cockchafer**	[kumbaŋ kokʃafer]
leech	**lintah**	[lintah]
caterpillar	**ulat**	[ulat]
earthworm	**cacing**	[ʧatʃiŋ]
larva	**larva**	[larva]

184. Animals. Body parts

beak	**paruh**	[paruh]
wings	**sayap**	[sajap]
foot (of bird)	**kaki**	[kaki]
feathers (plumage)	**bulu-bulu**	[bulu-bulu]
feather	**bulu**	[bulu]
crest	**jambul**	[dʒiambul]
gills	**insang**	[insaŋ]
spawn	**telur ikan**	[telur ikan]

larva	**larva**	[larva]
fin	**sirip**	[sirip]
scales (of fish, reptile)	**sisik**	[sisiʔ]

fang (canine)	**taring**	[tariŋ]
paw (e.g., cat's ~)	**kaki**	[kaki]
muzzle (snout)	**moncong**	[montʃoŋ]
mouth (of cat, dog)	**mulut**	[mulut]
tail	**ekor**	[ekor]
whiskers	**kumis**	[kumis]

| hoof | **tapak, kuku** | [tapak], [kuku] |
| horn | **tanduk** | [tanduʔ] |

carapace	**cangkang**	[tʃaŋkaŋ]
shell (of mollusk)	**kerang**	[keraŋ]
eggshell	**kulit telur**	[kulit telur]

| animal's hair (pelage) | **bulu** | [bulu] |
| pelt (hide) | **kulit** | [kulit] |

185. Animals. Habitats

| habitat | **habitat** | [habitat] |
| migration | **migrasi** | [migrasi] |

mountain	**gunung**	[gunuŋ]
reef	**terumbu**	[tərumbu]
cliff	**tebing**	[tebiŋ]

forest	**hutan**	[hutan]
jungle	**rimba**	[rimba]
savanna	**sabana**	[sabana]
tundra	**tundra**	[tundra]

steppe	**stepa**	[stepa]
desert	**gurun**	[gurun]
oasis	**oasis, oase**	[oasis], [oase]

sea	**laut**	[laut]
lake	**danau**	[danau]
ocean	**samudra**	[samudra]

swamp (marshland)	**rawa**	[rawa]
freshwater (adj)	**air tawar**	[air tawar]
pond	**kolam**	[kolam]
river	**sungai**	[suŋaj]

| den (bear's ~) | **goa** | [goa] |
| nest | **sarang** | [saraŋ] |

hollow (in a tree)	**lubang pohon**	[lubaŋ pohon]
burrow (animal hole)	**lubang**	[lubaŋ]
anthill	**sarang semut**	[saraŋ semut]

Flora

186. Trees

tree	**pohon**	[pohon]
deciduous (adj)	**daun luruh**	[daun luruh]
coniferous (adj)	**pohon jarum**	[pohon dʒʲarum]
evergreen (adj)	**selalu hijau**	[selalu hidʒʲau]
apple tree	**pohon apel**	[pohon apel]
pear tree	**pohon pir**	[pohon pir]
sweet cherry tree	**pohon ceri manis**	[pohon tʃeri manis]
sour cherry tree	**pohon ceri asam**	[pohon tʃeri asam]
plum tree	**pohon plum**	[pohon plum]
birch	**pohon berk**	[pohon bərʔ]
oak	**pohon eik**	[pohon eiʔ]
linden tree	**pohon linden**	[pohon linden]
aspen	**pohon aspen**	[pohon aspen]
maple	**pohon mapel**	[pohon mapel]
spruce	**pohon den**	[pohon den]
pine	**pohon pinus**	[pohon pinus]
larch	**pohon larch**	[pohon lartʃ]
fir tree	**pohon fir**	[pohon fir]
cedar	**pohon aras**	[pohon aras]
poplar	**pohon poplar**	[pohon poplar]
rowan	**pohon rowan**	[pohon rowan]
willow	**pohon dedalu**	[pohon dedalu]
alder	**pohon alder**	[pohon alder]
beech	**pohon nothofagus**	[pohon notofagus]
elm	**pohon elm**	[pohon elm]
ash (tree)	**pohon abu**	[pohon abu]
chestnut	**kastanye**	[kastanje]
magnolia	**magnolia**	[magnolia]
palm tree	**palem**	[palem]
cypress	**pokok cipres**	[pokoʔ sipres]
mangrove	**bakau**	[bakau]
baobab	**baobab**	[baobab]
eucalyptus	**kayu putih**	[kaju putih]
sequoia	**sequoia**	[sekuoia]

187. Shrubs

bush	rumpun	[rumpun]
shrub	semak	[semaʔ]
grapevine	pohon anggur	[pohon aŋgur]
vineyard	kebun anggur	[kebun aŋgur]
raspberry bush	pohon frambus	[pohon frambus]
blackcurrant bush	pohon blackcurrant	[pohon bleʔkaren]
redcurrant bush	pohon redcurrant	[pohon redkaren]
gooseberry bush	pohon arbei hijau	[pohon arbei hiʤʲau]
acacia	pohon akasia	[pohon akasia]
barberry	pohon barberis	[pohon barberis]
jasmine	melati	[melati]
juniper	pohon juniper	[pohon ʤʲuniper]
rosebush	pohon mawar	[pohon mawar]
dog rose	pohon mawar liar	[pohon mawar liar]

188. Mushrooms

mushroom	jamur	[ʤʲamur]
edible mushroom	jamur makanan	[ʤʲamur makanan]
poisonous mushroom	jamur beracun	[ʤʲamur bəratʃun]
cap (of mushroom)	kepala jamur	[kepala ʤʲamur]
stipe (of mushroom)	batang jamur	[bataŋ ʤʲamur]
cep (Boletus edulis)	jamur boletus	[ʤʲamur boletus]
orange-cap boletus	jamur topi jingga	[ʤʲamur topi ʤiŋga]
birch bolete	jamur boletus berk	[ʤʲamur boletus berʔ]
chanterelle	jamur chanterelle	[ʤʲamur tʃanterelle]
russula	jamur rusula	[ʤʲamur rusula]
morel	jamur morel	[ʤʲamur morel]
fly agaric	jamur Amanita muscaria	[ʤʲamur amanita mustʃaria]
death cap	jamur topi kematian	[ʤʲamur topi kematian]

189. Fruits. Berries

fruit	buah	[buah]
fruits	buah-buahan	[buah-buahan]
apple	apel	[apel]
pear	pir	[pir]

plum	**plum**	[plum]
strawberry (garden ~)	**stroberi**	[stroberi]
sour cherry	**buah ceri asam**	[buah tʃeri asam]
sweet cherry	**buah ceri manis**	[buah tʃeri manis]
grape	**buah anggur**	[buah aŋgur]
raspberry	**buah frambus**	[buah frambus]
blackcurrant	**blackcurrant**	[bleʔkaren]
redcurrant	**redcurrant**	[redkaren]
gooseberry	**buah arbei hijau**	[buah arbei hidʒʲau]
cranberry	**buah kranberi**	[buah kranberi]
orange	**jeruk manis**	[dʒʲeruʔ manis]
mandarin	**jeruk mandarin**	[dʒʲeruʔ mandarin]
pineapple	**nanas**	[nanas]
banana	**pisang**	[pisaŋ]
date	**buah kurma**	[buah kurma]
lemon	**jeruk sitrun**	[dʒʲeruʔ sitrun]
apricot	**aprikot**	[aprikot]
peach	**persik**	[persiʔ]
kiwi	**kiwi**	[kiwi]
grapefruit	**jeruk Bali**	[dʒʲeruʔ bali]
berry	**buah beri**	[buah beri]
berries	**buah-buah beri**	[buah-buah beri]
cowberry	**buah cowberry**	[buah kowberi]
wild strawberry	**stroberi liar**	[stroberi liar]
bilberry	**buah bilberi**	[buah bilberi]

190. Flowers. Plants

flower	**bunga**	[buŋa]
bouquet (of flowers)	**buket**	[buket]
rose (flower)	**mawar**	[mawar]
tulip	**tulip**	[tulip]
carnation	**bunga anyelir**	[buŋa anjelir]
gladiolus	**bunga gladiol**	[buŋa gladiol]
cornflower	**cornflower**	[kornflawa]
harebell	**bunga lonceng biru**	[buŋa lontʃeŋ biru]
dandelion	**dandelion**	[dandelion]
camomile	**bunga margrit**	[buŋa margrit]
aloe	**lidah buaya**	[lidah buaja]
cactus	**kaktus**	[kaktus]
rubber plant, ficus	**pohon ara**	[pohon ara]
lily	**bunga lili**	[buŋa lili]
geranium	**geranium**	[geranium]

hyacinth	**bunga bakung lembayung**	[buŋa bakuŋ lembajuŋ]
mimosa	**putri malu**	[putri malu]
narcissus	**bunga narsis**	[buŋa narsis]
nasturtium	**bunga nasturtium**	[buŋa nasturtium]
orchid	**anggrek**	[aŋgreʔ]
peony	**bunga peoni**	[buŋa peoni]
violet	**bunga violet**	[buŋa violet]
pansy	**bunga pansy**	[buŋa pansi]
forget-me-not	**bunga jangan-lupakan-daku**	[buŋa dʒʲaŋan-lupakan-daku]
daisy	**bunga desi**	[buŋa desi]
poppy	**bunga madat**	[buŋa madat]
hemp	**rami**	[rami]
mint	**mint**	[min]
lily of the valley	**lili lembah**	[lili lembah]
snowdrop	**bunga tetesan salju**	[buŋa tetesan saldʒʲu]
nettle	**jelatang**	[dʒʲelataŋ]
sorrel	**daun sorrel**	[daun sorrel]
water lily	**lili air**	[lili air]
fern	**pakis**	[pakis]
lichen	**lichen**	[litʃen]
greenhouse (tropical ~)	**rumah kaca**	[rumah katʃa]
lawn	**halaman berumput**	[halaman berumput]
flowerbed	**bedeng bunga**	[bedeŋ buŋa]
plant	**tumbuhan**	[tumbuhan]
grass	**rumput**	[rumput]
blade of grass	**sehelai rumput**	[sehelaj rumput]
leaf	**daun**	[daun]
petal	**kelopak**	[kelopaʔ]
stem	**batang**	[bataŋ]
tuber	**ubi**	[ubi]
young plant (shoot)	**tunas**	[tunas]
thorn	**duri**	[duri]
to blossom (vi)	**berbunga**	[berbuŋa]
to fade, to wither	**layu**	[laju]
smell (odor)	**bau**	[bau]
to cut (flowers)	**memotong**	[memotoŋ]
to pick (a flower)	**memetik**	[memetiʔ]

191. Cereals, grains

grain	biji-bijian	[bidʒi-bidʒian]
cereal crops	padi-padian	[padi-padian]
ear (of barley, etc.)	bulir	[bulir]
wheat	gandum	[gandum]
rye	gandum hitam	[gandum hitam]
oats	oat	[oat]
millet	jawawut	[dʒʲawawut]
barley	jelai	[dʒʲelaj]
corn	jagung	[dʒʲaguŋ]
rice	beras	[beras]
buckwheat	buckwheat	[bakvit]
pea plant	kacang polong	[katʃaŋ poloŋ]
kidney bean	kacang buncis	[katʃaŋ buntʃis]
soy	kacang kedelai	[katʃaŋ kedelaj]
lentil	kacang lentil	[katʃaŋ lentil]
beans (pulse crops)	kacang-kacangan	[katʃaŋ-katʃaŋan]

REGIONAL GEOGRAPHY

Countries. Nationalities

192. Politics. Government. Part 1

politics	politik	[politi']
political (adj)	politis	[politis]
politician	politisi, politikus	[politisi], [politikus]
state (country)	negara	[negara]
citizen	warganegara	[warganegara]
citizenship	kewarganegaraan	[kewarganegara'an]
national emblem	lambang negara	[lambaŋ negara]
national anthem	lagu kebangsaan	[lagu kebaŋsa'an]
government	pemerintah	[pemerintah]
head of state	kepala negara	[kepala negara]
parliament	parlemen	[parlemen]
party	partai	[partaj]
capitalism	kapitalisme	[kapitalisme]
capitalist (adj)	kapitalis	[kapitalis]
socialism	sosialisme	[sosialisme]
socialist (adj)	sosialis	[sosialis]
communism	komunisme	[komunisme]
communist (adj)	komunis	[komunis]
communist (n)	orang komunis	[oraŋ komunis]
democracy	demokrasi	[demokrasi]
democrat	demokrat	[demokrat]
democratic (adj)	demokratis	[demokratis]
Democratic party	Partai Demokrasi	[partaj demokrasi]
liberal (n)	orang liberal	[oraŋ liberal]
liberal (adj)	liberal	[liberal]
conservative (n)	orang yang konservatif	[oraŋ yaŋ konservatif]
conservative (adj)	konservatif	[konservatif]
republic (n)	republik	[republi']
republican (n)	pendukung	[pendukuŋ
	Partai Republik	partaj republi']

Republican party	**Partai Republik**	[partaj republi']
elections	**pemilu**	[pemilu]
to elect (vt)	**memilih**	[memilih]
elector, voter	**pemilih**	[pemilih]
election campaign	**kampanye pemilu**	[kampane pemilu]

voting (n)	**pemungutan suara**	[pemuŋutan suara]
to vote (vi)	**memberikan suara**	[memberikan suara]
suffrage, right to vote	**hak suara**	[ha' suara]

candidate	**kandidat, calon**	[kandidat], [tʃalon]
to be a candidate	**mencalonkan diri**	[mentʃalonkan diri]
campaign	**kampanye**	[kampanje]

| opposition (as adj) | **oposisi** | [oposisi] |
| opposition (n) | **oposisi** | [oposisi] |

visit	**kunjungan**	[kundʒʲuŋan]
official visit	**kunjungan resmi**	[kundʒʲuŋan resmi]
international (adj)	**internasional**	[internasional]

| negotiations | **negosiasi, perundingan** | [negosiasi], [perundiŋan] |
| to negotiate (vi) | **bernegosiasi** | [bernegosiasi] |

193. Politics. Government. Part 2

society	**masyarakat**	[maʃarakat]
constitution	**Konstitusi, Undang-Undang Dasar**	[konstitusi], [undaŋ-undaŋ dasar]
power (political control)	**kekuasaan**	[kekuasa'an]
corruption	**korupsi**	[korupsi]

| law (justice) | **hukum** | [hukum] |
| legal (legitimate) | **sah** | [sah] |

| justice (fairness) | **keadilan** | [keadilan] |
| just (fair) | **adil** | [adil] |

| committee | **komite** | [komite] |
| bill (draft law) | **rancangan undang-undang** | [rantʃaŋan undaŋ-undaŋ] |

budget	**anggaran belanja**	[aŋgaran belandʒʲa]
policy	**kebijakan**	[kebidʒʲakan]
reform	**reformasi**	[reformasi]
radical (adj)	**radikal**	[radikal]

power (strength, force)	**kuasa**	[kuasa]
powerful (adj)	**adikuasa, berkuasa**	[adikuasa], [berkuasa]
supporter	**pendukung**	[pendukuŋ]
influence	**pengaruh**	[peŋaruh]

regime (e.g., military ~)	**rezim**	[rezim]
conflict	**konflik**	[konfli']
conspiracy (plot)	**komplotan**	[komplotan]
provocation	**provokasi**	[provokasi]
to overthrow (regime, etc.)	**menggulingkan**	[məŋguliŋkan]
overthrow (of government)	**penggulingan**	[peŋguliŋan]
revolution	**revolusi**	[revolusi]
coup d'état	**kudeta**	[kudeta]
military coup	**kudeta militer**	[kudeta militer]
crisis	**krisis**	[krisis]
economic recession	**resesi ekonomi**	[resesi ekonomi]
demonstrator (protester)	**pendemo**	[pendemo]
demonstration	**demonstrasi**	[demonstrasi]
martial law	**darurat militer**	[darurat militer]
military base	**pangkalan militer**	[paŋkalan militer]
stability	**stabilitas**	[stabilitas]
stable (adj)	**stabil**	[stabil]
exploitation	**eksploitasi**	[eksploitasi]
to exploit (workers)	**mengeksploitasi**	[məŋeksploitasi]
racism	**rasisme**	[rasisme]
racist	**rasis**	[rasis]
fascism	**fasisme**	[fasisme]
fascist	**fasis**	[fasis]

194. Countries. Miscellaneous

foreigner	**orang asing**	[oraŋ asiŋ]
foreign (adj)	**asing**	[asiŋ]
abroad	**di luar negeri**	[di luar negeri]
(in a foreign country)		
emigrant	**emigran**	[emigran]
emigration	**emigrasi**	[emigrasi]
to emigrate (vi)	**beremigrasi**	[beremigrasi]
the West	**Barat**	[barat]
the East	**Timur**	[timur]
the Far East	**Timur Jauh**	[timur dʒʲauh]
civilization	**peradaban**	[peradaban]
humanity (mankind)	**umat manusia**	[umat manusia]
the world (earth)	**dunia**	[dunia]
peace	**perdamaian**	[perdamajan]
worldwide (adj)	**sedunia**	[sedunia]

homeland	tanah air	[tanah air]
people (population)	rakyat	[rakjat]
population	populasi, penduduk	[populasi], [pendudu']
people (a lot of ~)	orang-orang	[oraŋ-oraŋ]
nation (people)	bangsa	[baŋsa]
generation	generasi	[generasi]

territory (area)	wilayah	[wilajah]
region	kawasan	[kawasan]
state (part of a country)	negara bagian	[negara bagian]

tradition	tradisi	[tradisi]
custom (tradition)	adat	[adat]
ecology	ekologi	[ekologi]

Indian (Native American)	orang Indian	[oraŋ indian]
Gypsy (masc.)	lelaki Gipsi	[lelaki gipsi]
Gypsy (fem.)	wanita Gipsi	[wanita gipsi]
Gypsy (adj)	Gipsi, Rom	[gipsi], [rom]

empire	kekaisaran	[kekajsaran]
colony	koloni, negeri jajahan	[koloni], [negeri dʒʲadʒʲahan]
slavery	perbudakan	[pərbudakan]
invasion	invasi, penyerbuan	[invasi], [penerbuan]
famine	kelaparan, paceklik	[kelaparan], [patʃekli']

195. Major religious groups. Confessions

religion	agama	[agama]
religious (adj)	religius	[religius]

faith, belief	keyakinan, iman	[keyakinan], [iman]
to believe (in God)	percaya	[pərtʃaja]
believer	penganut agama	[penanut agama]

atheism	ateisme	[ateisme]
atheist	ateis	[ateis]

Christianity	agama Kristen	[agama kristen]
Christian (n)	orang Kristen	[oraŋ kristen]
Christian (adj)	Kristen	[kristen]

Catholicism	agama Katolik	[agama katoli']
Catholic (n)	orang Katolik	[oraŋ katoli']
Catholic (adj)	Katolik	[katoli']

Protestantism	Protestanisme	[protestanisme]
Protestant Church	Gereja Protestan	[geredʒʲa protestan]
Protestant (n)	Protestan	[protestan]

Orthodoxy	**Kristen Ortodoks**	[kristen ortodoks]
Orthodox Church	**Gereja Kristen Ortodoks**	[geredʒʲa kristen ortodoks]
Orthodox (n)	**Ortodoks**	[ortodoks]

Presbyterianism	**Gereja Presbiterian**	[geredʒʲa presbiterian]
Presbyterian Church	**Gereja Presbiterian**	[geredʒʲa presbiterian]
Presbyterian (n)	**penganut**	[peŋanut
	Gereja Presbiterian	geredʒʲa presbiterian]

Lutheranism	**Gereja Lutheran**	[geredʒʲa luteran]
Lutheran (n)	**pengikut**	[peŋikut
	Gereja Lutheran	geredʒʲa luteran]

| Baptist Church | **Gereja Baptis** | [geredʒʲa baptis] |
| Baptist (n) | **penganut Gereja Baptis** | [peŋanut geredʒʲa baptis] |

Anglican Church	**Gereja Anglikan**	[geredʒʲa aŋlikan]
Anglican (n)	**penganut Anglikanisme**	[peŋanut aŋlikanisme]
Mormonism	**Mormonisme**	[mormonisme]
Mormon (n)	**Mormon**	[mormon]

| Judaism | **agama Yahudi** | [agama yahudi] |
| Jew (n) | **orang Yahudi** | [oraŋ yahudi] |

| Buddhism | **agama Buddha** | [agama budda] |
| Buddhist (n) | **penganut Buddha** | [peŋanut budda] |

| Hinduism | **agama Hindu** | [agama hindu] |
| Hindu (n) | **penganut Hindu** | [peŋanut hindu] |

Islam	**Islam**	[islam]
Muslim (n)	**Muslim**	[muslim]
Muslim (adj)	**Muslim**	[muslim]

Shiah Islam	**Syi'ah**	[ʃi-a]
Shiite (n)	**penganut Syi'ah**	[peŋanut ʃi-a]
Sunni Islam	**Sunni**	[sunni]
Sunnite (n)	**ahli Sunni**	[ahli sunni]

196. Religions. Priests

| priest | **pendeta** | [pendeta] |
| the Pope | **Paus** | [paus] |

monk, friar	**biarawan, rahib**	[biarawan], [rahib]
nun	**biarawati**	[biarawati]
pastor	**pastor**	[pastor]

| abbot | **abbas** | [abbas] |
| vicar (parish priest) | **vikaris** | [vikaris] |

| bishop | uskup | [uskup] |
| cardinal | kardinal | [kardinal] |

preacher	pengkhotbah	[peŋhotbah]
preaching	khotbah	[hotbah]
parishioners	ahli paroki	[ahli paroki]

| believer | penganut agama | [peŋanut agama] |
| atheist | ateis | [ateis] |

197. Faith. Christianity. Islam

| Adam | Adam | [adam] |
| Eve | Hawa | [hawa] |

God	Tuhan	[tuhan]
the Lord	Tuhan	[tuhan]
the Almighty	Yang Maha Kuasa	[yaŋ maha kuasa]

sin	dosa	[dosa]
to sin (vi)	berdosa	[bərdosa]
sinner (masc.)	pedosa lelaki	[pedosa lelaki]
sinner (fem.)	pedosa wanita	[pedosa wanita]

| hell | neraka | [neraka] |
| paradise | surga | [surga] |

| Jesus | Yesus | [yesus] |
| Jesus Christ | Yesus Kristus | [yesus kristus] |

the Holy Spirit	Roh Kudus	[roh kudus]
the Savior	Juru Selamat	[dʒʲuru selamat]
the Virgin Mary	Perawan Maria	[perawan maria]

the Devil	Iblis	[iblis]
devil's (adj)	setan	[setan]
Satan	setan	[setan]
satanic (adj)	setan	[setan]

angel	malaikat	[malajkat]
guardian angel	malaikat pelindung	[malajkat pelinduŋ]
angelic (adj)	malaikat	[malajkat]

apostle	rasul	[rasul]
archangel	malaikat utama	[malajkat utama]
the Antichrist	Antikristus	[antikristus]

Church	Gereja	[geredʒʲa]
Bible	Alkitab	[alkitab]
biblical (adj)	Alkitab	[alkitab]

Old Testament	Perjanjian Lama	[pərdʒ'andʒian lama]
New Testament	Perjanjian Baru	[pərdʒ'andʒian baru]
Gospel	Injil	[indʒil]
Holy Scripture	Kitab Suci	[kitab sutʃi]
Heaven	Surga	[surga]
Commandment	Perintah Allah	[pərintah allah]
prophet	nabi	[nabi]
prophecy	ramalan	[ramalan]
Allah	Allah	[alah]
Mohammed	Muhammad	[muhammad]
the Koran	Al Quran	[al kurʔan]
mosque	masjid	[masdʒid]
mullah	mullah	[mullah]
prayer	sembahyang, doa	[sembahjaŋ], [doa]
to pray (vi, vt)	bersembahyang, berdoa	[bərsembahjaŋ], [bərdoa]
pilgrimage	ziarah	[ziarah]
pilgrim	peziarah	[peziarah]
Mecca	Mekah	[mekah]
church	gereja	[geredʒ'a]
temple	kuil, candi	[kuil], [tʃandi]
cathedral	katedral	[katedral]
Gothic (adj)	Gotik	[gotiʔ]
synagogue	sinagoga, kanisah	[sinagoga], [kanisah]
mosque	masjid	[masdʒid]
chapel	kapel	[kapel]
abbey	keabbasan	[keabbasan]
convent	biara	[biara]
monastery	biara	[biara]
bell (church ~s)	lonceng	[lontʃeŋ]
bell tower	menara lonceng	[mənara lontʃeŋ]
to ring (ab. bells)	berbunyi	[bərbunji]
cross	salib	[salib]
cupola (roof)	kubah	[kubah]
icon	ikon	[ikon]
soul	jiwa	[dʒiwa]
fate (destiny)	takdir	[takdir]
evil (n)	kejahatan	[kedʒ'ahatan]
good (n)	kebaikan	[kebajkan]
vampire	vampir	[vampir]
witch (evil ~)	tukang sihir	[tukaŋ sihir]
demon	iblis	[iblis]
spirit	roh	[roh]

redemption (giving us ~)	**penebusan**	[penebusan]
to redeem (vt)	**menebus**	[mənebus]
church service, mass	**misa**	[misa]
to say mass	**menyelenggarakan misa**	[mənjeleŋgarakan misa]
confession	**pengakuan dosa**	[peŋakuan dosa]
to confess (vi)	**mengaku dosa**	[məŋaku dosa]
saint (n)	**santo**	[santo]
sacred (holy)	**suci, kudus**	[sutʃi], [kudus]
holy water	**air suci**	[air sutʃi]
ritual (n)	**ritus**	[ritus]
ritual (adj)	**ritual**	[ritual]
sacrifice	**pengorbangan**	[peŋorbaŋan]
superstition	**takhayul**	[tahajul]
superstitious (adj)	**bertakhayul**	[bərtahajul]
afterlife	**akhirat**	[ahirat]
eternal life	**hidup abadi**	[hidup abadi]

MISCELLANEOUS

198. Various useful words

background (green ~)	**latar belakang**	[latar belakaŋ]
balance (of situation)	**keseimbangan**	[keseimbaŋan]
barrier (obstacle)	**rintangan**	[rintaŋan]
base (basis)	**basis, dasar**	[basis], [dasar]
beginning	**permulaan**	[pərmulaʔan]
category	**kategori**	[kategori]
cause (reason)	**sebab**	[sebab]
choice	**pilihan**	[pilihan]
coincidence	**kebetulan**	[kebetulan]
comfortable (~ chair)	**nyaman**	[njaman]
comparison	**perbandingan**	[pərbandiŋan]
compensation	**kompensasi, ganti rugi**	[kompensasi], [ganti rugi]
degree (extent, amount)	**tingkat**	[tiŋkat]
development	**perkembangan**	[pərkembaŋan]
difference	**perbedaan**	[pərbedaʔan]
effect (e.g., of drugs)	**efek, pengaruh**	[efek], [peŋaruh]
effort (exertion)	**usaha**	[usaha]
element	**unsur**	[unsur]
end (finish)	**akhir**	[ahir]
example (illustration)	**contoh**	[tʃontoh]
fact	**fakta**	[fakta]
frequent (adj)	**kerap, sering**	[kerap], [seriŋ]
growth (development)	**pertumbuhan**	[pertumbuhan]
help	**bantuan**	[bantuan]
ideal	**ideal**	[ideal]
kind (sort, type)	**jenis**	[dʒʲenis]
labyrinth	**labirin**	[labirin]
mistake, error	**kesalahan**	[kesalahan]
moment	**saat, waktu**	[saʔat], [waktu]
object (thing)	**objek**	[obdʒʲeʔ]
obstacle	**rintangan**	[rintaŋan]
original (original copy)	**orisinal, dokumen asli**	[orisinal], [dokumen asli]
part (~ of sth)	**bagian**	[bagian]
particle, small part	**partikel, bagian kecil**	[partikel], [bagian ketʃil]
pause (break)	**istirahat**	[istirahat]

position	**posisi**	[posisi]
principle	**prinsip**	[prinsip]
problem	**masalah**	[masalah]
process	**proses**	[proses]
progress	**kemajuan**	[kemadʒⁱuan]
property (quality)	**sifat**	[sifat]
reaction	**reaksi**	[reaksi]
risk	**risiko**	[risiko]
secret	**rahasia**	[rahasia]
series	**rangkaian**	[raŋkajan]
shape (outer form)	**bentuk, rupa**	[bentuk], [rupa]
situation	**situasi**	[situasi]
solution	**solusi, penyelesaian**	[solusi], [penjelesajan]
standard (adj)	**standar**	[standar]
standard (level of quality)	**standar**	[standar]
stop (pause)	**perhentian**	[pərhentian]
style	**gaya**	[gaja]
system	**sistem**	[sistem]
table (chart)	**tabel**	[tabel]
tempo, rate	**tempo, laju**	[tempo], [ladʒⁱu]
term (word, expression)	**istilah**	[istilah]
thing (object, item)	**barang**	[baraŋ]
truth (e.g., moment of ~)	**kebenaran**	[kebenaran]
turn (please wait your ~)	**giliran**	[giliran]
type (sort, kind)	**jenis**	[dʒⁱenis]
urgent (adj)	**segera**	[segera]
urgently (adv)	**segera**	[segera]
utility (usefulness)	**kegunaan**	[keguna'an]
variant (alternative)	**varian**	[varian]
way (means, method)	**cara**	[tʃara]
zone	**zona**	[zona]